LOST ON EVEREST

BBC

LOST ON EVEREST

The Search for

Mallory

&Irvine

PETER FIRSTBROOK

Published by BBC Worldwide Ltd,
Woodlands,
80 Wood Lane,
London W12 0TT

BBC Worldwide would like to thank the following for providing photographs and for
permission to reproduce copyright material. While every effort has been made
to trace and acknowledge all copyright holders, we would like to apologise
should there be any errors or omissions.

Alpine Club 4bl, 5bl; ©BBC 10b, 12, 13b, 14, 16; British Library (WD3114)2b;
Chinese Mountaineering Association 11; George Ingle Finch Photographic Archive 9;
John Noel Photographic Collection 1br, 4br, 6t, 7b, 15; Royal Geographic Society 1bl, 2t, 3t
(©Noel Collection), 3b, 4tl and tr, 5tl, tr and br, 6b (© Noel Collection), 7t, 8, 10t, 13t
(©Noel Collection); Salkeld Collection 1t.

ISBN 0 563 55129 1

Commissioning Editor: Sheila Ableman
Project Editor: Katy Lord
Designer: John Calvert
Picture Researcher: Liz Boggis
Maps by Oxford Designers and Illustrators

Set in Perpetua by Keystroke, Jacaranda Lodge, Wolverhampton
Printed and bound in Great Britain by Butler and Tanner Ltd, Frome & London
Jacket printed by Lawrence Allen Ltd, Weston-super-Mare

Contents

Bokhara
(Bukhara)

Kashgar
(Kashi)

_P a m i r s_

Oxus River

Hindu Kush

Chitral

Gilgit

K2

_K u n   L u_

Karakoram Range

Kabul

LADAKH

Peshawar

AFGHANISTAN

Rawalpindi

Indus River

Gartok
(Garyarsa)

Daba

Lahore

Niti Pass

Dehra Dun

▲
_Mount
Trisul_

PAKISTAN

Delhi

Agra

Karachi

I N D I A

Northern India and western Tibet, showing relevant landmarks
and geographical features.

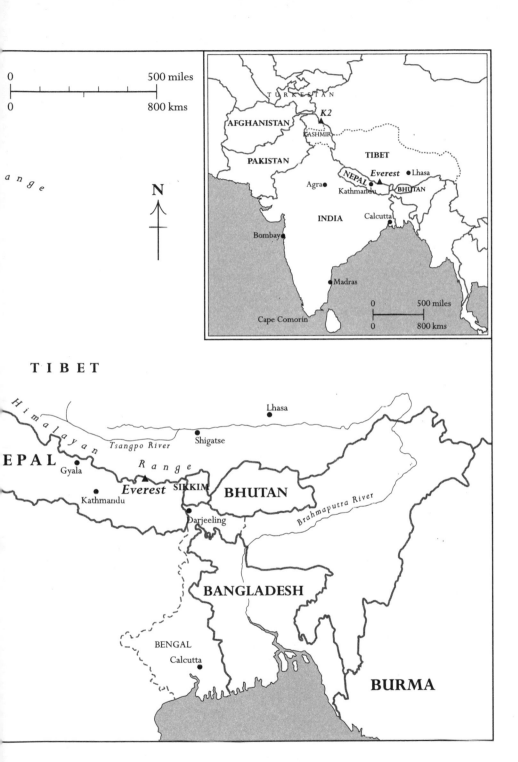

0

500 miles

0

800 kms

TURKESTAN

AFGHANISTAN

K2

KASHMIR

PAKISTAN

TIBET

NEPAL

Everest

Lhasa

Agra

Kathmandu

BHUTAN

INDIA

Calcutta

Bombay

Madras

Cape Comorin

0

500 miles

0

800 kms

N

ange

TIBET

Lhasa

Himalayan

Tsangpo River

Shigatse

Range

EPAL

Gyala

Everest SIKKIM

Kathmandu

BHUTAN

Darjeeling

Brahmaputra River

BANGLADESH

BENGAL

Calcutta

BURMA

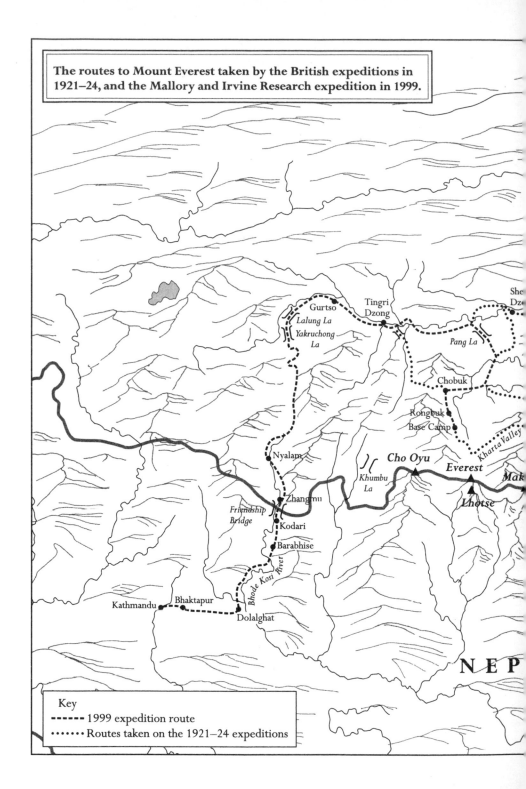

The routes to Mount Everest taken by the British expeditions in 1921–24, and the Mallory and Irvine Research expedition in 1999.

Gurtso
Lalung La
Yakruchong La
Tingri Dzong
She Dze
Pang La
Chobuk
Rongbuk Base Camp
Kharta Valley
Nyalam
Cho Oyu
Khumbu La
Everest
Mak
Zhangmu
Lhotse
Friendship Bridge
Kodari
Barabhise
Bhode Kosi River
Kathmandu
Bhaktapur
Dolalghat

N E P

Key
------- 1999 expedition route
········· Routes taken on the 1921–24 expeditions

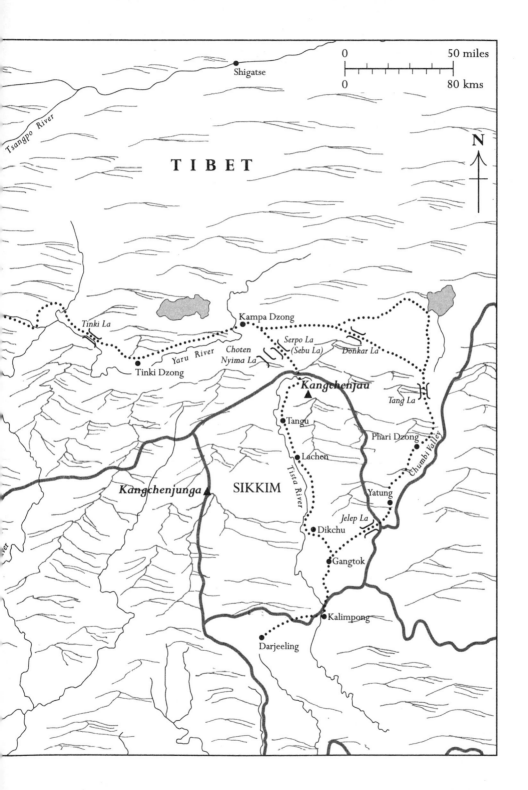

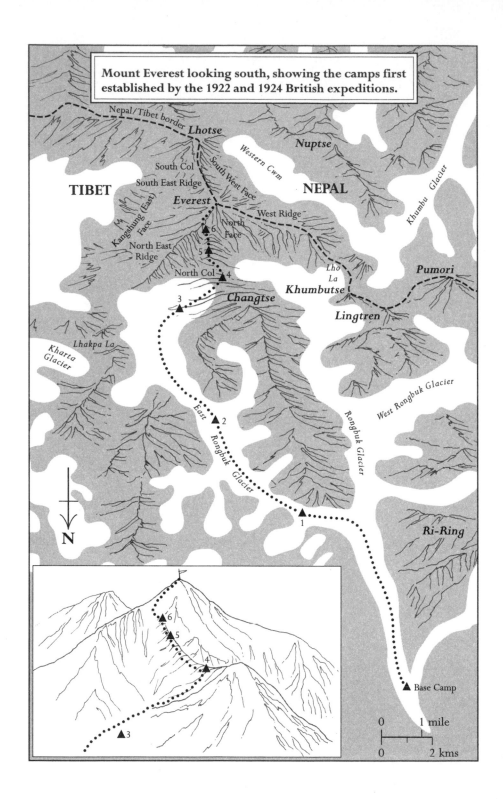

Mount Everest looking south, showing the camps first established by the 1922 and 1924 British expeditions.

Acknowledgements

In 1971 an American called Tom Holzel published an article about the Mallory and Irvine mystery and regenerated interest and debate about what happened to the two climbers in 1924. Since then, Holzel and the British historian Audrey Salkeld have kept the story alive with their writings, which are an invaluable source of information. Likewise, Jochen Hemmleb, himself inspired by their writings, did valuable research before our expedition.

No book on George Mallory could be written without reference to his three biographies – by David Pye, David Robertson and Dudley Green. Walt Unsworth's *Everest* is also an invaluable source of information about the mountain. The Alpine Club, the Royal Geographical Society and Magdalene College, Cambridge, all contain important documents, and I am grateful to the staff of all these for their help.

My gratitude also extends to those who risked their lives on the mountain: the climbers Conrad Anker, Dave Hahn, Jake Norton, Andy Politz, Tap Richards and Eric Simonson, and the Sherpas Ang Passang, Danuru, Dawa Nuru (Sirdar), Kami, Lakpa Rita, Panuru, Phinjo and Tashi.

My thanks also go to my film-making colleagues on the mountain: Liesl Clark, Ned Johnston, Thom Pollard and Jyoti Lal Rana, and especially to Graham Hoyland, who, for 30 years, dreamed of searching for Mallory's camera. At BBC Worldwide, Sheila Ableman and Katy Lord have been a constant support during the writing of this book.

From the beginning, the families of Mallory and Irvine gave their support to our documentary and handled the unexpected publicity in May 1999 with great dignity and patience; we should never forget that for them this is a family affair.

My final thanks go to my wife and children, for patiently putting up with me being away, yet again.

Every attempt has been made to obtain permissions to use the references quoted in the book, and I trust the task is complete. However, despite every care taken over checking the manuscript, my biggest concern is that mistakes might still have crept in. If so, the responsibility is mine, and I hope they are not so serious that they spoil what I hope you will find a fascinating story.

Dedicated
to the memory of

George Leigh Mallory
1886–1924

and

Andrew Comyn Irvine
1902–24

for Paula

Introduction

'Because it's there.'

George Leigh Mallory, 1923

*T*o crawl out of your tent in the morning in the Rongbuk Valley and turn to look south is to stare deep into history. Twenty kilometres (12 miles) away, but appearing much closer in the clean, dry Himalayan air, lies Mount Everest. The huge North Face of the peak dominates the valley, towering over its foreground neighbour Changtse – itself no Lilliputian at 7550 metres (24,770 feet).

Mount Everest – Chomolungma or 'Mother Goddess of the Earth' to the Tibetans – presides over the barren, rocky moonscape of the Rongbuk Valley like a giant's citadel; a fortress waiting patiently for the next assault. Everest is not technically the *hardest* peak to climb, but it is the highest. As such, the Mother Goddess weaves a magical spell, unique among mountains.

Over 1000 climbers have reached the summit, and several dozen have even succeeded without the use of supplementary oxygen. But all those who venture near the mountain understand the potential cost of their impudence; since 1922 more than 160 climbers have paid the ultimate price of their lives. Extreme altitude, intense cold and exposure to scything winds combine to make this a most hostile environment for mortals. The chances of making an attempt on the summit and *not* living to tell the tale are about one in six.

George Leigh Mallory and Andrew 'Sandy' Irvine were not the first to die on the mountain. Seven Sherpas were lost in an avalanche in 1922 and two Gurkhas died from frostbite and other complications in 1924. But the names of Mallory and Irvine are those remembered because they were the first to perish during a summit attempt. Their deaths shocked the nation; it was unbelievable that Mallory, the star of the mountaineering world, could have perished. He and his companion had disappeared without trace, leaving Britain in mourning. Since then, their names have been forever linked to the greatest mountaineering mystery of all time. Their story has taken on the same mythical status as Scott's race for the South Pole or Shackleton's epic voyage across the southern ocean to South Georgia.

For three-quarters of a century, the story of what happened to these two men has loomed large across the pages of history. It is a secret that Everest has guarded jealously.

On 29 May 1953, Edmund Hillary and Sherpa Tenzing Norgay climbed to the summit of Mount Everest and returned triumphant. Their well-planned ascent of the world's highest peak is still one of the great achievements of the post-war years, made all the more exciting when the news was announced on the eve of the coronation of Queen Elizabeth II. But there was always the nagging doubt that they might not have been the first to reach the top.

Hillary and Tenzing climbed the mountain from the Nepalese southern side. When he stood on the summit, Hillary admits to peering through his dark glacier glasses, looking for some evidence of the pre-war climbers. Not surprisingly, in that most extreme environment, he saw nothing but snow, ice and exposed rock jutting more than 8 kilometres (5 miles) above sea level.

When Mallory and Irvine attempted the summit 29 years previously, British high-altitude climbing was still in its infancy, and Everest a relatively unknown quantity. The British made a reconnaissance trip to the mountain in 1921, quickly followed by a determined attempt to reach the summit in 1922. The latter was a failure, but when they tried again two years later, they believed they had a good chance of success.

The 1924 British Everest expedition arrived in Darjeeling in March. At the time the only way into Tibet from India was to walk, and the expedition spent several weeks trekking to Base Camp, supported by a veritable army of porters and Sherpas. During May 1924, the expedition made several attempts on the summit, but none was successful. By early June, the summer monsoon was close and with it would come heavy snow, making any further climbing on the mountain too dangerous because of the risk of avalanche. The expedition had time for one final crack at the summit before withdrawing from the mountain. This last chance fell to the team's most experienced climber, George Mallory.

To the surprise of the other team members (and to historians since), Mallory chose the relatively inexperienced Andrew Irvine as his climbing partner. At 22 years old, Irvine was the youngest member of the expedition. He was an engineering student at Merton College, Oxford, and had a Blue in both rowing and squash, but little experience in mountaineering before going out to Everest. However, taking Irvine as a climbing partner had its advantages for Mallory: he was young, fit and enthusiastic; but most of all, his engineering skills enabled him to keep the fickle oxygen equipment working.

On 7 June 1924 the two men climbed up to a solitary two-man tent clinging precariously to the North Face of the mountain at 8170 metres (26,800 feet). It was here that Mallory and Irvine spent their last night together. They had everything working in their favour and the weather looked promising. There was good reason for optimism. Mallory had been to Everest on both previous expeditions and knew the mountain well. The problems of altitude were now better understood, and the bulky oxygen tanks – their key to the summit – were lighter and more reliable than ever.

Most important of all, Mallory had a fierce determination to succeed. He was 38 years old and knew this would be his last chance to be immortalized as the man who conquered Everest. Few of his fellow climbers on the expedition doubted either his ability or his conviction to succeed.

Early on the morning of 8 June 1924, Mallory and Irvine left Camp VI and climbed into history. A fellow team member, Noel Odell, was also on the mountain that day in support. He was the last person to see the two climbers alive – at 12.50 p.m., just 240 metres (800 feet) below the summit and still 'going strong for the top'. Within minutes, however, the two climbers had disappeared in a snowstorm and were never seen again. Odell's report of this last sighting has contributed to a passionate debate about whether they succeeded in reaching the summit.

The 1999 Mallory and Irvine Research Expedition — which comprised American and British climbers, together with a documentary film team — made world headlines when the news broke that Mallory's body had been found. We now know that the two climbers fell to their deaths on the North Face as they were coming down the mountain. But did they reach the summit before they died? Did they, for a few brief moments, have the satisfaction of looking around at the majestic peaks spread below them, in the certain knowledge that they were the first human beings to stand on the top of the world?

Over the years there have been a few tantalizing clues about what happened to the two climbers that day. Like a handful of pieces that make up an incomplete jigsaw, they are enough to intrigue but insufficient to enlighten. Apart from Odell's sighting, a British expedition in 1933 found an ice-axe lying on a gently sloping slab of rock. It was later identified as belonging to Andrew Irvine. But was it left there during a rest break, or dropped during a fall?

After World War II, Tibet was closed to Western climbers, thus preventing any further British attempts from the north. However, the southern approach to the mountain from Nepal was opened up, and it was here that Hillary's expedition successfully climbed to the summit in 1953.

Chinese and Russian teams, however, were still making attempts from the northern side. In 1979 a Japanese team supported by Chinese climbers made the first non-communist reconnaissance of the mountain since the war. A chance conversation between the leader of the Japanese team and Wang Hong-bao, a Chinese climber, revealed an astonishing story.

Wang told the Japanese climber that during an earlier expedition in 1975 he had stumbled upon the body of a climber on the North Face at approximately 8150 metres (26,730 feet), whom he was certain was English. He used sign language to indicate that the body was dressed in old-fashioned and tattered clothing, which suggested that it had rested in that position for some considerable time. The style of the clothing, the condition of the body and its location on the mountain suggested that it was one of the two lost British climbers from 1924, but nobody knew whether it was the body of Mallory or Irvine. The story rocked the climbing world. But Everest is good at keeping its secrets and tragedy struck again when Wang died in an avalanche the next day. Nobody could confirm his story.

This evidence was intriguing, but only hinted at what might have happened to the climbers. Mallory's friends were convinced that he would have continued to the top, come what may. He was a man driven to conquer Everest, almost regardless of the consequences. But without further evidence the mystery of what happened would remain unsolved.

The seventy-fifth anniversary of Mallory and Irvine's deaths fell in 1999 and seemed an appropriate time to take a fresh look at what happened on the afternoon of 8 June 1924. With a little intelligent deduction and new research into the whereabouts of the 1975 Chinese camp, we were confident that there was enough new information to make a search on the mountain worth while.

Hundreds of thousands of pounds and months of preparation brought a team of experienced climbers and a television documentary crew to the north side of Everest. It was a huge gamble for everyone concerned. The evidence was tenuous, the weather unpredictable. Illness, accidents, high winds or even a light covering of snow could have made a high-altitude search impossible. But we were lucky. At 11.45 a.m. on 1 May 1999 the climber Conrad Anker made mountaineering history by finding the body of the man who lived, and ultimately died, for Everest. He had found George Mallory.

CHAPTER ONE

'A Small Margin of Safety'

'There is no doubt that all his life he enjoyed
taking risks, or perhaps it would be fairer to say
doing things with a small margin of safety.'

David Pye about George Mallory

*I*n the summer of 1909, at the age of 23, George Mallory was invited ·
to go climbing in the Alps. He had just graduated from Cambridge
and although he was not a particularly experienced mountaineer,
his occasional climbing trips proved that he had a natural talent for the
sport. Two events in the mountains that summer give an interesting insight
into Mallory as a climber.

The first happened when he and his friends were making a traverse of the
Finsteraarhorn by its difficult southerly arête. The conditions were sunny but
very cold, and Geoffrey Winthrop Young, a very experienced alpine climber,
later recalled: 'The cold upon the very high and exposed cone was positively
numbing. It seemed to have curdled even the snow-skin upon the rocks ...
George gave me an extra shudder by suggesting – possibly in grave joke –
that we should cut his business short by glissading down the ghastly ice-
infinity of the western flank.'[1]

The climbers reached the summit, but it was not a day to linger, and
Mallory took over the lead to guide the party down the north face of
the mountain. He had not moved very far along the exposed ridge
before the more experienced Young noticed that Mallory had forgotten
to 'rope up'. Mallory was perched in a very exposed and dangerous position

with only the tiniest foothold cut into the icy slabs and with no protection should he slip. Nearly 2 kilometres (1 mile) below him lay the Finsteraarhorn glacier.

Young was horrified at the situation. Rather than risk startling Mallory by shouting across to him, he whispered instead for him to stay exactly where he was and not to move an inch. Meanwhile Young motioned to Donald Robertson, the second climber, to climb down carefully and attach the safety rope, which Mallory had clearly forgotten to tie before he started out after their rest on the summit. As Robertson nervously began to move down the ridge, he slipped and made such a racket that Mallory, alarmed at the sudden noise, spun around on the tiny step he had etched into the ice. Young was sure that Mallory would fall, and he could barely bring himself to look at the acrobatics being performed by the climbers perched high above the glacier.

But his anxiety was unnecessary. Mallory kept his balance and showed little concern about the serious situation in which he had recklessly put himself. But it was a chastened party that continued the long descent that afternoon. Afterwards, Young recalled: 'My panic was unnecessary, because the reassurance of a rope never meant anything to Mallory, who was as sure-footed and as agile in recovery as the proverbial chamois.'[2]

The second event happened just a few days later, around 6 p.m., at the end of a long day spent making an attempt on the unclimbed south-east ridge of the Nesthorn. Mallory had just taken over as the lead climber of the group and was trying to work his way around the fourth and final vertical pinnacle near the summit. At the time he was about 6 metres (20 feet) above Young; Donald Robertson was out of sight around the corner. On either side, the ridge disappeared below them in the evening gloom.

Mallory was faced with an overhang that was proving to be an awkward obstacle to further progress up the face. He made an energetic swing to get over the obstruction and in doing so he fell backwards off the rock face. He plunged 12 metres (40 feet) before Young realized what had happened and braced himself to check the fall with a belay. In a later account of the climb, Young wrote: 'I saw the boots flash from the wall without even a scrape; and, equally soundlessly, a grey streak flickered downward, and past me, out of sight. So much did the wall, to which he had clung so long, overhang that from the instant he lost hold he touched nothing until the rope stopped him in mid-air over the glacier.'[3]

Young was shocked by what had happened: 'At first there was nothing to do but hold on, and watch the pendulum movement of a tense cord straining over the edge and down into space. My first cautious shouts were unanswered. Then there came, from nowhere, a tranquil call to let out more rope, and to "lower away" ... He had not even let go of his ice axe during the fall. The whole incident had passed so swiftly and unemotionally – I had almost said with such decorum – that Donald, twenty feet below us, and round the corner on the north face, remained unaware that anything unusual had happened. Nor did we enlighten him at the time.'[4]

Mallory eventually appeared, completely unflustered, and climbed past Young and continued up the pitch. But, despite his nonchalance, it was a lucky escape for the young climber because they later found that the rope had a very low breaking strain. The three friends continued to complete the first ascent of the Nesthorn by this route and they did not return to their hotel until after midnight. Mallory later wrote to his mother: 'We were out twenty-one hours and were altogether rather pleased with ourselves, as we started in bad weather which afterwards cleared up beautifully.'[5] He made no mention of his near fatal fall.

These two incidents just days apart give a valuable insight into Mallory's character. Forgetting to tie on is an alarming lapse of memory for any climber who is attempting an exposed climb. Even more serious is that you endanger your climbing partners as well as yourself.

Admittedly Mallory was still something of a novice climber at the time, but basic safety procedures are drilled into you from your very first lesson, so the event says more about his chronic forgetfulness than his inexperience. He was often vague about practicalities and had to make a conscious effort to remember basic precautionary measures, which normally come naturally to experienced climbers. This problem stayed with him throughout his life and may even have cost him the position of climbing leader in 1924 on Everest, when he was one of the most experienced mountaineers of the day. General Charles Bruce, who led that expedition, once commented wryly: 'He is a great dear, but forgets his boots on all occasions.'[6]

However, Mallory's abilities on a mountain far outweighed his limitations.

His surefootedness on the icy arête as he swung around to see the cause of the commotion was an unambiguous demonstration of his balance and agility as a climber. As his mountain experience developed and improved over the years, many people were so impressed with his skill that they were convinced he would never fall; others thought he displayed a cavalier attitude at times, or at least that he was rash in some of his judgements.

This is the eternal enigma about Mallory and it perplexed climbers even before his death. Was he impulsive and absent-minded and therefore potentially dangerous on a mountain, or an exceptionally competent climber who rose far above the abilities of most other people?

A couple of years later, Mallory spent Easter at Pen-y-Pass in Wales, a regular spring meeting place for his climbing friends. That year there were several very experienced climbers in the party, including Dr Karl Blodig, a distinguished Austrian climber who had climbed most of the 4000-metre (13,120-foot) peaks in the Alps. On one particularly challenging climb up an ice chimney, Blodig watched Mallory tackle the difficult pitch. He later wrote: '... with the greatest dash and marvellous skill, [he] worked his way up the smooth surface until he disappeared from our view. Unanimous cries of "Hurrah" and "Bravo" hailed this extraordinary performance.'[7] Blodig continued to be impressed with Mallory's skill as a climber, but began to harbour doubts about his prudence and made a prophetic comment one evening when he said: 'That young man will not be alive for long!'[8]

Mallory was aghast at this opinion, and his friend, Cottie Sanders, leapt to his defence: 'He was prudent, according to his own standards; but his standards were not those of the ordinary medium-good rock climber. The fact was that difficult rocks had become to him a perfectly normal element; his reach, his strength, and his admirable technique, joined to a sort of cat-like agility, made him feel completely secure on rocks so difficult as to fill less competent climbers with a sense of hazardous enterprise ... I never saw him do a reckless or ill-considered thing on steep rocks. He hated the irresponsible folly and ignorance which led incompetent people into dangerous situations.'[9]

George Mallory was born on 18 June 1886 in Mobberley, Cheshire. It was then a leafy village some 24 kilometres (15 miles) south of Manchester.

Mallory's father, Herbert, was both clergyman to the local parish church in Mobberley and lord of the manor. He and his wife, Annie, had four children; Mary, George, Victoria (Avie) and Trafford (who later became an air vice-marshal in the Royal Air Force).

Mobberley was a charming and adventurous place for the children to grow up. There were trees to climb and the local brook was always a fascinating place to explore. Mallory's younger sister remembered her childhood there with affection: 'It was always fun doing things with George. He had the knack of making things exciting and often rather dangerous. He climbed everything that it was at all possible to climb. I learnt very early that it was fatal to tell him that any tree was impossible for him to get up.'[10]

Life for the Mobberley children was idyllic but undisciplined by the normal standards of late-Victorian England, and Avie recalled that they were unruly and misbehaved. On one occasion, at the age of seven, George was sent to his room for misbehaving in the nursery at teatime. A little later, he was nowhere to be found, until he was noticed climbing on the roof of Mobberley Parish Church. His one defence was that he *had* gone to his room – to fetch his cap.

Their father was a gentle man, but with a reputation for being rather distant and indifferent towards his parishioners. The Rev. Herbert Leigh Mallory was the youngest of 10 children, all of them born at Manor House in Mobberley. The family was related to the old Cheshire Leigh family of High Leigh, and for over 200 years the Mallorys had given Mobberley their rectors and lords of the manor. Herbert continued the tradition when he succeeded his father as rector of Mobberley parish in 1885. Whether he considered his job a true vocation or simply a convenient way of life is now impossible to tell, but his position in Mobberley seems to have been pre-ordained. What is in little doubt is that George was devoted to his father, who by all accounts was a friendly and compassionate man.

Mallory's impulsive and daring nature became apparent from quite an early age. One summer, when George was eight or nine, the family took a seaside holiday at St Bees in the English Lake District. The young George wondered what it would be like to be cut off by the tide and left stranded, surrounded by sea, so he climbed up on a large rock at low water and waited for the tide to come in. Unfortunately, he took no account of the fact that the rock itself would become submerged by the incoming tide and he soon found the water rising above his ankles. His grandmother implored a holidaymaker to go and rescue the boy, and the unfortunate volunteer waded out and made repeated attempts before finally being successful. By all accounts young George was quite untroubled by the incident.

On another occasion his mother caught him climbing a high iron pier and waited anxiously for him to climb down, which he apparently did with perfect composure. He once told his sister that it would be quite easy to lie between railway lines and let a steam train run over him (but fortunately he did not try the experiment). Another time he happily climbed up a drain-pipe and over the roof of his house with all the skill and ability of a born mountaineer. David Pye, a friend from Cambridge days and Mallory's first biographer, wrote: 'There is no doubt that all his life he enjoyed taking risks, or perhaps it would be fairer to say doing things with a small margin of safety. He always caught a train by five seconds rather than five minutes: a trait annoying to his companions, and not less so because he always justified it by not missing the train.'[11]

It was usual at the time for boys from even moderately wealthy middle-class homes to be sent away to boarding school. When the headmaster of his preparatory school in West Kirby died in 1896, George was sent to Glengorse, a boarding school in Eastbourne on the south coast of England. He seemed to be perfectly happy at the school, but he ran away with another boy after a couple of years, apparently for no other reason than that his friend did not want to run away alone. It was not long before an assistant master caught up with the two miscreants and he found the only luggage George had with him were his geometry books, neatly wrapped up in brown paper. It was agreed that if the two boys came back to Glengorse they would not be punished – a promise easily offered but inevitably broken when they returned. George was outraged by the deceit.

In 1900, when George was 14, he won a mathematics scholarship to Winchester College. Within days of arriving, he wrote to his mother: 'I like being here very much – ever so much better than Glengorse; and I like the *men* better, too. (Instead of chaps we always say men.) We have plenty of work to do, and I'm afraid I'm running you up a heavy book bill.'[12]

George was fortunate that his housemaster at Winchester was an experienced climber. Graham Irving climbed regularly with a colleague on the staff at Winchester, but when his friend died Irving looked to some of the more energetic, older boys at the school to train and accompany him on his Alpine excursions. Two boys in particular seemed most suitable – George Mallory and his friend Harry Gibson (who had previously visited the Alps and was an enthusiastic mountain walker). From this point onwards the young Mallory was taught to climb properly, and they called their little climbing group the Winchester Ice Club. Irving was the first president, and the schoolboy members were Harry Gibson, George Mallory, Guy Bullock and Harry Tyndale.

Mallory made his first climbing visit to the Alps in the summer of 1904 when he was 18. The group went to Bourg St-Pierre, intending to climb Mont Vélon, a modest mountain less than 3650 metres (12,000 feet) high and technically not much of a challenge. But it was a big undertaking for complete novices and both boys developed mountain sickness just 180 metres (600 feet) from the summit, forcing them to turn back. Despite this inauspicious start to his Alpine career, Mallory later succeeded in making two further climbs in the mountains with Irving. After they returned from his first successful summit, Mallory wrote to his mother: 'We went up the last 700 feet in fine form in half an hour. The Grand Combin is 14,100 feet, and of course the view from the top is perfectly ripping.'[13] Later they made a traverse of Mont Blanc from the Dôme hut to the Grands Mulets after a period of appalling weather, 'carried through after long imprisonment by storms on a few biscuits and scrapings of honey'.[14]

For many people, this summer climbing in the Alps might have seemed a baptism of fire. But it was enough of a success for Mallory to return the following year with another party of Winchester schoolboys, which included Guy Bullock, who later joined Mallory on the 1921 reconnaissance expedition to Everest. These two seasons in the Alps were to have an enduring influence on Mallory.

No doubt his housemaster also left a lasting impression on the young man. Graham Irving was an experienced but controversial climber. He was one of the first to advocate guideless climbing in the Alps, which in itself was a radical practice at the time and deplored by many older mountaineers. Even more controversial was Irving's habit of climbing solo on some of the easier routes. This was considered to be even more irresponsible and both of these approaches to climbing ran contrary to conventional wisdom in England at the time.

Some years later, in December 1908, Irving went to London to give a talk at the prestigious Alpine Club – the world's oldest mountaineering club, founded in 1857. His presentation was called 'Five Years with Recruits'. He knew that his climbing opinions were contentious and he expected criticism from the assembled ranks. His talk was later published in the *Alpine Journal*, and he wrote: 'To some of you it may seem sheer impudence to usurp the functions of the professional experts of Meiringen and Zermatt. It may even be that I shall be accused of corrupting the youth ...'[15]

As he had anticipated, his talk at the Alpine Club caused a storm of protest, and 14 members of the organization signed a disclaimer, denying responsibility '... for any encouragement which publication ... may give to expeditions undertaken after the manner therein described'.[16]

Back in England in the autumn of 1905, Mallory was determined not to lose the new skills he had acquired with Irving. His family had moved to a new parish in Birkenhead the previous year, and during one of his home visits he asked Harold Porter, a school friend, to help him climb on to the roof of the vicarage. Their plan was for Mallory to climb out of an upstairs window where he could get a grip on the overhanging eaves. Then, with an energetic kick, he intended to hoist himself up on to the roof of the house.

Unfortunately, as he swung his legs upwards, he kicked in a windowpane with a resounding crash and woke his mother who was resting in the adjacent bedroom. Annie Mallory rushed into her son's room to find his embarrassed young friend frantically paying out a rope. The other end of the rope was connected to her son, who by this time had taken off across the roof of the family house. Harold Porter later recalled: '... George sped over the roof to a known route of descent on the far side, leaving to me the embarrassing task of pacifying his agitated parent until his reappearance.'[17]

Once he returned to boarding school at Winchester, Mallory continued his extra-curricular exploits. On one occasion he climbed the tower of an old church in Romsey. On another, to celebrate his last day of the summer term, he scaled a tower by working his way up with his feet against the brickwork and bracing his shoulders against an adjacent chimney. There was a vertical drop of 15 metres (50 feet) to the paving stones below, and inevitably a group of schoolboys gathered to watch his exploits. One of the enthralled observers later recalled that seeing Mallory perched so high made him feel almost sick – another wrote that the ascent looked to him 'like magic'.

It is intriguing to speculate what effect Graham Irving's unconventional approach had on the young Winchester schoolboy. Here was an older man with great experience of the mountains and a passion for climbing them. He introduced Mallory to the Alps at an impressionable age and left him with a lifelong love of climbing. But Irving's style and technique were far in advance of the accepted wisdom of the day and he could only have fuelled Mallory's natural inclination to be an adventurous and unorthodox climber.

After Mallory's death, Irving speculated as to whether he was right to have introduced him to the mountains, and whether by doing so he might have contributed in some unforeseen way to his death. He wondered whether there was an inevitability that Mallory should climb mountains, but concluded that such a talented and energetic man could most certainly have excelled at any number of sports.

In October 1905 George Mallory went up to Magdalene College, Cambridge, to study history. In those days Magdalene was a small and friendly college of about 50 undergraduates, set apart from the other colleges on the opposite side of the River Cam. One of the first things Mallory did on arrival was to visit Arthur Benson, his tutor at Magdalene. Benson later wrote in his diary: '… a simpler, more ingenuous, more unaffected, more genuinely interested boy, I never saw. He is to be under me, and I rejoice in the thought. He seemed full of admiration for all good things, and yet with no touch of priggishness.'[18]

Mallory and his tutor became close friends. Benson encouraged his protégé to work hard and to read, among other things, Boswell's *Life of Johnson*. This started Mallory's fascination with the 18th-century biographer of Samuel Johnson. The new undergraduate worked hard on his essays but frequently failed to finish them on time. He also rowed for his college but, despite throwing himself into all the work and recreation that was on offer, he was not particularly happy in his first year. When he compared Magdalene with his time at Winchester, he found Cambridge 'shallow'.

But things began to look up for Mallory during his second year, when he started to make more friends. Many of these new acquaintances later proved to be very influential and they included Charles Darwin (whose grandfather wrote *On The Origin of Species*), the zoologist A.E. Shipley, the gifted young poet Rupert Brooke, the economist Maynard Keynes and his brother Geoffrey.

These university friendships became very important to Mallory, and one of his climbing friends, Cottie Sanders, once wrote that George and his friends: ' ... held personal relationships as so important that they held only a few other things as being of any importance whatever. Conventional inessentials simply had no meaning for them. They were extraordinarily attached to one another; they stuck closer than brothers; there was, literally, nothing they wouldn't do for one another.' [19]

Politically, these young men tended towards the liberal left, and Mallory joined the Cambridge Union Fabian Society, much to the concern of his father. But Mallory's main political interest was in support of votes for women, and he became college secretary on the committee of the University Women's Suffrage Association.

In his second year Mallory did poorly in his examinations, achieving only a third class in the History Tripos Part I; he called it 'a worthless performance'. Despite his poor results he developed a wide interest in poetry, literature and painting. He also grew his hair long and dressed strangely in 'black flannel shirts and coloured ties' – but he was not a complete aesthete and he never lost his love of the outdoor life.

Most vacations saw Mallory climbing with his brother Trafford, Geoffrey Keynes and others, usually in Wales or the Lake District. But he still retained his interest in rowing and became captain of the Magdalene Boat Club in 1907–8, a year in which the college did particularly well. His academic work also improved and he was awarded a second in his History Tripos part II.

Mallory enjoyed his final year at Cambridge, and in the spring the subject for the Member's Prize Essay was announced: it was to be on James Boswell. This was one of Mallory's favourite topics and he decided to enter the competition. In his essay he analysed Boswell's character writing: 'Herein lay the essence of his genius. The story of Boswell's life is the story of a struggle between influences and ambitions which led him towards the commonplace, and the rare qualities grafted deeply within him, which bore him steadily in an opposite direction.'[20] He concluded that, despite Boswell's formidable abilities, the biographer could very easily have slipped into a state of indifference had he not had the determination and aspiration to rise above mediocrity. Mallory's conclusions on Boswell are an interesting reflection on his own life and ambitions.

It was also in early 1909 that Mallory first met the experienced mountaineer Geoffrey Winthrop Young. Although a decade older than Mallory, Young was to become a lifelong friend and climbing mentor to the young undergraduate, and within weeks of meeting they were climbing together in Wales. It was during these meets at Pen-y-Pass that Mallory was introduced to some of the great pioneers of mountaineering, many already in their middle age. Among them was Oscar Eckenstein, who had twice been to the Karakorams, the first time in 1892 with the great English Himalayan explorer Martin Conway. Another climbing partner was Percy Farrar, who had 17 seasons of Alpine experience. He was later to become president of the Alpine Club, and it was Farrar who proposed that Mallory be included on the first expedition to Everest. Clearly, Mallory was beginning to get himself known in very influential circles.

During the summer of 1909 Mallory began to consider what he would do with his life. He wanted to write, but he realized there was little chance of earning a living this way. At one time he had considered following in his father's footsteps and going into the Church. In 1907 he wrote to Edmund Morgan, a friend from Winchester who later became a bishop: 'For me, whatever else I may believe, the personality of Christ will live . . . That there is a God I have never doubted. That conviction seems to be part of every feeling that I have.'[21]

However, during his time at Cambridge he began to question traditional religious ideology. He always continued to believe in the fundamentals of Christianity, but he began to have doubts about his suitability for ordination and confided in Benson, his tutor: ' . . . I'm at variance with so many parsons that I meet. They're excessively good, most of them, much better than I can ever hope to be; but their sense of goodness seems sometimes to displace their reason.'[22]

His dilemma over his future continued, but for the moment there was a more pressing opportunity. Geoffrey Young was planning another summer excursion to the Alps, and not for the last time Mallory put his life on hold for the chance to go climbing.

CHAPTER TWO

'Any Aspirations?'

'Party would leave early April and get back in
October. Any aspirations?'

Everest Committee invitation to George Mallory, 1921

T he summer of 1909 was a crucial period in Mallory's development as a climber. Despite his fall on the ascent of the Nesthorn and forgetting to rope up on the traverse of the Finsteraarhorn, he had learnt much as a climber. It was during this trip that he first met Cottie Sanders, who was to become a great admirer of his climbing abilities. The first time she saw him, she recalled: 'He was picturesque and untidy, in loose grey flannels with a bright handkerchief round his neck; but the things which chiefly aroused attention were his good looks and his complexion ... this young man's skin was clear and fair as a girl's.'[1] Mallory clearly made a big impression on the young woman. She found him polite, but shy and reserved, preferring to read a book than to socialize.

Mallory had also developed a reputation for being impractical; according to Miss Sanders: 'He was very vague and ramshackly about everything practical ... and [we] derived great amusement from Geoffrey Young's efforts to get George packed and breakfasted and off in time.'[2] On one occasion, Mallory was sent out to buy food for the party, but he noticed that Cottie Sanders had an alarm clock with her. He had never seen one before and became so absorbed with its novelty that he completely forgot about his shopping errand.

After returning from the Alps, Mallory had an accident that proved to be much more damaging than his tumble on the Nesthorn. It was September 1909 and he was out walking in Birkenhead with his sisters. They came to a disused quarry and Mallory, in a typically impetuous moment, could not resist clambering up the sandstone cliff. On getting to the top, the crumbly rock came away in his hand and he fell backwards, landing awkwardly on his ankle. He thought it was only a sprain but it took much longer to heal than expected and he wrote to Geoffrey Young: '... the said ankle refused for a long time to get any better and I hobbled about shamefully. Indeed it is still in a poor state and though I can walk well enough for a short distance, it is no good for the mountains....'[3] The injury never fully healed, and he was sent home from the trenches during World War I because the pain became intolerable. He later had an operation during which it was discovered that he had actually broken his ankle and the bone had not healed properly. His injury continued to give him problems, even as late as 1924 when he went to Everest.

Mallory continued to drift through life, not really clear what he wanted to do. The chance of a job at his old school, Winchester, came to nothing as he was not really qualified to teach mathematics, French and German. He spent the winter with the Bussy family in the south of France; Simon Bussy was a painter and a friend of Renoir. Mallory spent his time swimming in the Mediterranean and walking in the hills when his ankle would allow. He also heard that his essay on Boswell had not won the Member's Prize and he was understandably disappointed.

In February 1910 he toured northern Italy, visiting Florence, Pisa and Genoa, before staying with friends in Basel and then going on to Paris. He spent several weeks in the city, and worked hard at trying to improve his French by going to the theatre, reading, and sitting in on lectures at the Sorbonne. He missed the regular Easter climbing party in Wales, which in some ways was fortuitous because his friend Donald Robertson fell and fractured his skull. He died shortly afterwards in Bangor Infirmary.

Mallory's funds were running low and he was beginning to drift. It was not long before he came under pressure from his father to get himself a proper career. Despite his disappointment at not getting the teaching post at Winchester, he was still interested in becoming a schoolmaster and he got a temporary position teaching at the Royal Naval College in Dartmouth, which he enjoyed. With this experience, he spent the early summer applying for other teaching jobs, and attended several interviews before he was offered the probationary position of assistant master at Charterhouse on a salary of £270 a year.

As he was not due to take up his post until September, he agreed to escort a 15-year-old boy to Switzerland in August. The boy's parents presumably thought that a month walking and climbing would be good for 'character building', but the partnership was not a happy one. The young boy showed little enthusiasm for the mountains and sustained a fortuitous injury to his knee quite early on in the trip. Little was achieved and it was a frustrating month for Mallory, stuck in the mountains with his immobile charge. But by all accounts he took good care of the boy and never openly lost his patience.

On 21 September 1910 Mallory started work at Charterhouse, but the first few months were far from easy. The headmaster was a kindly man but discipline at the school was lax. Mallory was not much older than the more senior boys, and his youthful appearance frequently meant that parents mistook him for a pupil. His boyish looks, together with his limited teaching experience, also made it difficult for him to maintain control in the classroom. He continued to remain optimistic, however, and wrote to his mother: 'I am enjoying life here, though there are moments of doubt. My work is a good deal with small boys, who are much more difficult to teach and control; but it amuses me, and that is the great thing. Dreariness is fatal to success in teaching, and if I escape that I may learn to be of some use.'[4]

Mallory's main problem was that he relied more on enthusiasm than authority in the classroom, and an older colleague in the school was obliged to give him some gentle words of advice on how to maintain better control. However, there were occasions when he resorted to conventional discipline, as one ex-pupil recalled: '... one day, when I stank out a neighbouring Form by pouring ink on calcium carbide through the dividing door, [Mallory] seized a fragment of broken desk, bade me bend over, and left a strong impression of muscularity on my hindquarters.'[5] But Mallory was a conscientious teacher and among his other achievements he recognized and encouraged the poetic talent of Robert Graves, who was one of his pupils.

In the winter of Mallory's first year at Charterhouse, Geoffrey Young and Graham Irving proposed him as a member of the Alpine Club and he was elected on 5 December 1910. He spent New Year in Wales again, climbing with his friends, including Young and Cottie Sanders. By now his climbing talents were clear for all to see, and the admiring Miss Sanders wrote: 'He was never a showy climber; he did not go in for the minute precisions of style at all. On the contrary, he seemed to move on rocks with a sort of large, casual ease which was very deceptive when one came to try and follow him. When he was confronted with a pitch which taxed his powers, he would fling himself at it with a sort of angry energy, appearing to worry it as a terrier worries a rat till he had mastered it.'[6]

That summer, Mallory found himself short of funds again and his climbing plans were uncertain. His heart had also developed a worrying click, but by the end of July he was declared fit and healthy and he took off to the Alps with Graham Irving and Harry Tyndale. By now Mallory was becoming an accomplished ice climber himself and years later Tyndale wrote: 'He cut a superb staircase, with inimitable ease and grace and a perfect economy of effort. In watching George at work one was conscious not so much of physical strength as of suppleness and balance; so rhythmical and harmonious was his progress in any steep place, above all on slabs, that his movements appeared almost serpentine in their smoothness.'[7]

When Mallory returned to Charterhouse in September 1911 the old headmaster had retired and Frank Fletcher took over the position. Fletcher came from Marlborough, another English public school, and had a reputation for discipline and toughness. Although like Mallory he was a mountaineer and member of the Alpine Club, it took some time before the two men saw eye to eye.

Mallory's approach to teaching was unconventional and progressive for the time, and at odds with the rigid approach of the regime of the new head. He refused to accept the tradition of animosity between masters and boys and this often antagonized his colleagues and sometimes bewildered his pupils. Robert Graves always maintained that Mallory's teaching talents were wasted at Charterhouse. Following Graham Irving's example, Mallory also took the opportunity to take his boys climbing in Wales during the Easter vacation, but always with parental approval.

He spent the summer of 1912 in the Alps with Geoffrey Young, together with Humphry Owen Jones and Hugh Rose Pope – both climbers had often joined Mallory and Young in Wales for their Easter climbing parties. Jones had been married just a few weeks previously and he brought his new bride with him on their Alpine holiday. But it was not a good year for climbing and the weather was as bad as anyone could remember. Disaster struck when Jones and his wife, together with their climbing guide, were killed on the Gamba. The remaining climbers were devastated, and they buried the victims together in Courmayeur. In the middle of October, just a few weeks after returning to Charterhouse, Mallory had word that Pope had died on the Pic du Midi d'Ossau.

Mallory continued taking his pupils climbing and often wrote about how much he enjoyed the experience. Some of the boys began to call him 'Uncle George', but later dropped the 'Uncle'. He relished his pastoral vacations climbing in Wales and the Lakes; he was gaining confidence as a teacher and as a consequence he was much happier: 'My life even now is the most agreeable I know of. When we see the sun again in this green paradise, I shall effervesce into a spirit.'[8]

After spending the summer of 1913 sailing off the coast of Ireland rather than climbing in the Alps, Mallory was back at Charterhouse, still fighting the system and complaining that he disliked the 'mechanical atmosphere' of the school.

His publishers wrote that the sales of his Boswell book had not gone well and he would not make any money out of it – or as they phrased it with much greater Edwardian elegance, it had not reached 'a point affecting his pecuniary interest'.[9] But despite the setbacks and trials he remained irrepressibly happy – and the reason was about to become clear. George Mallory, 27-year-old assistant master at Charterhouse School, was falling in love.

Hugh Thackeray Turner was an architect who lived in a fine house built on a hill to the west of Godalming, overlooking the wooded valley of the River Wey and just a short distance from Charterhouse. Mallory became a frequent visitor to Westbrook, but it was not the refined proportions of the house and gardens that took his fancy, nor was it the walks in the woods or games of billiards he played with Turner. It was his daughters – Marjorie, Ruth and Mildred – who were the main attraction.

Mallory first met the Turner family when they attended a school play. Turner (who was a widower) and his daughters were later invited to a Shakespeare reading at Charterhouse, and after that Mallory became a frequent visitor at Westbrook. Turner was planning to spend Easter 1914 in Venice with the girls, and he asked Mallory to join them. For the first time in many years, he was to forgo the well-trodden climbs of Pen-y-Pass. Instead, he spent a week in Venice and fell hopelessly in love with Turner's middle daughter, Ruth. They became engaged on May Day in 1914.

Ruth was not Mallory's first love. While at Cambridge he fell in love with a doctor's daughter who lived near Birkenhead. She was just 16, but he promised faithfully that one day they would marry. Later, Mallory was involved for several years with Cottie Sanders, whom he first met in the Alps when he was 23. The relationship foundered a year before Mallory met Ruth, but he and Cottie remained the best of friends after she was married. (Cottie Sanders was also known as the novelist Ann Bridge.)

In one of life's coincidences, Rosamund Wills, an aunt of Ruth's, wrote to a friend: 'My niece, Ruth Turner, is engaged to be married ... [to] ... a young Charterhouse master, George Mallory – I hope he is good enough for her, but it is hardly possible.'[10] Her friend happened to be the newly married Cottie Sanders, now Lady O'Malley, and her amused response was that Ruth would be marrying one of the rarest spirits of his generation and that it sounded as though *she* might not be nearly good enough for *him*!

Ruth's father, however, would not be hurried into giving his final consent to the marriage. He saw a fine young man with whom his daughter was clearly in love, but how could he expect to support her on his modest earnings as an assistant schoolmaster? Was he intending to rely on his wife's private income? Mallory was appalled at the suggestion and replied that he couldn't possibly marry a girl who had her own trust fund. Mr Turner's rather more sagacious reply was that they couldn't possibly get married if she *hadn't*.

Turner decided it would be prudent to take his daughters away to Ireland for a vacation. The two young lovers continued to write almost every day. Faced with this devotion, Turner agreed to the union and the couple were married on 29 July 1914, with Mallory's father officiating at the ceremony and Geoffrey Young acting as best man.

Meanwhile, war had broken out on the Continent, so an Alpine honeymoon was out of the question. Instead, the newlyweds took off to the West Country for a camping holiday, where the sight of the two young people under canvas aroused such curiosity among the locals that the couple were briefly arrested on suspicion of being German spies.

With hostilities intensifying in France, there was little chance for the couple to settle down to a normal married life. Ruth went to work in a hospital in Godalming and Mallory continued his teaching at Charterhouse. However, he became increasingly uneasy with his situation, knowing his friends were already making the ultimate sacrifice. He wrote to his old tutor, A.C. Benson: '... there's something indecent when so many friends have been enduring so many horrors in just going on at one's job quite happy and prosperous.'[11]

Mallory's persistent enquiries about joining up were constantly thwarted by his headmaster. Fletcher happened to be chairman of the Headmasters' Conference Committee, and he had asked the government to clarify its policy on the release of schoolmasters for the war effort. General Kitchener's enigmatic reply from the War Office was that headmasters should use their own judgement over who could be spared for officer training. As a result, Fletcher blocked all Mallory's efforts to join up. He missed a Naval commission in the early months of 1915 and later a chance to join the Royal Naval Air Service.

It was now May 1915 and Mallory's frustration continued to grow like an insidious cancer. Ruth was expecting their first child in September and the primroses, daffodils, bluebells and anemones of spring surrounded their cottage at Charterhouse. He and Ruth were happier than they could possibly have imagined. Meanwhile, every one of his close friends had crossed the Channel to join the war against Germany. His brother Trafford had been in the trenches since March, Geoffrey Young had survived the Battle of Ypres, George Trevelyan was attached to the British Ambulance Unit in Italy, Hugh Wilson was with the Worcestershires and Geoffrey Keynes was in the Royal Army Medical Corps in France. Robert Graves had joined the Welch Fusiliers, Alan Goodfellow was training to be a pilot and Hilton Young was off to Serbia with a naval mission. George Mallory, meanwhile, was still an assistant housemaster at Charterhouse.

He and Ruth became parents on 19 September 1915 with a daughter, Frances Clare. Mallory continued working on new ways to teach history, but word began to filter back from the front and he grew increasingly unsettled. Rupert Brooke died of blood poisoning in April 1915, Jack Sanders died in the same month during the first German gas attack of the war, Harry Garret had been shot through the head in Turkey and Hugh Wilson was killed at Hébuterne in September. Mallory was torn between his role as husband and father and his patriotic duty to go to war.

Later that year, Mallory began making enquiries about a commission as an artillery officer. Fortuitously, this initiative coincided with Fletcher hearing of a possible replacement to take over his work as history master at Charterhouse. Very soon, Second Lieutenant George Mallory was off to war with the Royal Garrison Artillery. Surprisingly, given his very limited practical abilities, he found himself being instructed in the finer qualities of siege warfare and the deployment of the army's biggest howitzers. He crossed the Channel on 4 May 1916 and reported for duty at the 40th Siege Battery, just north of Armentières.

Among his duties as a young officer was to move forward to an observation post on the front line and report back on the accuracy of the battery's shelling. On these missions, which often lasted several days, he was accompanied by only a couple of signallers. Later, he was given charge of the battery and wrote home about his visits to the front lines: 'I have been rather depressed. The day before yesterday I went up to the trenches – an early start (not really that early – breakfast 7.15) to make sure of getting something done. The trenches were in a filthy state, owing to a more or less futile attack made by our men the night before. I don't object to corpses so long as they are fresh. With the wounded it is different: it always distresses me to see them.'[12]

In August 1916 the ankle he had injured seven years previously began to give him a sharp pain. His discomfort was increased when the autumn brought rain, reducing the trenches to a quagmire. He still retained a sense of order, however, and frequently read three or four books a week despite the conditions. Nine months later, when he eventually had his ankle examined by an army doctor, he was sent back to London for an operation. This time the bones healed much better and that summer he climbed in

Scotland and pronounced his ankle fit and well.

The Mallorys' second daughter, Beridge Ruth (named after her grandmother and mother), was born on 16 September 1917. With the new baby, Ruth was worried about money. Mallory had mentioned in a letter that he had ordered a book; Ruth's reply was brusque: 'You say do I mind but I am afraid this letter will not get to you in time to prevent you. I think I do mind. I don't see that we have any more right to go spending large sums of money on books than I have on cloths [sic]. I am trying very hard to be economical and it's not encouraging to have you spend £50 without even seriously consulting me.'[13] Fifty pounds was more than two months' salary for an assistant master at Charterhouse.

Mallory's joy over the birth of his daughter was eclipsed by the news that Geoffrey Young had been badly wounded in the battle for Monte San Gabriele and his left leg had been amputated above the knee. Mallory himself suffered an injury too, but in less valiant circumstances. Returning to his posting on a motorbike, he hit a pillar at the entrance to his camp and crushed his right foot. He spent the rest of 1917 'frittering away days and weeks in England as one can only do in the Army'.[14]

For most of the summer of 1918 Mallory was posted to Newcastle where he worked on the trials of a new supergun. In late September he returned to France and spent the last few weeks of the war in a battery near Arras. With the Armistice expected soon, he had plenty of time to reflect on his two years at war. He wrote to his father in mid-October: 'I should have liked to return home, if not a hero, at least a man of arms more tried than I have been; my share has been too small; my instinct now is to want more fighting for myself.'[15] This frustration may have contributed to Mallory's need to prove himself later in life and achieve something of significance.

Mallory spent the last day of the war with his old Cambridge friend Geoffrey Keynes, who was a surgeon at a clearing station just outside Cambrai. On 12 November 1918 Mallory wrote to Ruth: 'We celebrated peace in Cambrai last night at the Officer's Club – 5 of us from here, a very agreeable little party. It was a good evening altogether of the kind one would expect from the public school type of British officer and good of that kind, with much hilarity – no drunkenness. The prevalent feeling I make out, & in part my own, is simply the elation that comes after a hard game or race of supreme importance, won after a struggle in which everyone has expended himself to the last ounce. What a freedom it is now! I seem to be inundated by waves of elation & to be capable now of untroubled joy such as one hasn't known during these 4 years since the war began!'[16]

The slaughter was over. But not before 4 in every 10 undergraduates who had been at Cambridge with Mallory had died.

It is not unusual for those who return home from war to reassess their lives, and George Mallory was no exception. On the surface, things could not have been much better. He was unscathed, living happily with his wife and two young daughters and back at Charterhouse. His relationship with Fletcher had improved and he was teaching more English, which he greatly enjoyed.

Mallory, however, was still uneasy about the English public school system: he thought the separation of school and home was unhealthy; that the boys led an exclusive life with little chance to relate to others from different backgrounds; that work and play were seen as quite separate things; and that too much emphasis was given to team games and too little to other outdoor pursuits. Mallory's views are not unusual today, but in the early twentieth century they were decidedly radical.

For a while he considered establishing 'a school of the future' with Geoffrey Young, founded on their social idealism. He also became increasingly interested in politics and spoke of a new patriotism and a more civilized and just society. But his interest in social reform was more than post-war theorizing.

During the Christmas holidays he went to Ireland to see for himself the reality of the Anglo-Irish Troubles. He was not naive about the risks: he made sure that he carried no compromising letters when he went out, he did his best to avoid the Black and Tan patrols, and he made a point of keeping his hands in his pockets and never running in public in case he attracted unwanted attention.

One night the reality of the situation was brought home to him when he was woken by an intruder with a torch in one hand and a revolver in the other: 'Who are you? What's your name? Where were you born?'[17] Mallory recalls that he was eventually asked if he was a Protestant. When he replied that his father was a clergyman in the Church of England, the British Army patrol left without even searching his room. He came away realizing there were injustices on both sides, but overall he was sympathetic to the call for Irish independence.

Meanwhile, the mountaineers who had survived the war were keen to resume their climbing, and the tradition of Easter at Pen-y-Pass was reinstated. Geoffrey Young, with his one good leg, was among the first up the mountain and his climbing was said to be extraordinary. That summer Mallory went back to the Alps after a hiatus of seven years, and for the first time he found he enjoyed climbing on ice and snow more than on rock. Towards the end of August he joined forces with George Finch and they traversed the Matterhorn together. Finch was one of the finest and most experienced climbers in Europe at the time and he later played a significant but controversial role in the exploration of Everest.

Mallory wrote regularly to his old friend Geoffrey Young, who had stayed behind in England. Young considered that Mallory had matured over the years. 'His early idea of "leadership",' Young pronounced, with a germane reference to recent events, 'was to go "over the top" at the first rush. He lacked the detachment of an officer.'[18] Now, after his war experiences, he showed much clearer judgement.

The following year, Mallory was keen to return to the Alps, but Ruth was expecting their third child at the end of August. It was agreed, however, that he would go over in July, giving him plenty of time to get back for the birth of their child. Unsettled weather made the climbing disappointing and Mallory returned home on the morning of 21 August to find that his son had beaten him to it by half an hour. He was thrilled and declared that John was 'a thumping great bruiser of a boy'.

Not long after the war the idea of an expedition to Everest was resurrected. In March 1919 John Noel gave a presentation at the Royal Geographical Society (RGS) in which he described his clandestine journey to Everest in 1913. He had succeeded in making a covert visit across the border into Tibet to within 64 kilometres (40 miles) of the mountain before being turned back by Tibetan soldiers. It was heady stuff. 'Now that the poles have been reached,' he declared, 'it is generally felt that the next and equally important task is the exploration and mapping of Mount Everest.'[19]

Of course, the height and position of Everest had been mapped nearly 70 years previously by the Great Trigonometrical Survey of India, which had declared the world's highest mountain to be 8840 metres (29,002 feet) high. That was back in 1852, but no surveyor since then had managed to get closer to the peak than 160 kilometres (100 miles). The route to Everest ran through the strange and little-known country of Tibet, which made the thought of an expedition even more appealing. The audience at the RGS, which included the great and the good of both the RGS and the Alpine Club, was transfixed by the prospect.

There was more than just a sense of adventure and challenge attached to the proposal. National prestige was also at stake. Both the North and South Poles had been 'conquered' before the war, but on both occasions 'foreigners' had beaten the British to the prize. The consensus at the RGS on the night of Noel's talk was that this last great objective, the 'third pole', should be a British triumph.

Nepal, which gave access to the south side of the mountain, was closed to foreigners, so permission for access to the north side of Everest would have to be sought from the Tibetans. Meanwhile, Percy Farrar, the president of the Alpine Club, began to compile a register of potential climbers for the party. The first name on his list was that of George Mallory.

Farrar wrote to Mallory at the end of January 1921: 'It looks as though Everest would really be tried this summer. Party would leave early April and get back in October. Any aspirations?'[20]

CHAPTER THREE

'Higher in the Sky Than Imagination'

'Gradually, very gradually, we saw the great mountain sides and glaciers and arêtes, now one fragment and now another through the floating rifts, until far higher in the sky than imagination had dared to suggest the white summit of Everest appeared.'

George Mallory, 1921

One day in 1852, according to legend, an Indian surveyor called Radhanath Sikdhar rushed into the office of Sir Andrew Waugh, the Surveyor General of India. Sikdhar was head of the Computing Office of the Grand Trigonometrical Survey (GTS) of India and he had news that had been eagerly awaited for several years. 'Sir,' gasped the surveyor, 'I have discovered the highest mountain in the world!'[1]

The painstakingly laborious work of measuring the high peaks of the Himalayas had at last produced a winner. The GTS had discovered a mountain calculated to be over 8840 metres (29,000 feet) high. The discovery was the start of a long love affair between the British and Everest, but it would not be until 1921, when the first British reconnaissance arrived at Everest, that climbers could test their skills on the flanks of the great mountain.

Radhanath Sikdhar and Michael Hennessy, the young assistant to the Surveyor General, were given equal credit for the 'discovery' of this giant. In reality, many people at the Grand Trigonometrical Survey (located in Dehra Dun, about 145 kilometres (90 miles) north of Delhi) had been slavishly working for a long time to calculate the height of the world's tallest mountain – until now known only as Peak XV. But would anybody back in Britain believe them?

The extraordinarily high altitudes claimed for the newly discovered Himalayan peaks were being dismissed as preposterous by certain 'learned' men back in Europe, who maintained that it was impossible for a mountain to be any higher than about 7620 metres (25,000 feet). They were certainly going to be sceptical about a mountain that towered to over 8840 metres (29,000 feet).

During the mid-nineteenth century, the British were embarked upon a major project to survey the whole of the Indian subcontinent, from Cape Cormorin in the south to the towering Himalayas in the north. This was neither an academic nor an altruistic exercise, but an objective with very real political and strategic objectives.

Throughout the eighteenth and nineteenth centuries the British had consolidated their control over the Indian subcontinent, but they constantly had their eye on the greater political landscape, and particularly on the other superpowers of the day. In this case they were most concerned about Russia's attempts to expand her influence into central Asia, and particularly into the Hindu Kush (eastern Afghanistan), the Pamir (southern Tadzhikistan) and Tibet. Although very little was known about these countries by either the Russians or by the British, their position at the very heart of Asia was enough to make them a strategic priority for both superpowers.

The purpose of the GTS was not only to make a grid survey of the whole of the Raj, but also to calculate the great meridian arc from Cape Cormorin to the Himalayas, a north–south distance of nearly 2900 kilometres (1800 miles). Only by making this calculation could the theoretical sphere of the Earth be computed, and it was only with this measurement that the height of the Himalayan peaks could be determined. In its day this was the most ambitious scientific measurement ever attempted anywhere in the world, and involved a survey that created a highly accurate framework of survey-triangles across the whole subcontinent.

This formidable project was started in 1802 by William Lampton, a British Army officer, and was continued after his death by Colonel George Everest. Born in 1790 in Brecknockshire, but educated in England, Everest was a lean and wiry man with deep-set eyes. He was a stickler for detail and accuracy, and had a temper that burnt on a very short fuse. Under his leadership, the Grand Trigonometrical Survey completed its topographic work over most of the Indian subcontinent, and this remarkable achievement laid the foundation for the measurement of the Himalayan peaks.

The survey of the Himalayas proper did not begin in earnest until Everest retired having lived and worked in India for over 25 years. He was knighted in 1861 and died in 1866. Although he surveyed India as far north as the Himalayas, there is no evidence that he ever set eyes on the mountain that was later to carry his name.

The biggest problem in mapping the Himalayan peaks was access. British surveyors were barred from the countries to the north of India: Tibet and Nepal were both autonomous kingdoms, and any attempt by British topographers to venture into these countries would have been dangerous. The Himalayan peaks therefore had to be measured from trigonometrical stations positioned on British-Indian territory, sometimes as far away as 240 kilometres (150 miles).

Colonel Andrew Waugh continued in the wake of Sir George Everest, and began the first detailed measurement of the Himalayas in 1847. These surveying campaigns were complex and sometimes hazardous projects, and life was not easy for the early surveyors, working as they did with fastidious care and attention to detail. British surveying parties became a common sight south of the Himalayas and these expeditions were mounted with all the planning of a modest military campaign.

Dozens of men were involved: half-naked Indians took turns to push the measuring wheel, others carried tents, supplies and equipment, a company of armed sepoys gave protection to the convoy from bandit attack, and the British officers sweated in their heavy regulation uniform. Year on year, in monsoon downpours and under the searing Indian sun, they went about their methodical work. As the Himalayan peaks were observed from such a distance, good visibility was essential and this often restricted the period when these extended observations could be made to between October and December, when the high atmospheric moisture of the monsoon period had passed.

Local environmental conditions took a harsh toll on Waugh and his team. They suffered from headaches, snow blindness, altitude sickness and cold. Several were struck by lightning during violent thunderstorms. Cloud would often prevent measurements being taken for weeks and consequently food and supplies would run short. In addition the men faced danger from bandits, jungle fever, tigers, bears and snakes.

The work itself was physically demanding and mentally taxing. The bulky, cumbersome theodolites, which were used to measure angles, weighed more than 45 kilograms (100 lb). They needed a dozen men to carry them over rivers and glaciers, up steep hills and across deep ravines. Yet they were precision instruments of great delicacy and any small knock could destroy their accuracy. When they were set up, allowances had to be made for a number of variables including altitude, the curvature of the Earth, the refraction of light over long distances, and even for the mass of nearby mountains. Yet their accuracy was remarkable and a series of measurements made over hundreds of miles would rarely err by more than an inch or two per mile of baseline.

In the autumn of 1847, the surveying team was concentrating on the measurement of a peak called Kangchenjunga, then considered to be the highest in the world. Beyond and to the north, another majestic peak could be observed which was perhaps even higher. They called the unknown mountain 'Peak B' and soon Waugh began to have doubts that Kangchenjunga was the highest in the Himalayas. He arranged for additional measurements to be made of the mystery mountain.

Readings were taken from six different directions, but none was closer than 170 kilometres (105 miles). These long distances, compounded by the antics of light reflected off snowfields and glaciers, made it all but impossible to get the same theodolite reading twice in succession. It took several years of lengthy and tedious computations at the survey headquarters to confirm that Peak B was significantly higher than Kangchenjunga.

By 1852 the calculations were complete. Peak IX (Kangchenjunga) was indeed a very big mountain, measuring 8628 metres (28,307 feet). But the most exciting news was about Peak B, since renamed Peak XV. It measured 8840 metres (29,002 feet) above sea level. With characteristic Victorian caution, Waugh declared that Peak XV *might* be the tallest mountain in the world, and he eventually made the discovery public in 1856. He chose to name it after his predecessor, a man who had contributed so much to the survey of India. It must be said that George Everest was greatly embarrassed by the accolade and went to his deathbed still wishing that the mountain had been given a local name.

It later transpired that the mountain had many alternative names: Tschoumou-Lancma was inscribed on a French map dated 1733, and other names include Jo-Mo-Glan-Ma, Devadhunga, Chinpopamaqi, Kangchen Lemboo Geudyong and the Turquoise Mountain. The Chinese call it the Great Headache Mountain, and the Nepalese name is Sagarmatha; but perhaps the most elegant name of all is from Tibet – Chomolungma, meaning Goddess Mother of the World.

There is controversy to this day over the precise height of Everest because of variations in snow thickness and deviations in gravity and light refraction. In the 1950s the original calculation was revised upwards to 8848 metres (29,028 feet). There is still no certainty, however, that this is the correct height. Colonel S.G. Burrard of the Grand Trigonometrical Survey once remarked: 'All observations are liable to error; no telescope is perfect; no levelling instrument entirely trustworthy; no instrumental graduations are exact; no observer is infallible.'[2]

This is prudent advice for any surveyor, but what nobody realized at the time was that the Himalayas are actually growing higher, sometimes by as much as 2.5 centimetres (1 inch) a year, which is fast by geological standards. Inevitably erosion and landslides take their toll, but Mount Everest and all the mountains around it are slowly getting taller.

Burrard's words rang particularly true when the British surveyors began to discover discrepancies in their calculations on reaching the foothills of the Himalayas. For example, the distance between the town of Kaliana and Kalianpur, nearly 640 kilometres (400 miles) to the south, was first measured by triangulation, and then checked by direct surface measurement. The two results differed by almost 150 metres (500 feet), which was an unacceptable margin of error for the GTS.

This dilemma became known as the Indian Puzzle, and after months of speculation, the surveyors eventually discovered where the problem lay. They had reasoned that if the Earth's mass was homogeneous, its gravitational attraction would be uniform and the plumb bob under the theodolite would hang perfectly perpendicular to the surface of the planet.

However, the Earth is *not* uniform, and the surveyors allowed for this by estimating that the huge mass of the Himalayas would deflect the plumb line on their theodolite by a quarter of a degree. This, as it turned out, was over-generous: the mountain range *did* deflect the plumb line, but only by *one-twelfth* of a degree of arc.

This simple error was easily corrected, but it nevertheless had a profound effect and began to influence thinking on the geological formation of mountains. The French scientist Pierre Bouguer originally proposed the idea that mountains are made from rock which is *less dense* than the surrounding lowlands. If this were true, it could account for the gravitational pull near the Himalayas being less than anticipated.

These findings from the Survey of India led to a much greater understanding of the nature and structure of mountain ranges and to the development of the theory of *isostasy*, from the Greek words meaning 'equal standing'. This theory proposes that a mountain range has a 'root', much like that of a tooth, which penetrates as deeply into the gum as it projects above it. Subsequent gravity measurements supported the idea that there is indeed a reduced mass of rock under mountains – a root of lighter material. For this reason the surveyor's plumb bob was deflected less than had been anticipated.

No less fascinating than the problems of measuring Everest accurately is the question of why the mountain exists at all. Around 100 million years ago, when dinosaurs still dominated the world, the continent of India was a big island mass in the southern hemisphere. It had just begun to break away from a much larger super-continent called Gondwana, which included the continents of Africa, South America, Australia and Antarctica.

As Gondwana broke up, the five main continents as we know them began to move towards their present-day positions by a process geologists call seafloor spreading. This works like a giant, global conveyor belt, moving these vast continental 'plates' over the surface of the planet like pieces of a huge jigsaw. In the case of India, the continental plate moved northwards at the geologically breakneck speed of about 10 centimetres (4 inches) a year. The Indian plate crossed the Equator around 70 million years ago and eventually collided with the northern continent of Europe and Asia.

As it continued to push northward, India squashed and thickened the margins of the two continents in the process, not unlike pushing a rug against a wall. The result of this continental confrontation was the Himalayan mountain range, a buckled and jumbled mixture of ancient rocks from the Eurasian and Indian geological plates, mixed up with much younger sedimentary rocks left over from the ancient ocean that previously lay between India and Asia. The process of collision between these two continental plates continues today, which is why the Himalayas are still growing in height.

Out of this cataclysmic event Mount Everest was born – a huge, triangular pyramid with three ridges running up to the summit, below which are three broad faces – the North Face, the South West Face and the Kangshung (or East) Face. Dividing these three faces are three ridges, which provide the most frequently used routes to the summit – the North East Ridge, the West Ridge and the South East Ridge.

Geologically, the mountain is a mixture of very different rocks. The lower levels comprise mainly metamorphic rocks, which have been altered by heat or pressure (or sometimes both). These are predominantly coarse-grained schists, mainly gneisses and migmatites. Further up the mountain is granite, an igneous rock produced by the slow cooling of hot molten rock, which is commonly found in the heart of big mountain ranges.

At the very top of the mountain are sedimentary rocks – clays, silts and the carbonate (chalky) remains of marine animals – thrust up from the warm, tropical Tethys Ocean to the very roof of the world by these dynamic mountain-building forces. This layer is known as the Yellow Band by Everest climbers. The very top of the pyramid comprises a much purer limestone mixed with sandy layers. Ironically, when climbers pose at the summit of the world's tallest mountain they are standing on marine fossils which are 50 million years old.

The ongoing clash between the continents has many repercussions, not least of which are devastating earthquakes. But it has also created a landscape of incomparable grandeur and contrast: giant mountains and vast high-altitude plains, plus some of the world's largest rivers and most formidable glaciers. It is a land scorched by searing heat and numbed by freezing cold; hurricane-force winds and snowstorms bombard the high mountains, yet hidden valleys are still nurtured by gentle breezes and warm rain.

Tibet had intrigued and captivated Europeans since the fourteenth century. It was a country of mysterious religious practices and supported a society that had changed little for hundreds of years. Imposing mountains guarded the region as effectively as the stone walls of any citadel, and the high passes giving access to the country were as easily defended as any castle gate. To the European explorer and adventurer it represented the ultimate challenge.

CHAPTER FOUR

'The Game Is Well Worth the Candle'

'The expedition is full of hazard but *le jeu vaut bien la chandelle* [the game is well worth the candle].'

Letter from William Moorcroft, shortly before his death; 1825

J ust as nature abhors a vacuum, so the expanding British Empire of the nineteenth century could not tolerate blank spaces on the world map. By the second half of the nineteenth century, Britain controlled and ruled huge swathes of the globe, including the jewel in Queen Victoria's Imperial crown, India. But to the north of the subcontinent lay a stubbornly blank part of the planet – the Himalayas. It was a challenge that could not be resisted for long.

Existing accounts of the region came from pre-nineteenth-century travellers and were of little help to the early British explorers. Buddhist monks made pilgrimages from China to India between the fifth and seventh centuries and later wrote about their travels, but the British knew nothing of these writings until the 1860s.

One of the first descriptions of Tibet came from a Franciscan friar in the fourteenth century called Odoric. Whether he wrote from first-hand experience or simply reported tales he had heard during his travels in Asia is something historians still dispute, because his account of Lhasa is a lurid mixture of fantasy and fact.

In the late sixteenth century, Jesuit priests journeyed from Goa to the court of the Mogul Emperor Akbar in Agra. There they became excited by stories from wandering holy men who spoke of people living beyond the mountains who seemed to follow religious practices similar to those of the Roman Catholic Church.

The Jesuits decided to make an attempt to find this mysterious community in 1603, but it ended in failure. Another attempt was made in 1624, led by Father Antonio de Andrade, head of the Jesuit mission to the Mogul Court. This small group headed north disguised as Hindu pilgrims, but their subterfuge was discovered near the border and they were ordered back. Undaunted, they tried again and made a dash for a remote high pass into Tibet, only to find themselves struggling through deep snow and blinding snowstorms at nearly 5500 metres (18,000 feet). They were perplexed to find themselves very short of breath and were unwilling to accept the local explanation that this was caused by poisonous air. Andrade recorded: 'According to the natives, many people die on account of the noxious vapours that rise. It is a fact that people in good health are suddenly taken ill and die within a quarter of an hour.'[1] This is probably the first written account of altitude sickness.

Through a combination of devout faith and extraordinary stamina, the Jesuits succeeded in crossing the Himalayas. Their reports give graphic descriptions of their hardships, but are vague on geographical detail. During the final stages of what was the first recorded climb of a Himalayan pass by Europeans, a blizzard struck the small party: 'Our feet were frozen and swollen so much that we did not feel it when later they touched a piece of red-hot iron.'[2]

Father Andrade succeeded in reaching the ancient kingdom of Gugé in western Tibet, but he found no Christians. Although the people there were deeply religious and many aspects of worship were superficially similar to Christianity – for example, their chants and vestments – they also drank from human skulls and used thigh bones for trumpets. Convinced that this was not a lost Christian civilization, Andrade established a mission there, but his success at converting the Tibetans to Christianity was disappointing. He returned to Goa in 1630, but died four years later, apparently poisoned by a colleague who objected to the enthusiasm with which he embraced the Inquisition. Despite his untimely end, he can lay claim to being the first true European explorer to venture into the Himalayas.

In 1712 a young Jesuit priest called Ippolito Desideri persuaded the Pope to back another expedition to Tibet. On arriving in India he found a country in much greater chaos than in Andrade's day, with the great Mogul Empire in disarray. Nonetheless, he and his party struggled to cross the high mountain passes and on one occasion the priest lost his sight from snow blindness. Their porters chose this moment to strike and established (for the first time) what has become a familiar and time honoured tradition on all the best Himalayan expeditions. The solution has also become part of Himalayan convention. Desideri's colleague slipped the Sherpa leader some extra cash and 'soothed them with soft words'.[3]

Desideri travelled throughout Tibet until he was ordered back to Rome in 1727. There, he set about compiling a study of the country's religion, history, geography and culture, but he died before he could publish his *Historical Sketch of Tibet*. The manuscript was lost after his death and a copy of it did not reappear until 1875, long after it could have been useful to the British.

By the time of Desideri's death, Britain had become the dominant colonial nation in India, and from this point on exploration of the Himalayan region was an almost exclusively British affair. Most notable among the travellers attracted to the region was the eccentric Dr William Moorcroft, who is credited with being the father of modern exploration of the Himalayas. He remains an obscure individual, preferring to write more of his achievements than of himself. But there is no doubting his energy and enthusiasm, nor the obstinate, eccentric and controversial side of his character. He has been called a spy, a genius, an adventurer and a horse dealer. These descriptions all have a grain of truth about them, but essentially Moorcroft was a new breed of traveller for whom the main pleasure was the journey itself. As such, he embodied the enterprising spirit of nineteenth-century British explorers who became the heroes for George Mallory's generation.

As a young man in the 1790s Moorcroft began to study medicine at the Liverpool Infirmary, but a local outbreak of cattle plague convinced him that veterinary surgery was the profession of the future, and he moved to Paris to study. He returned as the first qualified vet in Britain, set up a practice in London and quickly became very successful and wealthy. He also invented a machine to mass-produce horseshoes, but the enterprise was a total disaster and he lost his fortune.

Soon afterwards he became a vet for the British East India Company, charged with the task of improving the company's horse stock in India. Moorcroft tackled the work with an enthusiasm that took his employers by surprise. Within a short time, and on the flimsiest of excuses, he set off to central Asia, claiming that he needed to find horses to improve the breeding stock.

He made the first of his two great journeys in 1812 in the company of an Anglo-Indian cartographer called Hyder Young Hearsey. They devised a plan to 'penetrate into Tartary', but Moorcroft informed his employers that he was simply making a 'journey into the hills' in search of 'new blood from the Hill strains' and 'goats bred for the sake of their hair'.[4] The two men set off disguised as Hindu pilgrims called Mayapori and Haragiri, accompanied by 50 servants and two Indian surveyors. One of the surveyors was required to measure the distance they travelled by taking double strides measuring exactly 4 feet. As a mapmaker, Hearsey also took with him a compass and thermometer, which was used to measure the temperature of boiling water to estimate altitude. (The temperature at which water boils falls with increasing height, and this phenomenon can be used as a rough estimate of altitude.)

The road to Tibet was not easy. To enter the country the team had to trek through the Niti Pass in Garwhal (just to the west of the present-day frontier of Nepal). On approaching the pass, Moorcroft sent a gift on to the Tibetan governor at Daba. When he arrived at the border he found that his offering had been returned, accompanied by a detachment of troops sent to prevent the party from entering the country.

Moorcroft was undeterred and through a combination of cunning and good fortune the party eventually gained access to Tibet. When the East India Company discovered Moorcroft's true destination they were not entirely convinced he was looking for good breeding stock, as the only horses available in Tibet were wild *kiangs* which were quite unsuitable for breeding. He partly redeemed himself by returning with 50 goats, whose wool created quite a profitable shawl industry for the company – but by now he had acquired a reputation for 'running over the country in quest of phantoms'.[5]

As soon as the irrepressible Moorcroft returned home, he announced his plans to travel to the legendary city of Bokhara in western Turkestan. It took him seven years of badgering to persuade the company to let him make the journey, by which time he was 55 years old. Even Moorcroft realized this would be his last great adventure. He did indeed reach the fabled city of Bokhara, but he insisted on continuing his journey into central Asia, with disastrous consequences.

Within weeks Moorcroft and his two English companions were dead. Some say they were poisoned by Russian agents, others that they were robbed and shot. Whatever the cause, it was a tragic end to a colourful and enterprising Englishman who travelled widely and contributed so much to the understanding of the region. Perhaps his most appropriate epitaph comes from a letter he sent from Turkestan shortly before his death: 'The expedition is full of hazard but *le jeu vaut bien la chandelle* [the game is well worth the candle].'[6]

The British were not alone in their fascination for the Himalayas. In 1854 three Bavarian brothers – Adolf, Robert and Hermann Schlagintweit – went to work for the British East India Company on the recommendation of Baron Humboldt (arguably the greatest traveller of his day) and backed by the King of Prussia. Their arrival caused much dismay to those working on the Grand Trigonometrical Survey of India. After all, the British had hundreds of surveyors scattered throughout the country. What were three Germans doing wandering around the sensitive northern frontier?

When the Schlagintweit brothers arrived in Bombay, the editor of the *Bombay Times* noted that they were well off for equipment, but he questioned whether they knew how to use it properly. He also remarked that they smoked so heavily that he doubted they would ever reach Calcutta alive. Eventually, however, they did, and they went on to travel widely throughout the Himalayas.

In 1855 Adolf and Robert Schlagintweit travelled up into the Johar Valley, where they recruited Mani Singh Rawat and his two younger cousins, Dolpa and Nain. These three Bhotian hillmen accompanied the Schlagintweits north to Gartok, and eventually on to Ladakh, but they were later to play a much greater role in the exploration of Tibet under the British.

The German brothers successfully crossed the Karakoram Pass and explored the Kun Lun Mountains to the north of the Tibetan high plateau. They were the first to traverse the entire mountain range between India and Turkestan and the first to recognize that the Karakorams and Kun Lun were separate mountain systems. The following year, 1857, Adolf Schlagintweit failed to return from an expedition in the north. He had blundered into a civil war and was executed just outside Kashgar.

In 1861 the two surviving brothers offered to dedicate their work to the Royal Geographical Society, but they were turned down on the grounds that the society had neither commissioned nor encouraged them. Clearly, the British were suspicious and resentful of these 'outsiders', which could be why they have never been given the full credit they deserve. The detailed reports of their travels have never been translated into English, so their achievements will probably remain in the relatively obscure recesses of history.

The middle of the nineteenth century saw the consolidation of British rule in India and increasing tension with Tsarist Russia (the British called this conflict the Great Game and a Russian minister once referred to it as 'this tournament of shadows'). Consequently, a detailed geographical knowledge of the region to the north of India was essential if the British were to thwart Russia's expansionist plans. By now, however, Tibet had firmly closed her borders to foreigners. To get round this restriction, the British decided to train local people and send them on covert missions into the country.

Captain Thomas G. Montgomerie, a surveyor in the Great Trigonometrical Survey of India, was given the task of training a group of agents to infiltrate Tibet. His first problem was picking the right people – presumably an immutable problem in establishing *any* spy network – and he scoured the local bazaars for natives who were willing to volunteer for this uncertain (and dangerous) task. His initiative brought poor results: 'Any number of men were willing to volunteer for such a service, and if their own accounts are to be believed, they are all well fitted for the task. But a very little enquiry, however, reduces the number of likely men nearly to zero; many cannot write, others are too old, and have no ideas beyond those of trade, and nearly everyone has special ideas as to what pay and rewards they are to get, and generally have special stipulations to make; all, however, apparently thinking nothing of the risks and exposure involved.'[7]

Chastened, Montgomerie adopted a different approach and selected candidates recommended to him from the Indian Education Service. Only two recruits survived the two years of rigorous training; they were the cousins Nain Singh and Mani Singh, the very men who had travelled with the Schlagintweits several years previously. Nain Singh was a young schoolmaster from one of the high valleys in the Himalayas – a *pandit*, or educated man: this word became corrupted by the British to 'pundit', a generic term used to describe all the subsequent recruits. The men were paid the modest salary of 16 rupees a month, rising in due course to 20 rupees.

Rudyard Kipling has told tales of the pundits and their exploits many times, most famously in *Kim*, where the pundits are involved in the political struggle between the British Raj and Tsarist Russia. In fact the pundits have never really been granted full credit for their achievements during that confrontation. This is partly because of the covert nature of their work, but also because their exploits have been considered 'unpatriotic' in post-independence India. Yet it was through the hardships and risks they endured in Tibet that the rest of the world came to realize the full extent and diversity of the country.

Disguise, secrecy and political subterfuge were all part of the pundit's training. This included instruction in surveying techniques and the use of a compass, and they were also drilled to take 2000 paces to the mile, each stride measuring exactly 80 centimetres (31.5 inches). To keep count of their paces, the pundits carried a special 'rosary' containing 100 beads. In this way, the British measured vast tracts of the Himalayas.

The pundits learnt how to memorize information by constant repetition as they walked their route, chanting aloud as the Tibetans chant their prayers. They were taught how to hide their notes and measurements in the form of written prayers concealed inside specially adapted Buddhist prayer-wheels, which they carried with them constantly.

No proper spy network would be complete without code names. Nain Singh was known as the Chief Pundit or 'No. 1'. His cousin Mani Singh was 'the Patwar' or 'G–M'. When Nain Singh's second cousin, Kalian Singh, later joined the group, he became known as 'Third Pundit' or 'G–K'.

On their first mission in 1865, Nain and Mani Singh had orders to proceed through Nepal into Tibet and continue to the capital, Lhasa, whose location was still a matter of speculation. Despite the years of training and preparation things did not go smoothly. The pundits tried to enter Tibet disguised as Bisahari horse-dealers from the Punjab. But the border guards had been alerted and stopped them, pointing out that it was the wrong time of year for horse-trading, and that they were also in the wrong place.

Mani Singh gave up and returned home, but later entered Tibet by another route. Nain, however, was made of sterner stuff and persevered with the mission, successfully entering Tibet disguised as a Ladakhi trader. Although robbed of most of his money he managed to keep his all-important surveying tools.

Joining a caravan of Ladakhi traders, this time disguised as a pilgrim, Nain's apparent devotion to religious rituals proved a cover for his other activities: his fellow travellers watched him recite his 'prayers' as he walked by day, and regarded his eccentric night-time rituals with bewildered tolerance. When the party travelled by boat, they thought nothing of their pilgrim's insistence on striding along the river bank instead, rosary in hand and counting the beads as they slipped through his fingers.

Nain Singh arrived in Lhasa in January 1866. He hired a couple of rooms which became his secret observatory. He poured mercury into a beggar's bowl and used its level, reflective surface as an artificial horizon so that he could take sextant readings from his window. From his measurements he was able to establish the precise location of the city. He also measured the temperature of boiling water and thus calculated the altitude of the city to be 3420 metres (11,220 feet) above sea level – an estimate that was only out by 3.5 per cent.

The precarious nature of his existence in Lhasa was brought home to him when he witnessed the public beheading of a Chinese man who had arrived in the city without permission. On 21 April 1866 he left the city and joined another Ladakhi caravan, heading west along the great River Tsangpo. Ever conscientious he furtively noted distances and bearings and traced the course of the river for more than 800 kilometres (500 miles).

Nain Singh arrived back at the survey headquarters in Dehra Dun at the end of October, having been away for 21 months. He had surveyed 2000 kilometres (1250 miles) of trading routes between Nepal and Lhasa, made many important cartographic measurements and returned with vivid and lucid descriptions of Tibet, particularly its capital, Lhasa. After many other successful missions, Nain Singh was awarded the Royal Geographical Society's gold medal as the explorer who 'has added a greater amount of positive knowledge to the map of Asia than any individual of our time'.

Over the next 20 years more pundits were trained for more covert missions into the north, with varying degrees of success. Hari Ram, the legendary M–H, set off from Darjeeling and crossed into Nepal. He reached Shigatse (Xigazê) in southern Tibet and explored the high mountain massifs around Everest. He also made his way to Lhasa, returning with descriptions and data on nearly 48,000 square kilometres (19,200 square miles) of previously unknown territory.

For absolute devotion to duty, nothing can eclipse the story of Kintup or K–P, who was sent north into Tibet to discover whether the great Tsangpo River flowed into the Brahmaputra. He and his companion were disguised as a manservant and Mongolian lama respectively. They were instructed to head north to the Tsangpo, then travel as far east as possible, documenting the region as they went. They were told to then prepare 500 specially marked logs, which would be tossed into the Tsangpo at the rate of 50 a day for 10 consecutive days. Observers positioned on the Brahmaputra would watch out for the logs, and their appearance would prove beyond doubt that the two great rivers were confluent.

It was a clever idea, but as with many of the pundit forays into Tibet, it became much more complicated than anyone could possibly have imagined. The Mongolian lama proved to be anything but godly and he frittered away the survey's funds on women and alcohol long before they reached the end of the mission. The holy man wasted four months in just one village, where Kintup had to use his own funds to buy his 'master' out of an entanglement with another man's wife.

They arrived later than scheduled at the Tsangpo after seven months' trekking through Tibet, but they did manage to get as far as Gyala and travelled a short distance into the magnificent gorge cut by the great river. Kintup faithfully recorded all his observations, including a magnificent waterfall 45 metres (150 feet) high. However, the novelty of working covertly for the Survey of India seems to have worn off for the lama, and he decided to return home to Mongolia – but not before secretly selling Kintup as a slave to a local headman.

Kintup had no option but to work in servitude, but after several months he managed to escape and loyally headed back to the Tsangpo to complete his mission. Unfortunately the headman sent a party after him with orders to bring him back to the village. Kintup was eventually caught, close to the monastery of Marpung, where he flung himself on the mercy of the abbot and explained how he had been betrayed by the lama and sold into slavery. The abbot took pity on the pundit and agreed to buy him from the headman for 50 rupees, but only on condition that Kintup worked off his debt.

Even though Kintup was still in bondage, he was determined to complete his mission. Several months passed before he asked his abbot for leave of absence to make a pilgrimage. Greatly impressed with his apparent devotion, the abbot agreed and Kintup was able to return secretly to the Tsangpo. Here he prepared his 500 logs, which he cut exactly 30 centimetres (1 foot) long, according to his instructions. He attached a special tag to each log, which, despite his ordeal, he had still managed to retain. Unfortunately he was now too late to meet his pre-arranged deadline, so there was no point in releasing the logs without first getting word back to headquarters to inform them of the delay. So Kintup carefully hid his consignment in a cave and returned to the monastery to continue his servitude.

A few more months passed and Kintup asked if he could make a second pilgrimage, and the abbot once more agreed. This time Kintup headed for Lhasa, where he sought out a trader he knew from Sikkim. Despite his natural aptitude as a spy, Kintup was uneducated and illiterate, so he asked his friend to write a letter on his behalf to the head of the survey back in Dehra Dun: 'Sir, The Lama who was sent with me sold me to a village headman as a slave and himself fled away with Government instruments that were in his charge. On account of this the journey proved a bad one. However, I, Kintup have prepared five hundred logs according to the order of Captain Harman, and am prepared to throw fifty a day into the Tsangpo from Bipung in Pemako from the fifth to the fifteenth of the tenth Tibetan month of the year called *Chuluk*....'[8]

The wife of his Sikkimese friend took the letter with her to Darjeeling, and Kintup returned to the monastery once again. When nine months had passed and the time for releasing the logs was close, Kintup asked the abbot if he could go on yet another pilgrimage. The abbot was so impressed at this extraordinary devotion that he granted his servant his freedom. In no time, Kintup was off across the mountains to the Tsangpo. On the appointed date he released 50 logs, and did the same thing for the next nine days. He then made his way back to the survey headquarters having been away for over four years.

Sadly, there was no hero's welcome waiting for Kintup on his return. First, he heard news that his mother had died heartbroken during his absence, thinking that her son had perished in Tibet. Next, he discovered that his letter had not reached its intended recipient at Dehra Dun, so his logs had floated down the Brahmaputra unannounced and unnoticed. Then he learned that the course of the Tsangpo had been obtained by other means, so his long journey and four years of torment had been in vain.

The final indignity, however, was that nobody at the survey headquarters believed his amazing story. His 'dogged obstinacy' was noted with approval, but his report was largely regarded as a figment of his imagination. With this astonishing rebuff, Kintup sank into obscurity and poverty, apparently scraping a living as a tailor in the backstreets of Darjeeling, his loyalty unrecognized and unrewarded.

Nearly 30 years later, a British frontier officer travelling in the region surveyed by Kintup was struck by the remarkable accuracy of his official report. Colonel Eric Bailey became convinced that Kintup must have been telling the truth, so he returned to Dehra Dun and lobbied hard for a pension for the pundit. The application was refused, but Kintup was awarded a lump sum of 1000 rupees. Shortly afterwards, he died, still in obscurity but at least with the satisfaction that he had been vindicated.

During the 1880s a new breed of Himalayan visitor came on the scene – the true predecessors of Mallory and Irvine. The Himalayan climber had arrived. Mountaineering as a sport emerged during the middle of the nineteenth century, when British, French and German climbers, with their predominantly Swiss guides, began to climb the more serious and challenging routes in the Alps. The summit of the Matterhorn was reached in 1865, and within a few years all the other main Alpine summits had been climbed. European climbers then began to look further afield for new and tougher challenges – the Rockies and Andes in the Americas, the Caucasus, the high African peaks and, inevitably, the vast ranges of the Himalayas.

Surprisingly, it was a Hungarian rather than a Briton who made the first visit to the Himalayas with the express intention of climbing. Unfortunately Maurice von Déchy was taken ill and achieved very little. He was followed in 1882 by the British climber W.W. Graham, accompanied by a number of Swiss guides. They intended to climb in the Kangchenjunga region, but Graham's account of his activities is so full of discrepancies that they are still a source of dispute today. The great soldier-explorer Francis Younghusband wrote: 'I had spoken [in 1885] with an officer of the Survey of India about Graham's reported ascent to about 24,000 feet on Kabru, and he has assured me that Graham must have mistaken his peak, for no man could go so high: 22,000 was the limit ... The highest peak of the Himalaya must for ever lie outside the range of human capacity.'[9]

In 1892, William Martin Conway pushed into the heart of the Karakorams with a small climbing party and became the first European to cross the mountain range into China. By profession Conway was an art critic, but his burning ambition was to make a name for himself as an explorer. He became one of the great climbing pioneers of his age, and arguably the greatest mountaineer of his day. Having decided that K2 was beyond his ability, he tackled Pioneer Peak, which at 6890 metres (22,600 feet) still set a new height record for a climber.

News of this triumph stimulated a great deal of interest back in London and marked the beginning of a new epoch in climbing aspirations. Inevitably, there was speculation about whether Everest itself could be climbed. One man who always maintained that it could was Clinton Dent, who wrote as early as 1885: 'I do not for a moment say that it would be wise to ascend

Top: George and Ruth Mallory during the early years of their marriage. Ruth's aunt called her 'a soul of the most crystal wisdom, simplicity and goodness'.

Above: Andrew Irvine was only 22 years old when he went to Everest – 12 years younger than the average age of the expedition members.

Right: Captain John Noel in 1913, in the disguise he adopted on his covert journey into Tibet.

Above: Climbers coming down the North Col in 1922, the year that seven sherpas were killed in an avalanche on 7 June.

Below: Sir George Everest, supervising the construction of a survey station in India, dated 1834. At the time, he was Superintendent of the Grand Trigonometrical Survey of India.

Above: George Finch (standing right) gave frequent demonstrations in the use of the oxygen apparatus during the 1922 expedition.

Right: *En route* to Everest. It took the climbers over a month to walk from Darjeeling to the Rongbuk Valley, and every night they had to pitch a new camp.

Sir George Everest (1790–1866) never
lived to see the mountain which now
bears his name.

Dr A.M. Kellas was a leading authority on
high-altitude physiology, but died in Tibet
in 1921 before reaching Everest.

Geoffrey Winthrop Young was a very
experienced alpine climber and became
George Mallory's friend and mentor.

Noel E. Odell was the last person to see
Mallory and Irvine alive, at 12.50 p.m. on
8 June 1924.

Arthur R. Hinks was joint secretary to the Everest Committee and a major influence throughout the 1920s and 30s.

Edward F. Norton was a very popular choice as leader of the 1924 Mount Everest Expedition.

John Percy Farrar was a leading British climber in his day and in his later life became president of the Alpine Club.

Howard Somervell was a doctor by training and a leading climber on the 1922 and 1924 expeditions.

Above: The 1924 expedition; left to right: Irvine, Mallory, Norton, Odell, MacDonald; (front row) Shebbeare, G. Bruce, Somervell, Beetham.

Below: Base Camp in 1922 and 1924 was situated behind a moraine ridge, which gave some protection from the incessant wind. The North Face is in the background, 20 kilometres (12 miles) to the south. John Noel (foreground) was in charge of photography and filming on both expeditions.

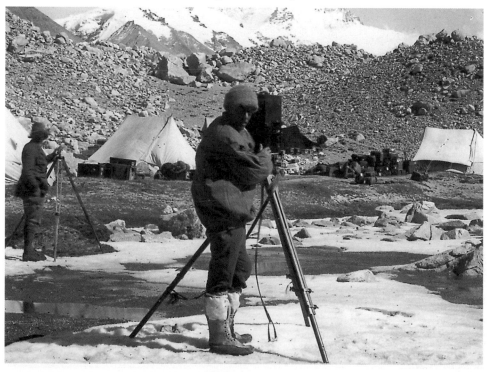

Above: Andrew Irvine was an engineering student from Merton College, Oxford, and took responsibility for maintaining the oxygen equipment in 1924.

Below: The North East Ridge photographed in 1924. Odell estimated that he saw Mallory and Irvine at 8600 metres (28,230 feet), which suggests they were between the First and Second Steps. However, the original notation suggests they were between the Second and Third Steps, or approximately 8660 metres (28,400 feet).

George Mallory and Edward Norton, photographed by Howard Somervell in 1922, climbing at an altitude of just under 8200 metres (26,900 feet). All three were climbing without supplementary oxygen.

Mount Everest, but I believe most firmly that it is humanly possible to do so; and, further, I feel sure that even in our own time, perhaps, the truth of these views will receive material corroboration.'[10]

Conway's expedition included a young lieutenant in the 5th Gurkhas, the Honourable Charles Granville Bruce. Affectionately known as Charlie or Bruiser to his friends, he was a great bear of a man, very strong, bawdy and adventurous. According to mess-room legend, he once simultaneously threw three Gurkhas out of a wrestling ring.

Bruce was involved in numerous frontier campaigns in India, which led to his developing an interest in mountaineering. Conway's 1892 campaign in the Karakorams was Bruce's first experience of a proper climbing expedition and, despite falling ill with malaria, he threw all his energies into the project. Bruce was already beginning to think about Everest.

In 1893 there was a chance meeting between Bruce and Francis Young-husband in Chitral, a British garrison town on the North-West Frontier. Although only 30 years old, Younghusband had already made a name for himself with some remarkable journeys in Asia, including one across the Gobi Desert and another across the formidable Mustagh Pass. In Chitral the two men climbed together and Bruce proposed that he and Younghusband should organize an expedition to Everest. Nothing came of their plans immediately, as the need to keep order on the Indian border took prece-dence, but the seed of an idea had germinated and their ambitious plans for Everest were never forgotten.

Meanwhile, the newly appointed Viceroy of India, Lord Curzon, began to wonder privately about the feasibility of an expedition to Everest. George Curzon was not a mountaineer, but he was an experienced traveller. He had met and befriended Younghusband in Chitral, and he also raised the idea of an expedition to Everest with William Douglas Freshfield, then president of both the Alpine Club and the Royal Geographical Society. Curzon later made a formal request to the Nepalese during an official visit to the country, but nothing came of the idea as global politics began to preoccupy him.

Curzon became obsessed with the perceived threat to Tibet from Tsarist Russia, and the Great Game was beginning to be played with an even greater intensity. Curzon was convinced that the Russians were making preparations to invade the Tibetan high plateau from the north, so he raised a small army under the leadership of Colonel Younghusband. Tibet was still under the rule of the Chinese, who were finding it difficult to govern the country effectively. The intervention by the British – initially a diplomatic mission to secure understandings on frontier and trade relations – soon turned into a military campaign. Tibetan resistance to the British was met with force, and the Dalai Lama fled from Lhasa to Mongolia.

The British settled the dispute with the Tibetans within a year by making an agreement that excluded the Chinese. But by 1906 the Chinese had negotiated a new treaty with Britain and sought direct control of Tibet using force. The Dalai Lama again fled the country, this time seeking refuge in India. The débâcle turned Tibetan indifference into enmity against their eastern neighbours, and the Chinese were eventually expelled from Tibet. The country declared itself independent and effectively functioned as an autonomous nation until China 'liberated' the country in 1951.

For Britain the outcome could not have been better. Russian territorial ambitions were stopped at the Tibetan border and the Chinese no longer had influence in the country. The British settled their differences with Tibet and now had a strong diplomatic presence in Lhasa. The stage was set for Curzon to realize his dream of mounting an expedition to Everest.

Others too were harbouring similar aspirations. During Younghusband's march on Lhasa in 1903, a young officer by the name of J. Claude White took the first photograph of Everest in which the East Face could be clearly seen. A year later, Cecil Rawling, another young army officer, was leading a small detachment of troops at Gartok in western Tibet and he reported seeing the North Face and the North Ridge of Everest from a distance of about 110 kilometres (70 miles). He was spellbound by what he saw and from then on harboured secret ambitions to climb the mountain.

Once the political situation in Tibet had settled down, Curzon wrote to Freshfield in his capacity as President of the Royal Geographical Society: 'I want to bring up again a question which I think I mentioned to you while in India. It has always seemed to me a reproach that with the second highest mountain in the world [K2] for the most part in British territory and with the highest mountain in a neighbouring and friendly state, we, the mountaineers and pioneers par excellence of the universe, make no sustained and scientific attempt to climb to the top of either of them ... Would you care to interest yourself at all in such an expedition? It occurs to me that it might be done by the Alpine Club and the RGS in combination ...'[11]

Curzon considered his plan carefully and outlined how they could use local Sherpas and where the camps would be positioned for the summit attempt: 'Camps would be instituted and gradually pushed forward until one day the advance camp would be placed on a spot from which a dash could be made for the summit.'[12] He estimated the cost of the venture at £5000–£6000 and suggested that the government of India could contribute half.

The Alpine Club considered the proposal and voted the sum of £100 to support the venture – not quite what Curzon had in mind. However, when the Viceroy's plan became more widely known, a wealthy member of the Alpine Club, A.L. Mumm, offered to fund an expedition from his own finances to mark the fiftieth anniversary of the AC. But this generous offer came too late as, once again, politics intervened.

Curzon resigned as Viceroy of India in 1905, but his successor, Lord Minto (himself a member of the Alpine Club), was supportive of his expedition. However, John Morley, the new British Secretary of State for India, blocked the plans on diplomatic grounds. Morley was an elderly, dry, austere man who was privately referred to by his Cabinet colleagues as 'Aunt Priscilla'. He wholeheartedly disapproved of Curzon's policy in Tibet, especially Younghusband's march on Lhasa, and was determined to use his position to prevent any further incursions into the territory. His justification was that an expedition to Everest would contravene the new Anglo-Russian treaty.

Morley's high-handed decision caused a furore in London. Sir George Goldie, then president of the RGS, resorted to publishing the correspondence in *The Times* and wrote acrimoniously: 'I leave it to others to comment on the regrettable interposition by a Liberal Government of a Himalayan barrier to the advance of knowledge in this direction.'[13] Not for the first time did the hurdle of politics prove to be as insurmountable as the mountain itself.

Turning their sights away from Everest, Mumm's team (which now included Charlie Bruce and Tom Longstaff) focused its attention on Garhwal instead, where there were no problems over access. The team made a successful ascent of Trisul, and in doing so set a new altitude record of 7120 metres (23,360 feet), which remained unbroken for the next 21 years.

One small Everest hurdle was crossed in 1907 when the Nepalese allowed Naatha Singh, who was working for the Survey of India, access to Dudh Kosi. He mapped the peaks on his way into the region and was the first visitor to the valley which years later became the southern gateway to Everest. He even managed to travel beyond Lobuche, and mapped the end of the Khumbu glacier.

In 1913, however, a young officer serving with the East Yorkshire regiment stationed in Calcutta took up the flagging Everest initiative. Every summer Lieutenant John Noel's regiment would withdraw from the stifling plains of northern India, and he used this opportunity to take off into the mountains with local Sherpas to investigate the trails and passes leading into Tibet. Noel set off from Gartok along the Tista River towards the Serpo La. He expected that the pass would be guarded, so he turned west into the lesser-known region of Lhonak and crossed into Tibet by a remote pass called Chorten Nyima La, at an altitude of 5700 metres (18,700 feet). Fortunately the Tibetan border guards did not watch this pass and he entered Tibet successfully, hoping to find a high-level route to the eastern flanks of Everest.

In the best traditions of earlier explorers, he dyed his hair and darkened his skin to disguise himself as an Indian: 'To defeat observation I intended to avoid the villages and settled parts generally, to carry our food, and to keep to those more desolate stretches where only an occasional shepherd was to be seen. My men were not startlingly different from the Tibetans, and if I darkened my skin and my hair I could pass, not as a native – the colour and shape of my eyes would prevent that – but as a Mohammedan from India. A Moslem would be a stranger and suspect in Tibet, but not as glaringly so as a white man.'[14]

Crossing the dry, sun-scorched Tibetan plateau, Noel found that his map was hopelessly inaccurate and that an extra mountain range blocked his way. Despite the hardships and disappointment, he pressed on and climbed the Langu La. Here he could see the Himalayas stretching out for miles before him: 'Presently, while watching the panorama, the shifting clouds revealed other high mountain masses in the distance; and directly over the crest of Taringban appeared a sharp spire peak. This, through its magnetic bearing by my compass, proved itself to be none other than Mount Everest. A thousand feet of the summit was visible.'[15]

Noel was only about 100 kilometres (60 miles) from Everest, but other mountains blocked a direct approach. His small party tried to skirt the obstacles, but they were stopped by Tibetan soldiers and ordered to leave the country. They were lucky to get away with their lives: 'There was nothing to be done but to turn our backs on the approaches to Everest ... Within forty miles, and nearer at that time than any white man had been! I leave you to imagine my chagrin and disappointment.'[16]

As 1914 approached, political events again intervened in the story of Everest. World War I was to decimate a generation of young men, and it would be many years before eyes looked up once again to the distant summit of the mountain.

CHAPTER FIVE

'An Adventurous Aspect Altogether'

'It has come to appear now, with the help of
Ruth's enthusiasm, rather as the opportunity of a
lifetime ... The future bears rather an
adventurous aspect altogether.'

George Mallory to his sister Avie, 1921

S hortly after George Mallory was demobilized from the British Army
in France, the Royal Geographical Society and the Alpine Club
rekindled the flame of an Everest campaign at a special meeting in
March 1919. Tragically, the pool of young and talented climbers from which
an expedition could be mounted was much smaller than before the war, but
there were some hopeful developments. Both China and Russia were in the
midst of political revolutions and had too many internal problems to worry
about a British climbing expedition travelling through Tibet. The Chinese
had withdrawn their garrison from Lhasa and the relationship between the
British and Tibetan governments was good.

John Noel was invited to talk at the RGS, and his timely presentation was
intended to start the campaign for an assault on the mountain with a rallying
call: 'Now that the poles have been reached,' he declared, 'it is generally felt
that the next and equally important task is the exploration and mapping of
Mount Everest.'[1] Everest was often referred to as the 'third pole' and

enthusiasm for the venture began to build.

An expedition committee was set up comprising members from both the RGS and the AC, but it was an uneasy partnership. The geographers wanted to survey the region; the mountaineers wanted to climb the mountain. Despite their differences, the committee agreed a list of 11 resolutions which defined the purpose of their initiative. Resolution 1 stated: 'That the principal object of the expedition should be the ascent of Mount Everest, to which all preliminary reconnaissance should be directed.'

Resolution 9 made it clear that no public announcement should be made until the Indian government had given its consent, but despite this several accounts of a forthright speech that Younghusband made about climbing Everest appeared in the newspapers the very next day. He had spoken openly to the meeting about what the endeavour would and would not achieve and *The Times* reported: 'Although there was no more use in climbing Everest than kicking a football about, or dancing, [Younghusband] believed the accomplishment would do a great deal of good.'[2]

The *Observer* focused on the financial aspect and claimed to quote Young-husband's own words 'Whilst, however, climbing Mount Everest will not put a pound into anyone's pocket, it will take a good many pounds out, the accomplishment of such a feat will elevate the human spirit and will give man, especially us geographers, a feeling that we really are getting the upper hand on Earth, and that we are acquiring a true mastery of our surroundings. … If man stands on Earth's highest summit, he will have an increased pride and confidence in himself in the struggle for ascendancy over matter. This is the incalculable good which the ascent of Mount Everest will confer.'[3] Other papers were openly hostile, claiming further loss of the Earth's mystery would 'queer the pitch for posterity'.[4]

Despite the poor press coverage, the committee set about its tasks with enthusiasm. Francis Younghusband, Charlie Bruce, Charles Howard-Bury and Percy Farrar met at the India Office in London on 23 June 1920 to discuss the matter in detail. Just two days later, Howard-Bury left for India to continue the negotiations over there.

Lieutenant-Colonel Howard-Bury of the 60th Rifles was not a member of the Alpine Club, nor was he a climber, but he had travelled in the

Karakorams and had been censured by Curzon for making a secret journey into Tibet in 1905. Consequently, his experiences in the Himalayas and his political and social connections made him a useful mediator. He spent nearly six months in India (at his own expense), cajoling and persuading various British officials, and his patience was eventually rewarded when he obtained the Tibetan government's consent for the proposed expedition. In London the Everest Committee was jubilant and made a public announcement on 10 January 1921. This time the newspapers were much more positive.

The RGS and AC lost no time in setting up a special expedition committee and the day-to-day administrative duties fell to Arthur Hinks, reputedly a cantankerous and boorish member of the RGS, who was to dominate the Everest Committee for the next 20 years. Hinks was a skilled mathematician, a cartographer and a leading authority on map projections, but he was sadly lacking in diplomacy, was often contemptuous of others, and was frequently rash and outspoken. Nor did he know much about mountaineering or travelling in remote regions, and he frequently clashed with the expedition members about the difficulties and dangers of being out in the field. Noel Odell once noted that he '... always rubbed people up the wrong way' and that 'He considered his word should be taken as gospel – and sometimes it simply wasn't gospel'.[5]

Hinks's other weakness was that he had an intrinsic dislike of publicity. This was a serious problem for the Everest Committee, which relied on self-promotion for much of its funding. His other responsibilities included cataloguing pictures from the expedition, negotiating with publishers and dealing with enquiries from the public. Few considered him suitable for the job.

Meanwhile, the search began to find the best team for the expedition. It was already decided that the project would be spread across two years, with a reconnaissance in 1921 followed by a proper attempt on the mountain in 1922. Despite almost universal support for Charlie Bruce to lead the expedition, he was unable to do so, having just taken up another appointment.

Instead, the committee invited Howard-Bury to lead the reconnaissance. Despite his lack of experience as a mountaineer he had other qualities in his favour, not least his ability to organize men. Being independently wealthy, he was also prepared to pay his own expenses, which came in particularly useful when the cashier employed by the committee absconded with £717 of the expedition's funds.

The Everest Committee had estimated that the joint cost of the 1921 and 1922 expeditions would eventually be about £10,000, with about one third allocated to the reconnaissance. The money was raised through private donations: over £3000 came from the Alpine Club (more than the RGS managed to raise, despite having many more members) and individual donations came from many other quarters including King George V, who gave £100, the Prince of Wales (£50) and the Viceroy of India (750 rupees).

Howard-Bury was formally appointed expedition leader on 24 January 1921, and the committee issued the following statement: 'The main object this year is reconnaissance. This does not debar the mountain party from climbing as high as possible on a favourable route, but attempts on a particular route must not be prolonged to hinder the completion of the reconnaissance.'[6] It was a formidable task to organize such a large expedition within just a few months, especially as it involved travelling for several weeks across the cold and arid Tibetan plateau to a region hitherto unexplored by Europeans.

Other members of the team included Henry Morshead and Edward Wheeler, both professional surveyors and experienced mountaineers. The Geological Survey of India also added Dr A.M. Heron, whose geological activities were to upset the Tibetan authorities so much that he was banned from the expedition the following year.

Top of Farrar's shortlist for the climbing team were George Finch and George Mallory. 'I have two,' declared Farrar confidently, 'who will get to the top, I'll guarantee.'[7] Finch, along with his brother Max, was an experienced Alpine climber with a fine record, but he was not a universally popular choice among the British climbing establishment: he was neither a member of the Alpine Club, nor had he been to a public school or university in Britain. Finch was born in Australia but spent most of his life living in Europe, and he spoke better German than he did English. People thought he was rakish, outspoken, uncompromising and overly self-confident – in other words, he was not considered a gentleman.

By contrast, Mallory fulfilled all of the requirements expected by the conservative members of the Alpine Club. Although he was not as accomplished or experienced as Finch, he was nevertheless a fine rock climber at the peak of his abilities. He had also assiduously cultivated his friends and acquaintances ever since he had been at Magdalene, and he was a longstanding member of the Alpine Club.

When Mallory received Farrar's invitation from the Alpine Club to participate in the Everest reconnaissance, he was, perhaps surprisingly, torn over the decision. He wrote to his friend David Pye: 'I am faced with a problem which throws all others into the background – Everest?'[8] Mallory had become increasingly frustrated with the limitations of teaching at Charterhouse and had already decided to leave, but he had a wife and three young children to support. How could he risk what he held most dear for the sake of adventure?

It was his old friend Geoffrey Winthrop Young who eventually persuaded Mallory to take part, claiming that it would be not only an exciting adventure, but a valuable experience that could also bring him celebrity status. This would stand him in good stead should he later decide to take up a writing career. It must have been a very persuasive speech because it took Young only 20 minutes to convince both George *and* Ruth that it was the right decision.

In a letter to his sister Avie, Mallory wrote: 'I hope it won't appear to you a merely fantastic performance. I was inclined to regard it as such when the idea was first mooted a few weeks ago, but it has come to appear now, with the help of Ruth's enthusiasm, rather as the opportunity of a lifetime.... . The future bears rather an adventurous aspect altogether ...'[9]

On 9 February 1921 the Everest Committee invited Mallory to luncheon in Mayfair. Colonel Farrar was there, together with Sir Francis Young-husband and the Scottish mountaineer, Harold Raeburn, who had been appointed climbing leader despite being 56. Mallory had already decided to accept their invitation to join the expedition, but he sat patiently and heard out Younghusband's eloquent and persuasive case for him to join the team. When the president of the RGS finally offered the young climber the position, Mallory's response took Younghusband by surprise: 'But when the invitation was made he accepted it without visible emotion. He had the self-confidence of assured position as a climber. He had neither exaggerated modesty nor pushful self-assertiveness.'[10]

Despite his deadpan response at the luncheon, Mallory was thrilled at the prospect. The following day he wrote to Geoffrey Young: 'I lunched with Farrar yesterday to meet Raeburn and Younghusband, and the old boy made me a formal offer which I accepted. It seems rather a momentous step altogether, with a new job to find when I come back, but it will not be a bad thing to give up the settled ease of this present life ... I expect I shall have no cause to regret your persuasions in the cause of Everest; at present I'm highly elated at the prospect and so is Ruth: thank you for that.'[11]

It was a decision that led to his untimely death and ultimately to his immortality as the man who sacrificed all for Everest.

From the very start, the 1921 reconnaissance was fraught with personal conflict between the different team members. Throughout the expedition Raeburn suffered from chronic ill-health and gastric trouble and this made him irritable and short-tempered. Mallory, who was usually tolerant of others, wrote to his wife: 'I saw and still see Raeburn as a great difficulty ... He is evidently touchy about his position as leader of the Alpine party and wants to be treated with proper respect. And he is dreadfully dictatorial about matters of fact, and often wrong ... His total lack of *calm* and sense of humour at the same time is most unfortunate.'[12]

Nor did Howard-Bury have any time for the irascible Scot. On one occasion, Raeburn forgot to collect the expedition mail and Howard-Bury wrote back to Hinks in London: 'Can you imagine anyone being such a fool?'[13] On another occasion he confided in Hinks: 'Raeburn has become old and a great responsibility ... he is [also] very obstinate.'[14] This rancour between the climbing leader and the expedition leader continued throughout the trip.

The discord among the climbers, however, started even before the party left for Tibet. The problem began over George Finch. His expedition medical found him to be in poor physical condition: he was anaemic, sallow, flabby, underweight and his mouth was 'very deficient in teeth'. Finch's medical problems were compounded by malaria, which he had contracted during the war and from which he had not made a full recovery. Finch was devastated when he was told that he was dropped from the team and made his feelings clear. He was aware of his unpopularity with the climbing establishment and he thought his rejection was part of a shabby, underhand conspiracy to get him off the expedition. Finch remained bitter over his rejection and never forgave the committee.

It was proposed to replace Finch with 48-year-old William N. Ling, an old climbing partner of Raeburn's. Mallory was appalled at the prospect and immediately wrote to Hinks: 'The substitution of Ling for Finch though it may make little difference in the earlier stages of climbing will in all probability very materially weaken the advance party ... I have all along regarded the party as barely strong enough for a venture of this kind ... You will understand that I must look after myself in this matter. I'm a married man & I can't go into this bald-headed.'[15] In the same letter he also raised doubts about the inclusion of Henry Morshead from the Survey of India because '... we know very little about him as a mountaineer'.[16]

Hinks suspected that Percy Farrar, president of the Alpine Club, whom he loathed, had motivated Mallory's letter. Hinks's tactless and brusque reply did nothing to endear him to Mallory: 'The fact that you have been in close touch with Farrar all along has no doubt made you imbibe his view which is hardly that of anybody else, that the first object of the Expedition is to get to the top of Mount Everest this year. Raeburn has been given full liberty to get as high as possible consistent with the complete reconnaissance of the mountain, and it is left at that.'[17] On the subject of Morshead, Hinks was no less forthright: 'I suspect you will find him a hard man to keep up with when he has been in the field for several months on his survey work, which is I should imagine the best possible training.'[18] Mallory was furious at these patronizing remarks, but in the end the bickering stopped when Ling turned down the offer to go on the expedition.

Seizing his opportunity, Mallory proposed to Younghusband that his old climbing friend Guy Bullock should join the party. Although Farrar had reservations about his lack of experience, Bullock proved to be a popular choice. He managed to get on with everybody – even Raeburn – and Howard-Bury wrote admiringly of his '... placid temperament and an ability to sleep under any conditions'.[19]

Prior to the team's departure, an exclusive contract had been made with *The Times* in London and the *Philadelphia Ledger* in the USA to publish the expedition telegrams, and with the *Graphic* to print the expedition photographs. These arrangements guaranteed that the project would be financially secure, but Hinks had a deep distrust of the press and publicity. He demanded that expedition members should sign a binding contract drawn up by him '... not to hold any communication with the press or with any press agency or publisher, or to deliver any public lecture, or to allow any information or photograph to be published either before, during or after the expedition without the sanction of the Mount Everest Committee'.[20] Hinks made it clear that he expected this restriction to continue in perpetuity.

Most of the expedition members were deeply unhappy with these conditions and Mallory was one of the first to object, concerned that signing the contract would restrict his ambitions to become a writer. In the end, however, the committee was resolute and backed Hinks. Mallory and the rest of the team therefore capitulated.

Given this unfortunate start, it is not surprising that the difficulties continued. There were just nine men in the party, two of whom were substitutes. Leading the expedition was Howard-Bury, supported by Raeburn as climbing leader: both men were already at loggerheads. The geologist A.M. Heron joined Morshead and Wheeler (two officers from the Survey of India) as a non-climbing member of the team. Mallory and Bullock formed the tiny but experienced core of climbers, though they had no previous knowledge of the Himalayas. The expedition doctor was the renowned climber Alexander F.R. Wollaston, supported by Dr Alexander Kellas, who was an expert in high-altitude physiology and the only person on the team capable of speaking the local languages. The average age was 44.

Within a short time of reaching Asia Mallory found himself unable to tolerate Howard-Bury, whose conservatism clashed with his own liberal tendencies. In a letter to his wife, Mallory wrote: '... . I don't find myself greatly liking him. He is too much the landlord with not only Tory pre-judices, but a very highly developed sense of hate and contempt for other sorts of people than his own...'[21] A later letter added: 'I felt I should never be at ease with him – and in a sense I never shall be. He is not a tolerant person. He is well informed and opinionated and doesn't at all like anyone else to know things he doesn't know.'[22]

These were early days in Everest exploration and little was known about what equipment and clothing were required. Mallory was unhappy with the arrangements and wrote to Geoffrey Young: 'Raeburn unfortunately was put in charge of the mountaineering section and is quite incompetent ... such a vital matter as tents has not been thought out and no proper provision for cold and great heights came with Raeburn's scheme of things.'[23]

The men were given a grant of £50 towards their gear (later raised to £100 'if necessary'), but the choice of clothing was left to personal preference. They took tweeds and greatcoats as protection against the piercingly cold wind on the Tibetan plateau, woollen scarves and cardigans, home-knitted socks and their leather Alpine climbing boots. When George Bernard Shaw saw photographs from the early Everest expeditions he said the climbers looked like a group on a picnic in Connemara, surprised by a snowstorm.

All told, it was a scruffy and cheerless group that made its way to Darjeeling. The one exception was Howard-Bury, who arrived from his country estate in Ireland grandly fitted out at his own expense with the very best Donegal tweed and Kashmir wool puttees, neatly bound below the knee. Within weeks of being blasted by the incessant Tibetan winds, he was indistinguishable from the rest of the team.

George Mallory was in a dark mood for much of his solitary sea journey to India: he was lonely and missed his wife. After disembarking at Calcutta he travelled north by train to Darjeeling, where the group assembled at the beginning of May. He was unable to shake off his sense of foreboding. Everyone was aware of the discord developing between Howard-Bury and Raeburn and Mallory got on with neither man.

But there were lighter moments. Mallory became friendly with Dr Kellas, who had spent the previous month exploring the mountains around Kangchenjunga. One evening the Governor of Bengal hosted a formal banquet for the expedition. Kellas arrived late and dishevelled, having walked several miles from a nearby village. 'I love Kellas already,' Mallory wrote to his wife. 'He is ... altogether uncouth. His appearance would form an admirable model to the stage for a farcical representation of an alchemist. He is slight in build, short, thin, stooping, and narrow-chested...'[24]

A chemist by training, but a high-altitude physiologist by inclination, Kellas probably knew as much as anyone at the time about the effects of altitude on the human body. It was he who discovered that the Bhotias and Sherpas were particularly suited for a high-altitude expedition. What nobody realized at the time, however, was that Kellas had pushed himself too far in the weeks running up to the expedition. He had lost over a stone in weight and was physically exhausted; at 53 he was the second oldest man on the team.

The expedition divided into two groups, with Morshead and his surveyors going ahead into northern Sikkim and then over the Serpo La to Kampa Dzong in Tibet. The others took a longer but easier route over the Jelep La and then made a wide arc around to join them. The Indian Army had supplied mules for the journey, but these sluggish animals were quite unsuited for the first stage of the trek through the dank, semi tropical forests of Sikkim and they were sent back after just five days. From then onwards the team had to rely on whatever hill mules and yaks they could find locally. They also experienced further delays from the torrential pre-monsoon rains that fell during May.

Once over the Jelep La, the main party moved into more agreeable surroundings with a moderate climate, not unlike the Alpine valleys the party were used to in Europe, except here they travelled through forests of rhododendrons, flowering clematis and wild roses. Next they began to climb to an altitude of about 4800 metres (15,750 feet) on to the flat, arid, high-altitude desert of the Tibetan plateau. In these harsher conditions everyone except Mallory came down with gastroenteritis and other stomach disorders. Raeburn was taken very ill and on two occasions he fell off his horse and was kicked and rolled upon by the animal.

However, it was Dr Kellas who suffered most. On top of his poor physical condition, dysentery sapped his strength to the point where he could no longer walk and had to be carried on a rudimentary stretcher. A small group of Tibetans was engaged specifically for this purpose, and his entourage would arrive at the evening halt a couple of hours after the main party. Despite his condition, he seemed bright and cheerful and it was generally assumed that he was recovering.

It therefore came as a great shock to everyone when news reached Kampa Dzong on 5 June that Kellas had died from a heart attack as he was carried over the last pass. Mallory wrote to his old friend David Pye: 'The most tragic and distressing fact about his death is that no one of us was with him. Can you imagine anything less like a mountaineering party? It was an arrangement which made me very unhappy, and which appalls [sic] me now in the light of what has happened. And yet it was a difficult position. The old gentleman (such as he seemed) was obliged to retire a number of times *en route* and could not bear to be seen in this distress, and so insisted that every one should be in front of him.'[25] It was a sombre little group that gathered to lay Kellas to rest in a shallow, rocky grave on a hillside overlooking the great Tibetan plain.

As the expedition doctor, Wollaston was concerned that he might be held responsible for the death of Kellas, so he decided to take no further chances. Raeburn was already displaying similar symptoms, so Wollaston decided to escort him back to Lachen in Sikkim, where Swedish missionaries could look after him until he made a full recovery. Nobody on the expedition raised any objection to Raeburn's departure.

Now reunited with the surveying party, the team took several more days to reach Everest. Minus two of their most experienced climbers, Mallory realized that if any climbing were to be achieved on Everest that year it would be up to Guy Bullock and himself.

As the expedition travelled west across Tibet, it moved into uncharted territory. The surveying team was kept busy mapping and calculating angles, heights and distances as they went. Finally, they arrived at Tingri Dzong, an important trading centre, which was to act as their base camp. About 65 kilometres (40 miles) to the south they could see Everest rising majestically above the Tibetan plain. 'Looked at from here,' Howard-Bury noted, 'it is certainly a very wonderful mountain, as it seems to stand up all by itself, but from this side it looks far too steep to be climbed.'[26]

It was decided that Morshead would remain in Tingri to map the area, while Wheeler and Heron would make topographic surveys around Khumba La, a high pass to the west used by traders from Nepal. Wollaston stayed at Base Camp with Howard-Bury, and set up a photographic darkroom. Meanwhile Mallory and Bullock headed south to find the best route to Everest.

On 13 June the two climbers explored the Yaru Gorge and climbed a small cliff 300 metres (1000 feet) high, which gave them a commanding view of the mountains to the south. At first, dark monsoon clouds hid the great peaks from view, but 'Presently the miracle happened,' recalled Mallory. '...A preposterous triangular lump rose out of the depths; its edge came leaping up at an angle of about 70° and ended nowhere. To the left a black serrated crest was hanging in the sky incredibly. Gradually, very gradually, we saw the great mountain sides and glaciers and arêtes, now one fragment and now another through the floating rifts, until far higher in the sky than imagination had dared to suggest the white summit of Everest appeared. And in this series of partial glimpses we had seen a whole; we were able to piece together the fragments, to interpret the dream.'[27]

The countryside was a dry and barren land of sand dunes alternating with mudflats and saltflats surrounded by bare, brown hills. Sandflies and gnats irritated the men whenever there was a temporary lull in the fierce, cold wind, but the two climbers persevered and on 25 June they entered the Rongbuk. Mallory wrote: 'The Rongbuk Valley is well constructed to show off the peak at its head; for about 20 miles it is extraordinarily straight and in that distance rises only 4,000 feet, the glacier, which is 10 miles long, no more steeply than the rest ... At the end of the valley and above the glacier, Everest rises not so much a peak as a prodigious mountain-mass ... To the discerning eye other mountains are visible, giants between 23,000 and 26,000 feet high. Not one of their slenderer heads even reaches their chief's shoulders; beside Everest they escape notice – such is the pre-eminence of the greatest.'[28]

By 29 June, Mallory, Bullock and their Sherpas established an Advanced Base Camp further up the valley at 5200 metres (17,060 feet), where they could explore the side valleys that fed the main glacier. From his observations Mallory judged that the only practical route to the summit was from the North Col, a depression below the North Face which forms a saddle between Everest and Changtse to the north. But how could they gain access to the North Col?

On 1 July the men moved south down the main Rongbuk Glacier, which seemed to offer a direct route to the mountain. In fact, it led to a snow corrie underneath the towering North Face of Everest. To the east of the Rongbuk, the North Col towered over the glacier, but the route up was very steep and broken. Mallory judged that it was too difficult and dangerous to attempt from that side, so he hoped the other side might offer a safer and more practical route. Bullock and Mallory decided to try the western arm of the Rongbuk to see if this offered an alternative route to the summit, and they climbed a peak 6844 metres (22,500 feet) high, which lay to the north-west of Everest. Mallory later noted: 'We moved very slowly, keeping up muscular energy and overcoming lassitude by breathing fast and deep. It was a colossal labour.'[29]

Both climbers wanted to name the peak Mount Kellas, but it was later given its local name of Ri-Ring. From the excellent view it gave them, they decided the best way to the North Col was from the east, up the Kharta Valley. Sadly, they were mistaken and wasted many weeks searching for access to the North Col.

Mallory has since been criticized for missing the obvious route. What he and Bullock had failed to realize was that a small glacier (now called the East Rongbuk Glacier) flows north along the eastern side of Changtse and then turns west to join the main Rongbuk Glacier. Mallory and Bullock had pitched their first camp opposite this small valley, where a river still tumbles down from a gap in the side of the valley and disappears into an ice cave in the main glacier. The two climbers must have looked up at the valley many times as they passed up and down the Rongbuk, but never realized that it offered the easiest way to the North Col. Ironically, they always intended to investigate the side valley to see where it might lead, but never quite found the time.

For several weeks the two climbers searched for possible routes to the North Col. During their excursions up the West Rongbuk, Bullock came close to crossing to Nepal over the Nup La. Throughout this time Mallory took many photographs, but unfortunately he confirmed his lack of practical ability by putting the plates in the camera the wrong way around and ruining the pictures. It would be several days before he found out about his blunder.

It was now beginning to dawn on Mallory and Bullock that the geography of the region was very different from their first impressions gained from the summit of Ri-Ring. They were also beginning to realize that the monsoon period was not the best time to be on Everest, as most of the annual fall of snow is deposited during the summer months, increasing the danger from avalanches. Their Mummery tents proved to be too small and lightweight for use in anything other than good weather, so the sturdier Whymper tents were brought further up the glacier to make life more comfortable.

The supply of food and fuel to the camps was not satisfactory, and Mallory frequently complained about the ineffectiveness of the Primus stoves, which would not work in the cold and draught of their tiny tents. Other equipment also proved to be inadequate for the task. Bullock brought his clothes out to Everest in a suitcase and wrote in his diary: 'There was at least 6 in. [15 centimetres] of snow before I got in. Having only brought one coat, which was wet, spent the evening in a sweater. Luckily I had two.'[30] At the time, Bullock was camped at 6100 metres (20,000 feet) in temperatures which can easily plunge below -20°C (-4°F) at night.

Mallory and Bullock decided to withdraw from the Rongbuk area and try their luck further east. Before they left a runner arrived with the frustrating news that Mallory had ruined the photographic plates: 'I have had a bitter blow,' he wrote to his wife. 'All the photos taken up here with the quarter-plate – practically all I have taken – have gone wrong. Apparently I put the plates in the wrong way round. I knew nothing about plates and followed instructions given me by Heron. I have taken enormous trouble over these photos: many of them were taken at sunrise from places where neither I nor anyone else may go again ... I am determined to replace them as far as possible...'[30]

At the end of July Mallory and Bullock joined the main expedition in the Kharta Valley, in a delightful location discovered by Howard-Bury. It was mild and green, with trees and flowers, and well protected from the incessant Tibetan wind. Their plan was to survey a route up the Kharta Glacier, but again the climbers were thwarted in their attempt to gain access to the North Col. This time the porters complained about their rations (a tradition on Everest that continues to this day). Added to this, the weather turned against them, which delayed things further.

Mallory also experienced a rare bout of illness: 'On August 7, as we toiled over the nevé in the afternoon, I felt for the first time a symptom of weari-ness beyond muscular fatigue and beyond the vague lassitude of mountain sickness. By the time we reached the moraine I had a bad headache. In the tent at last I was tired and shivering and there spent a fevered night.'[32]

For some time now, Guy Bullock had been tormented by the possibility that the unnamed glacier to the east of Changtse might turn west to enter the main Rongbuk Glacier. Mallory also remembered the river which joined the Rongbuk Valley, but he did not believe that a small tributary could drain such a sizeable glacier and he dismissed Bullock's theory. Howard-Bury later sent one of Wheeler's topographic sketches up to their camp, and the drawings coincided exactly with Bullock's belief that the mystery glacier did indeed merge with the main Rongbuk. But it was still only a possibility that needed confirmation. Mallory remained sceptical.

After a brief rest to recover their strength, Mallory and Morshead, with Sherpa support, moved west up the Kharta Glacier and climbed up to the pass called Lakpa La. Unfortunately it was now well into the monsoon season and visibility at the top was so poor that they could barely see to make a safe descent on the other side. Mallory, however, was now sure that they had found the key to approaching the North Col and they named the hidden glacier the East Rongbuk.

Their return that day was an exhausting trek, and they finally staggered into their tents at 2 a.m. Mallory was jubilant and wrote to Ruth: '. . . whatever may happen to the glacier whose exit we have yet to find, we have found our way to the great mountain ... As we came down the long, weary way, my thoughts were full of this prospect and this success. I don't know when I have allowed myself so much enjoyment from a personal achievement ...'[33]

From his writings, there is little doubt that the idea of climbing Everest was now exerting a very powerful influence on Mallory. For the first time in his life he had a clear ambition, but he felt that success or failure on the mountain rested on him alone. He later wrote to Geoffrey Winthrop Young: 'The whole thing is on my shoulders – I can say this to you. Bullock follows well and is safe; but you know what it means on a long, exhausting effort to lead all the time ...'[34] Mallory was unsettled by the extraordinary influence the mountain was beginning to hold over him.

It was now the middle of August and the climbers had to plan their final reconnaissance on the mountain. The monsoon, however, brought bad weather and they were stuck in their camp at 5250 metres (17,224 feet) for three weeks waiting for conditions to improve. They had been three months on the Tibetan plateau and they understood little of the long-term effects of spending such a long time at high altitude. Although they might not have fully realized their predicament, they were physically and mentally exhausted.

Not surprisingly, living in close proximity for such a long period was beginning to have an effect on friendships. In particular, Mallory was becoming irritated by Bullock, and wrote to Ruth on 1 September: 'We weren't getting on quite happily. We had rather drifted into that common superficial attitude between two people who live alone together – competitive and slightly quarrelsome, each looking out to see that he doesn't get done down in some small way by the other.'[35] The two men eyed each other, checking that no advantage was taken, and Mallory complained that Bullock was lazy and did not attend to the many small things that needed to be done. Nor did Mallory make an easy companion. He was on an emotional rollercoaster, with his spirits up one day and down the next. Fortunately Bullock was phlegmatic and maintained a steady good humour throughout the long expedition.

It was around this time, as they were climbing the Lakpa La, that the climbers chanced upon giant footprints in the fresh snow, which the Sherpas immediately identified as those of the *yeti*. For the British climbers, this was their first encounter with an enduring Himalayan legend. The locals were convinced of their existence and told tales of how they killed men and carried off their women. The creatures, apparently, had jaws so powerful they could bite through the neck of a yak and drink its blood. The name 'yeti' comes from Nepal and is derived from *ya-te*, meaning 'man of high places', but they are also called *nitikanji* or 'snow men', which gave rise to the popular European name of the Abominable Snowman.

By the middle of September, Raeburn had returned from his convalescence in Sikkim and was able to rejoin the climbing group. On 20 September the weather improved sufficiently to allow Mallory, Morshead and 15 Sherpas to pitch a camp at Lakpa La. Mallory had a clear view of the slopes that led up to the North Col and it seemed a daunting prospect: the steep face of snow and ice looked more difficult than he had imagined, about 300 metres (1000 feet) high and heavily crevassed.

Two days later, Mallory, Bullock and Wheeler set off together, with Morshead, Wollaston and Howard-Bury following behind in support. The team were exhausted and spent the night on Lakpa La in temperatures that plummeted to -34°C (-30°F). Wollaston and Howard-Bury had a bad night and retreated to Base Camp with the assistance of Morshead.

The rest of the group descended from Lakpa La to the East Rongbuk and battled up towards the head of the glacier, before pitching their camp at 6700 metres (22,000 feet). Above them towered the North Col, ready and waiting to be tackled the following day. Mallory later wrote to David Pye: 'At the last camp, under the North Col, we spent two nights; an unforgettable place too ... it was so flat and the world was so big; but at the same time the great cliffs on three sides of us were a felt presence. And down there ... the wind found us out; there was never a more determined and bitter enemy.'[36]

The fierce, post-monsoon wind constantly buffeted their inadequate tents and the climbers had a second bad night with little or no sleep. The following morning they continued towards the base of the North Col but they were soon labouring in the thin air. They made slow progress in the deep monsoon snow, finally arriving at a low platform on the North Col after an exhausting four and a half hours. Mallory recalled 'Even where we stood under the lee of a little ice cliff [the wind] came in fierce gusts at frequent intervals, blowing up the powdery snow in a suffocating tourbillion. On the col beyond it was blowing a gale. And higher was a more fearful sight.'[37]

The climbers debated what to do next. Wheeler had lost all feeling in his feet and wanted to return to Base Camp, which he did the next day. Mallory, however, wanted to push on despite the terrible conditions. Bullock realized how important this last attempt was for Mallory, and despite the bad weather he agreed to accompany him up another 600 metres (2000 feet). The two climbers set off together, leaving the others behind at the camp, but they were soon forced to turn back when hit by the full force of the icy wind. Nobody could survive for long in those conditions. Bullock later conceded: 'I was prepared to follow M if he wished to try and make some height, but was glad when he decided not to. It was lucky he didn't as my strength proved to ebb nearly at an end.'[38]

The decision was finally made to withdraw from the mountain on 24 September. The ice-cold Himalayan autumn had beaten the small group of climbers. This was as far at the expedition was going to get in 1921, but at last the road to Everest was clear for all to see.

As the exhausted party worked their way down the lower slopes of the

North Col, they noticed that an avalanche had wiped out some of the tracks they had made earlier that morning. It was a prophetic sign and an indication of how unstable the North Col could become. Mallory later wrote in the expedition account: 'Here our feet undoubtedly found a solid bed to tread on, but the substance above it was dubiously loose. It was my conviction at the time that with axes well driven in above us we were perfectly safe here. But on the way down we observed a space of 5 yards or so where the surface snow had slid away below our tracks. The disquieting thoughts that necessarily followed this discovery left and still leave me in some doubt as to how great a risk, if any, we were taking. But it is natural to suppose that at a higher elevation or in a cooler season, because the snow adheres less rapidly to the slopes on which it lies, an avalanche of new snow is more likely to occur.'[39]

The warning signs were clear. Loose snow above an underlying bed of ice is a very dangerous combination and this small avalanche was a warning that any climber ignores at his peril. Mallory did not, however, learn from the experience: a year later he disregarded similar danger signs, this time with much more serious consequences when a bigger avalanche caught his party during a similar descent of the North Col, with significant loss of life.

CHAPTER SIX

'It's an Infernal Mountain'

'The mountain has taken his toll among us; but
lord, how much worse it might have been! ...
David, it's an infernal mountain, cold and
treacherous ... Perhaps it's mere folly to go up
again. But how can I be out of the hunt?'

George Mallory to his friend David Pye, 1 June 1921

B y the time the expedition members had returned by ship to
Marseilles, the climbers had been away for six months, so Ruth
Mallory travelled to the French port to meet her husband off the
ship. For most of their marriage they had lived apart, so they took the
opportunity to take a short holiday together in France. Back in London the
1921 reconnaissance was considered a great success. The team had surveyed
the mountain from three sides and identified a practical route from the
north. Before the climbers had even left India, the Everest Committee was
already talking of another attempt on the mountain the following year, and
before he got home Mallory received a letter of invitation from
Younghusband to take part.

In the midst of the euphoria, however, Arthur Hinks struck a sour note.
He wrote in a fury to Howard-Bury about his dissatisfaction with the survey
work on the mountain: 'Is it possible that the surveyors never sent anyone
to make a reconnaissance sketch of the neighbourhood of the mountain. I
should have thought that this would have been the very first thing they would
do, and I am appalled by the prospect, which seems quite likely now, of
having no map upon which to describe the first year's work ... What has

happened to the big rock peak photographed both by Kellas and Sella ... north of Makalu? Has it fallen down since last December, and if not why is it not in your photographs.'[1] He also sent some of Mallory's expedition letters in confidence to Norman Collie, the president of the Alpine Club: 'Enclosed are copies of further letters from Mallory which will both interest you and amuse you ... they give one the impression that Mallory is a little impractical. He cannot make primus stoves work when other people can.'[2]

Mallory, however, was despondent. He regarded the reconnaissance trip as a failure because they had neither climbed the mountain nor made even a determined attempt. Discord in the team had also left its mark, and he wrote to his friend David Pye: 'Never mind Everest and its unfriendly glories. I'm tired of travelling and travellers, far countries and uncouth people, trains and ships and shimmering mausoleums, foreign ports, dark-skinned people, and a garish sun.'[3]

Mallory also wrote to his sister, Avie, doubting the chances of being able to raise a new expedition so quickly: 'They've had thoughts of organizing an expedition for next year; but I've said it's no use going out except early in the spring, to climb before the monsoon. They can't possibly organize another show so soon, particularly as I've also said that it's barely worth while trying again, and anyway not without eight first-rate climbers. They can't get eight, certainly not soon, perhaps not even the year after. Hinks (Hon. Sec.) already wants to know whether I'll go again. When they press for an answer, I shall tell them they can get the other seven first . . . I wouldn't go again next year, as the saying is, for all the gold in Arabia.'[4]

With characteristic insensitivity and unseemly haste, the Everest Committee nominated Charlie Bruce as the 1922 expedition leader, before Howard-Bury had even left India. Not surprisingly, Howard-Bury took this hasty announcement as an indictment of his leadership.

Bruce, now 56, had impeccable credentials for his appointment: he had spent many years in the region on military service and had climbed with the great Himalayan pioneers, including William Conway in 1892 and Albert Mummery in 1895. As a result, the 1922 expedition was altogether a more professional affair.

Bruce chose Edward Strutt to be his deputy, a solid, traditional mountaineer, who, when he was a commissioner in Danzig, became infamous for rescuing the Austrian royal family from a revolutionary rabble. Unfortunately, Bruce and Strutt were opposites in character and never really hit it off during the expedition. The 56-year-old Bruce was later to write with ill-concealed sarcasm: 'It may possibly be that we are a little too young for him.'[5]

George Finch was also invited to join the team, this time having passed the expedition medical. Having been rejected the previous year, he had taken off to the Alps and made several impressive first ascents, including a particularly difficult route on Mont Blanc. Finch was arguably the most accomplished climber on the 1922 team, but his exploits in the Alps had earned him a reputation for living rough in the mountains, and Bruce once wrote of him: 'A convincing raconteur of quite impossible qualifications. Cleans his teeth on February 1st and has a bath the same day if the water is very hot, otherwise puts it off until next year'.[6]

It was a much younger and fitter team that was chosen in 1922. Once again the medical profession was well represented, and included a London surgeon, Howard Somervell, who was an experienced climber with seemingly inexhaustible energy and a double first in natural history from Cambridge. Bruce declared that he was an '... absolute glutton for hard work ... wonderful goer and climber. He takes a size 22 hat. That is his only drawback.'[7] (Bruce's comment refers to Somervell's ego, rather than the dimensions of his head.)

Another climbing doctor was Arthur Wakefield, who once held the record for covering the most Lakeland summits in 24 hours. In 1905 he ran 94 kilometres (59 miles) and made an ascent of over 7000 metres (23,500 feet) in a little over 22 hours. His record remained unbroken for 15 years.

Edward Norton, an army major, joined the team with limited high-altitude experience, but proved to be a great Himalayan climber. The official expedition doctor was Tom Longstaff, who had extensive experience of the Himalayas, but made it clear from the outset that he had no interest in climbing. He had no illusions about what lay ahead: 'Everest is a forbidding mountain. It has no athlete's grace of form but the brutal mass of the all-in wrestler, murderous and threatening. Technically I cannot agree that it is an easy peak, as has been so often said. The strata of the upper slopes of the north face slant downwards like tiles on a roof. Too often they are covered with powder-snow, for above 25,000 feet snow hardly melts; nor does it solidify; it must either evaporate or be blown away by the terrible winds which scourge the mountain.'[8]

John Noel was placed in charge of filming and photography. He was the very man who had got so close to Everest in 1913 and whose speech to the RGS launched the current expeditions. The superb 35mm black and white film shot by Noel in both 1922 and 1924 is a unique record of the expeditions and still sells well today, at a price that would astonish those team members back in the 1920s.

Two Gurkha officers, Geoffrey Bruce (Charlie Bruce's nephew) and John Morris, were also included, together with five Gurkha soldiers. Neither of the officers had any climbing experience, but they had served together during the Afghan War of 1919 and were able to speak Nepali to the soldiers. Both men turned out to be excellent team members.

Bruce also wanted A.M. Heron to return with the 1922 expedition as the official geologist, but he had unwittingly upset the Tibetan government by digging holes in the ground, through which the Tibetans believed demons would escape. Official complaints from the Tibetans were sent to the committee, and Hinks wrote to the unfortunate geologist, offering little understanding or support: 'I suppose you are the member of the party whose mining work has been objected to by the Tibetans, and has been the subject of an official letter to us. It disturbed the demons which live in the ground, and the Jonpens [local leaders] were very much afraid of them breaking out.'[9]

Poor Heron was quite taken aback by this reproach and did his best to defend his corner: 'I have to plead "Not Guilty" to the charge of being a Disturber of Demons. I did no mining and the gentle hammer tapping … I am sure, [was] insufficient to alarm the most timid of the fraternity.'[10] The story later escalated and Heron was accused of digging up precious stones. When the same charge was subsequently levelled at the whole expedition, Bruce had little option but to use Heron as a scapegoat and exclude him from his plans.

With such a strong, young team, albeit with only six proper climbers instead of the eight that he preferred, George Mallory decided to join the expedition. He knew that much had been learnt from the 1921 attempt and the new expedition was better organized. This time there would be no shortage of funds, as the committee had a significant surplus left over from 1921, and enthusiasm in London for a return to Tibet would ensure there was more to come.

It was decided that the expedition should arrive in Tibet much earlier in the year, in order to miss the worst of the monsoon, so there was frenetic preparation to get everybody on a steamer to India before the end of March. Ideas about clothing for the climbers had altered little from those of 1921, except for the addition of a long, leather waistcoat, which they thought might keep out the wind. This proved to be inadequate and windproof smocks were later substituted. (George Finch was far ahead of the game when he designed for himself a quilted jacket made from thin balloon material and goose down.)

Much greater care was also taken with footwear, which included ski boots (with as few nails as possible to avoid the conduction of heat from the feet), supplemented with crampons for high-altitude climbing. At lower levels, high moccasins from Canada, felt boots with lambskin uppers and Norwegian fur-lined shoes gave better protection against frostbite.

Bruce was also aware that the food in 1921 was generally awful and had contributed towards poor morale, so he made sure that there were some culinary highlights during the next expedition. He introduced a more varied and appetizing menu, which included Harris's tinned sausages, Hunters hams, Heinz spaghetti, herrings, sardines, sliced bacon and tinned quail, as well as claret and champagne. This had the desired effect and did much to supplement the staple diet of potatoes and yak meat.

There was also a debate about whether or not to use oxygen. Oxygen systems had been developed by Professor Dreyer at Oxford University for the Royal Air Force. When Finch paid him a visit, Dreyer's advice was direct and to the point: 'I do not think you will get up without,' he announced to his visitor, 'but if you do succeed you may not get down again.'[11]

Dreyer obviously made a considerable impression on Finch, who tried an experiment in a decompression chamber. He performed simple physical exercise, both with and without the heavy equipment, and the difference in his performance was so marked that the committee set aside £400 for the apparatus and oxygen supplies. Finch, together with Farrar, Somervell and

Collie, became great advocates of the system in 1922 and believed that oxygen was indispensable. Others, including Mallory, Longstaff and Hinks, would not hear of it, and thought the systems too complicated and heavy to use on the mountain. Mallory argued that the use of 'English air' offended his romantic notion of the purity of man's struggle against a mountain and he believed it was science undermining natural forces. Instead, he preferred to rely on acclimatization to get him to high altitude.

The argument over the use of oxygen was to continue for some time, but it was a divisive issue even before the expedition left London. Hinks treated the whole matter as a joke: 'This afternoon we go to see a gas drill. They have contrived a most wonderful apparatus which will make you die of laughing,' he wrote to Bruce. '... I would gladly put a little money on Mallory to go to 25,000 feet without the assistance of four cylinders and a mask.'[12] Their united opposition to oxygen actually brought Mallory and Hinks closer together, much to the chagrin of Farrar, who was becoming increasingly irritated with Hinks.

By now, Hinks was more than happy to air opinions in print, and did so in a way that incensed Farrar, chairman of the committee. Writing anonymously, Hinks implied that the Everest Committee was disproportionately influenced by cranky boffins and wayward climbers: 'The party was equipped this year with oxygen at the strong desire of a section of the climbers who had convinced themselves, or had been convinced, that they would never reach the summit without it. The Committee, feeling bound to supply whatever in reason might be demanded ...'[13] It was a biased article, as Hinks had ignored the fact that Mallory was really the only climber on the expedition who did not favour the use of oxygen.

Farrar wrote to Hinks with more than a touch of irritation: 'I will say quite frankly that I do not like the somewhat satirical tone of your article ... solely for the reason that it may tend to minimise the opinion of the members of the Expedition in the value of oxygen. If I were one of them I should conclude from your paper that the Committee attached small importance to it and were inclined to jeer.'[14] Hinks's reply was curt: 'I should be especially sorry if the oxygen outfit prevents them going as high as possible without it. If some of the party do not go to 25,000 ft to 26,000 ft without oxygen they will be rotters.'[15]

The article also upset Finch, whose scientific training led him to conclude that the use of oxygen was a logical and essential aid to climbing at high altitude. He later wrote in his account of the expedition: 'Personally I feel certain [Everest] will never be climbed without oxygen. But there existed another force of oxygen antagonists, largely unscientific, who were willing enough to admit that oxygen might, indeed, have its uses, but condemned it on the ground that its employment was unsporting and, therefore, un-British. The line of reasoning of these anti-oxygenists is somewhat hard to follow ...'[16] Hinks was furious with Finch and the row rumbled on.

The oxygen equipment was certainly heavy and cumbersome. It comprised a frame which supported four steel cylinders, tubes, a regulator valve and two different types of face-mask. Each full oxygen bottle weighed 2.6 kilograms (5½ lb) and the whole contraption weighed 14.5 kilograms (32 lb). The committee ordered 10 sets, which included four spares. The apparatus proved to be very delicate and unreliable, and despite every care being taken, only three of the original 10 sets worked when the equipment arrived at Base Camp.

The team members sailed to India on the SS *Caledonian* at the beginning of March. It was a much more enjoyable voyage than Mallory had experienced the previous year; the men were relaxed and enjoyed each other's company. Noel spun yarns of his travels in exotic places, and even the rather serious Strutt recounted stories of how Curzon had tried to get him court-martialled. Finch ran his oxygen classes, and even Mallory began to come around to thinking that '... [oxygen] will serve us well enough and without physiological dangers from a camp at 25,000 feet'.[17]

Before the party had even assembled in Darjeeling, it faced its first medical emergency. On arrival in Calcutta, Norton played a game of 'pig-sticking' (hunting wild boar with a spear). He was something of an expert at the sport, but on this occasion the exertion left him with a bad case of haemorrhoids. Fortunately for him it proved unnecessary to operate.

By the time they assembled in Darjeeling, the expedition had swelled to include over 400 pack animals and 100 local porters. The entourage included 40 climbing porters, eight photographic porters, 10 oxygen porters, an interpreter, a cobbler, a tent-mender, several first-class cooks, and a sirdar, or headman, to keep them all in order. The expedition was travelling with much more scientific apparatus than in 1921. Noel's camera equipment alone arrived in Darjeeling in a box 12 metres (40 feet) long, and he spent some time 'scouring the country for an adequate mule'.

There was little doubt that this expedition would cost significantly more than the 1921 attempt, and Bruce was constantly cabling back to Hinks for more funds. He got short shrift from Hinks, however, who merely urged him to be more economic. Charlie Bruce took little notice and confided in Younghusband that the cost of 1922 was not going to be double that of 1921 (which had been their estimate) but could be *four* times as much. In the end, the expedition came out £750 overdrawn. The Alpine Club refused to guarantee further funding, so the RGS had to finance all of the overspend.

Meanwhile, back in India – financial problems aside – things were actually going rather well for Bruce. He knew the region well, looked after his Sherpas and was even able to speak directly to them in Nepali. He was always careful to make friends with the local people as he passed through their villages, and he took great pleasure in presenting each headman with a bowler hat, to the delight of the recipient and to the hilarity of the assembled throng. The team members were also getting on well with each other and they all held Charlie Bruce in the highest regard.

Mallory was already beginning to display his usual signs of chronic absent-mindedness. In his account of the expedition, John Morris recalled that: 'Mallory was the most absent-minded man I have ever known.'[18] Each of the climbers had a personal servant, but Mallory's tent was always in such a mess that his Sherpa could never understand that he actually wanted to keep these pieces and was always tempted to throw everything away. 'After the first few days,' recalls Morris, 'we took turns to see that none of his kit was left behind.'[19]

The expedition was split into two groups: the first left Darjeeling on 26 March and the second a few days later. Their route through Sikkim and then up on to the Tibetan plateau was the same as in 1921, but this year they were several weeks earlier, so the conditions were much bleaker and the ground still frozen hard. The two parties met at Phari Dzong on 7 April, before moving on through Kampa Dzong and Shekar Dzong.

While *en route*, Mallory and Somervell decided to climb Sangkar Ri, 6246 metres (20,490 feet) high: 'We were neither of us well acclimatised at the time,' wrote Somervell, 'moreover I had a severe attack of dysentery, and frequent halts and slow progress were necessary for me. Mallory could, I think, have got to the top without me, but instead he chose the safety of a party of two. In his place I should continually have said to my companion, "Come along now, don't be slow," and so on, but Mallory was absolutely patient, and while one could see his eagerness to get on one could see far more clearly his infinite consideration for his slow companion.'[20]

The expeditions reached the Rongbuk Valley on 30 April, much earlier than in 1921, but still three or four weeks later than modern expeditions now arrive. The abbot of the monastery gave Bruce and his men a warm welcome and bestowed his blessing on the climbers and their porters. But he also offered a warning: 'The country is a very cold one; only those who come for religious purposes can live here – it is difficult for the others. Moreover, the deity of the place is a very terrible one, so please take care of yourselves as much as possible.'[21]

Rongbuk is a holy place and the monastery itself is one of the most sacred sites in Lama Buddhism. Bruce was sensitive to the religion and customs of the people, and rigidly enforced a rule that no animals would be slaughtered in the valley. When the abbot asked Bruce why they had come to climb Chomolungma, the local name for Everest, Bruce avoided a trite Western rationale for the expedition. Instead, he explained it was a pilgrimage; as Chomolungma was the highest mountain in the world, it was the one place on Earth where a man could get closest to heaven.

Clearly Bruce was not only a fine military man, but an accomplished diplomat as well.

The expedition began what is now a well-established routine for all climbing expeditions to the North Face. Base Camp was established a short distance from the glacier snout at about 5180 metres (17,000 feet). On 4 May Strutt, Norton, Morshead and Longstaff set off to the East Rongbuk to find the best route up the glacier and to decide on the positions for the intermediate camps. These were established at intervals of approximately 5–6 kilometres (3–4 miles), which is about as far as a loaded porter can travel in a day when ascending 600–750 metres (2000–2500 feet). Camp I was situated at 5425 metres (17,800 feet) at the entrance to the East Rongbuk; Camp II was on the glacier itself at 6000 metres (19,800 feet); and finally Camp III (Advanced Base Camp) at 6400 metres (21,000 feet) was established in the great bowl at the head of the glacier.

Mallory and Somervell were chosen to make the first attempt up the North Col, which they climbed on 13 May with the support of one Sherpa. Mallory was excited at the prospect: 'The General's new plan is for Somervell and me to go straight through to No. 3 camp (the one below the North Col) and at once cut steps up on to the Col, establish a camp there two days later, and then get as high up the mountain as we can – a tremendous undertaking at this stage.'[22]

The conditions on the North Col were very different from the previous year. The snow was crusted and the thin icy shell broke easily underfoot to reveal dangerously unstable powder below. Mallory and Somervell did not find the climb particularly challenging, but the route had been carefully chosen to give the heavily laden Sherpas coming later the easiest possible way to the top. As they climbed, they hammered wooden stakes into the snow and attached fixed ropes. These formed temporary but effective handrails for climbers coming later.

The two climbers established Camp IV at the top of the col at an altitude of about 7000 metres (23,000 feet). This was the highest that man had ever spent the night, and from here they had a clear view up the North Ridge, which was their route towards the summit.

So far, all this climbing had been achieved without oxygen. This was partly because there were not enough porters available, but also because most of the equipment was not working properly when it reached Base Camp. Over the next week, equipment and provisions (including oxygen) gradually worked their way up the East Rongbuk Glacier from Base Camp to the North Col. For Somervell and Mallory, there was little to do but wait, and they spent the days reading and talking. Somervell wrote about the time they spent together: 'These many days of companionship with a man whose outlook on life was lofty and choice, human and loving, and in a measure divine, still remain for me a priceless memory ... He hated anything that savoured of hypocrisy or humbug, but cherished all that is really good and sound.'[24]

By the third week in May, the camp on the North Col was fully provisioned, with five small Mummery tents to accommodate four climbers and up to nine Sherpas. Living at 7000 metres (23,000 feet) brought special problems. One morning the men had planned to have tinned spaghetti for breakfast, but the tins 'instead of being gently nursed during the night against the warmer parts of the body, had been left in the cold snow'.[24] Thawing breakfast took a considerable time.

At last, the climbers were ready for the first attempt on the summit. The organization was left to George Mallory, but not for the first time, he underestimated the mountain and the effort that was required to climb it. His plan was to establish one small camp halfway between the North Col and the summit. This meant that the heavily laden porters had to climb 900 metres (3000 feet) to Camp V, before returning to Camp IV for the night. The following day, the climbers would make an attempt on the summit from Camp V and return all the way to Camp IV before nightfall.

At 5 a.m. on the morning of the 20 May, Mallory tried to rouse the party for an early start. All nine Sherpas, suffering varying degrees of altitude sickness, had tied their tent flaps from the inside and would not come out. When they were eventually cajoled to emerge, only four were fit to climb. Mallory, Somervell, Norton and Morshead were therefore not able to leave until 7.30 a.m. – late by present-day standards. As they headed up the North Ridge, the col dropped away on their left to the East Rongbuk, and on their right to the main Rongbuk Glacier. None of the men was using oxygen but Mallory felt optimistic: 'Major Morshead . . . seemed the strongest of the party, went first; and we proceeded at a satisfactory pace. It was a fine clear morning. Perhaps after all we should camp at 26,000.'[25]

As the morning wore on, it became apparent that conditions were not ideal. A breeze began to build and the temperature began to fall. As they paused to put on more clothes, Norton's rucksack slipped and tumbled out of sight down towards the glacier. Before long, they found themselves struggling into a full gale, which stripped the heat from their bodies. Mallory led the party off to one side so that they could shelter in the lee of the ridge. They had managed to climb 600 metres (2000 feet) in three and a half hours, but there was no question of going any further that day.

There was no obvious place for them to pitch their tents, so they had to search for a suitable site. The porters were sent back to Camp IV before the conditions deteriorated further, while the four climbers had a simple meal and crawled into their sleeping-bags for a restless night at 7600 metres (25,000 feet). By morning, the men were in poor shape. Norton's ear was frostbitten and 'three times the normal size'[26] and Mallory reported 'three of my fingers were touched by frost'.[27] But it was Morshead's condition that gave him most concern; he had been late putting on his sledging suit the previous day and was showing signs of hypothermia.

It had snowed during the night and this made the conditions even more difficult. The climbers left at 8 a.m. without any discussion over whether they should continue in these conditions. After just a few minutes Morshead had a change of heart and decided he could not go on, thinking he would only hold them back. Mallory, Somervell and Norton continued, and Morshead returned to spend the day waiting alone in one of the small, green tents. That decision probably saved his life.

Mallory was also having doubts about how much longer they could continue: 'In the light of subsequent events it would seem that the margin of strength to deal with an emergency was already small enough. I have little doubt that we could have struggled up perhaps in two hours more to the North-east shoulder, now little more than 400 feet above us. Whether we should then have been fit to conduct our descent in safety is another matter.'[28] The climbers continued, but they were clearly at the limits of their endurance and had no hope of reaching the summit, so they decided to turn back. They were still a long way short of the top, but higher than any man had ever climbed before. Their actual altitude has since been confirmed as 8225 metres (26,985 feet) – even higher than their estimate.

During their return, Mallory tried to find a new line down the mountain in fresh snow, which he thought would make the descent easier for the exhausted party. But the new route proved to be even more dangerous, so they struggled back to the original one. They reached Camp V at 4 p.m., very late in the day to continue their descent. Despite resting during the day, Morshead was in poor physical condition and badly frostbitten. Nobody was really fit to continue, nor did anyone relish the idea of spending a second night at Camp V. Estimating that it would take a little over an hour to get down to the North Col, they decided to risk it, with the hapless

Morshead being helped for much of the way.

Fresh snow covered their tracks from the previous day and they had trouble keeping to their route. Mallory led most of the way, cutting new steps in the snow; occasionally Norton would take the lead, giving Mallory a rest. Somervell followed behind as anchorman, giving the party protection and keeping an eye on Morshead, who found the going increasingly difficult.

As they crossed a snow couloir, Morshead slipped. Somervell was caught off balance and he too was jerked off his position, taking Norton with him as he fell. Within a blink, all three men were sliding down the couloir towards the glacier 800 metres (2500 feet) below them. Mallory was cutting a step at the time and instinctively realized what was happening. He plunged his ice-axe into the snow and wrapped his rope around the shaft in an attempt to arrest their fall. Somervell, too, was trying to arrest his slide with his ice-axe, and together they brought the men to a halt. They counted their blessings; nobody was injured, there was still an hour of daylight left and Camp IV was only a short distance away.

By this time Morshead's condition had deteriorated dangerously and he was beginning to hallucinate. Norton took responsibility for guiding and supporting him as best he could. Darkness came and the temperature fell; fortunately there was no wind. Eventually they found the snow staircase leading down to the col and were confident they were on the right track. Somervell lit a lantern to give them a glimmer of light as they crossed the treacherous ice. They had only 200 metres (600 feet) to go, but exhaustion and darkness made it a very dangerous final stage. A short distance from their tents, their candle burnt out and '....we groped for some time along the edge of the precipice and then began to go down at a steep slope, in some doubt as to whether this were the way. Suddenly someone hooked up the rope from under the snow. We knew then that we could reach our tents.'[29]

The climbers, exhausted, frostbitten, hungry and seriously dehydrated, crawled into their tents at Camp IV at 11.30 p.m. It had taken them over seven hours to descend 600 metres (2000 feet). Unfortunately, their problems were not over. Owing to a misunderstanding, the Sherpas had taken all the pans and cooking utensils back to Advanced Base Camp during the day, so the debilitated climbers had nothing in which to melt snow. It was a very dangerous mistake with potentially fatal consequences. In the event, Norton found a solution, as Mallory recalled: 'He opened a tin of jam and a tin of [condensed milk], and mixed these in a mug with snow. I followed his example. The result he thought delicious; to me it seemed disgusting, but at least it could be swallowed.'[30]

The following day, the men made their way down the North Col to Camp III, badly in need of liquid: Somervell alone is reputed to have drunk 17 cups of tea. Their climb had been an extraordinary achievement. They had gone higher than anyone had ever managed before and survived a potentially disastrous crisis. Mistakes had certainly been made. They had been too ambitious to try a summit attempt with just one camp above the North Col. Mallory was satisfied with what they had achieved, but he was concerned about Morshead's condition: 'We can't know yet what the damage will be. I suppose it was stupid or careless for us to be caught like this.'[31]

These were early days on Everest and an understanding of physiology and the limits of endurance at high altitude was virtually non-existent. The climbers knew that they had underestimated the mountain, and the end of this first attempt on the summit of Everest marked the beginning of the use of oxygen.

When the four climbers were up on the North Col, George Finch was at Base Camp, frustrated with the state of the oxygen equipment. Many parts had been damaged and the valves in the face-masks were making breathing very difficult. Finch wrote: 'With feelings akin to dismay, suspicions that I had already formed at Camp I were confirmed; not one of the ten oxygen apparatus was usable ...soldered joints leaked; washers had become so dry that the other joints could no longer be made gastight, and several of the gauges were out of action.'[32] Not surprisingly, the other climbers had little faith in the equipment.

Undeterred, Finch adapted the system, using glass T-pieces and toy football bladders which he had bought in Darjeeling. The repairs owed more to Heath Robinson than modern technology, but they worked well enough and allowed the apparatus to be used.

The day after Mallory's party returned to Advanced Base Camp (ABC) they met Finch and Geoffrey Bruce, together with the Lance-naik Tejbir Bura of the 6th Gurkhas, on their way to re-supply the North Col with oxygen and other equipment. The climb by Bruce and Finch up to the North Col on 22 May was the first trial with Finch's repaired oxygen equipment and the results were remarkable. With the use of 'English air', the climbers made an astonishing ascent to Camp IV in just three hours, and returned in 50 minutes. Finch even had time to take 36 photographs on the way.

On 24 May Finch, Geoffrey Bruce, Tejbir Bura and John Noel started out again for the North Col with the intention of continuing to the summit. They used oxygen and found the going easy. They had a sleepless night at Camp IV and felt lethargic the next morning. Noel suggested that they try a few whiffs of oxygen and he immediately felt rejuvenated. Finch did the same, and he too felt much better. They had discovered an additional benefit of oxygen, which would later save their lives.

Twelve porters left at 8 a.m. carrying oxygen and camping equipment. Bruce, Finch and Tejbir left an hour and a half later, carrying 14-kilogram (30-lb) loads; this was more than the Sherpas, but they had the advantage of breathing oxygen. By the time the climbers reached 7470 metres (24,500 feet), they had caught up with the porters. Just after midday, it began to snow and the wind freshened, so Finch called a halt for the day at 7800 metres (25,600 feet), some 150 metres (500 feet) short of their objective. This allowed the porters time to return to the North Col, and the British climbers spent another bad night on the mountain.

Once it got dark, the wind rose and the buffeting became so violent that the climbers were lifted clear of the ground during the gusts, only to be dumped unceremoniously back on to bare rock during the lulls. Added to that, the fastenings on the inside of the tent door had torn and the men had to hold the flaps together all night to stop their tent and its occupants from becoming airborne. Needless to say, sleep was impossible. George Finch wrote: 'Terrific gusts tore at our tent, and occasionally the wind would force its way underneath the sewn-in ground-sheet and lift it up at one side or the other. When this happened, our combined efforts were needed to hold the ground-sheet down, for we knew that, once the wind got a good hold upon it, the tent would belly out like a sail, and nothing would save it from stripping away from its moorings and being blown, with us inside, over the precipice on to the East Rongbuk Glacier.'[33]

Dawn brought a little respite from the storm, which began to moderate by midday. Exhausted and now short of rations, the climbers should have retreated from the mountain, but they were determined to stay up on the ridge. That afternoon Noel and six Sherpas climbed up to their camp with hot tea and soup.

The decision by Finch, Bruce and Tejbir to stay on the mountain was heroic, but it was the wrong decision. They had gone for over 36 hours without proper sleep or food in very low temperatures, and they now faced another night on the mountain. Incredibly, the men resorted to smoking that evening, which passed the time and helped relieve their hunger pangs. No doubt they were also encouraged by Finch's theory that smoking made breathing easier at high altitude.

As darkness fell, it became bitterly cold and Finch could feel numbness enveloping his body. He knew it was the onset of frostbite. Bruce, too, was looking gravely ill – and this was his very first climb. Finch realized that they were now in a desperate, possibly fatal, situation. It was at this point that he remembered the remarkable effect that oxygen had had on them two days previously. He took a few deep breaths from the cylinder and the effect was extraordinary and immediate. He passed the apparatus to Bruce and then Tejbir and saw them revive before his eyes. They breathed oxygen throughout the night and all three slept soundly and remained warm. Finch recalled: 'There is no doubt whatsoever that oxygen saved our lives that night; without it, in our well-nigh exhausted and famished condition, we would have succumbed to the cold.'[34]

The following day they were feeling very much better, and decided to make an attempt on the summit. They were away by 6.30 a.m., with the two British climbers carrying 18 kilograms (40 lb) and the Gurkha 22 kilograms (50 lb). Carrying the lion's share proved too much for Tejbir and he collapsed only 100 metres (300 feet) above their overnight camp. He retired to the tent and Bruce and Finch knew that their summit bid was now hopeless, but the two climbers were determined to push on for as long as possible. Unroping, so that they could move more quickly, they set off towards the North East Ridge.

Incessant buffeting from the rising wind forced the climbers off the ridge to seek protection on the vast North Face of Everest. Things immediately became more difficult for them as they worked their way across the Yellow

Band, the distinctive strip of marine limestone that circles the top of the mountain like a wedding ring. The immense, outward-sloping limestone slabs are always slippery, especially when covered with soft, unstable snow.

At around 8200 metres (26,900 feet) they decided to head up to the ridge again. They had not climbed more than 100 metres (300 feet) before Bruce staggered to a halt and cried out that he was getting no oxygen. Finch turned round just in time to catch his companion as Bruce began to fall backwards down the North Face. The glass tube in Bruce's supply mechanism had broken. Fortunately Finch was carrying a spare, but before he could repair the system he had to alter his own so that they could both share the oxygen supply. At an altitude 8320 metres (27,300 feet), they were the highest that man had ever climbed. They realized, however, that this was as far as they would get on this attempt. Bitterly disappointed, they withdrew from the mountain.

For Geoffrey Bruce, it was an extraordinary and unique achievement. He had come to Everest with no previous mountaineering experience and set a world altitude record on his very first climb. No other climber has since achieved this.

It is also interesting to compare the speed of these two attempts in 1922. From ABC, Mallory and Somervell climbed to 8120 metres (26,800 feet) in 14¾ hours without oxygen, an ascent rate of 120 metres (393 feet) per hour. Finch and Bruce climbed to 8320 metres (27,300 feet) in 12¼ hours with oxygen, a rate of 155 metres (517 feet) per hour, a figure that would be even higher if they had not spent time traversing the North Face. The advantages of using oxygen at high altitude were clear to even the most fervent sceptic.

The two climbing parties returned exhausted to Base Camp. Longstaff gave everyone an examination and declared them all medically unfit to climb, except Somervell, who seemed to have suffered no ill-effects. Finch and Strutt had strained their hearts, while the unfortunate Morshead was in great pain and distress with severe frostbite: although he put on a show of being cheerful, Somervell noticed he would slip away by himself and cry like a child. He later had a toe and several fingers amputated in India. Mallory also had frostbitten fingers, and his heart was showing signs of irregularities.

Both Mallory and Finch took umbrage over their medical examinations and insisted they were capable of another attempt on the summit. Mallory's frustration was clear when he wrote to Ruth: 'Longstaff, who has been very busy telling us all how ill we are since we came down, was strongly of the opinion that the expedition had done enough & had better shut up shop, reported me medically unfit not only on account of my finger but on account of my heart ...'[35] The long weeks on the mountain were beginning to take their toll and the climbers were irritable, Mallory included: '[Longstaff] is in one of his moods of bustling activity, when he becomes tiresome, interfering and self-important.'[36]

Finch tried to go up to Advanced Base Camp but felt too ill to go beyond Camp I. He returned to England early with Strutt, Longstaff and Morshead. When Hinks got wind of their departure, he wrote to Charlie Bruce with ill-concealed contempt: '[Even if] the oxygen experts want to come home I should myself have been glad to hear that some of you propose to stay and do further geographical work [and that] the party would not be in too much of a hurry to come home *en masse*.'[37]

Bruce replied to Hinks, explaining his concerns: 'It is also cruelly hard. The shortness of time, early monsoon, etc, disablement of climbers ... frankly I am afraid of Everest under the present conditions with the monsoon only within days of us.'[38] Hinks had little sympathy for the situation; he wrote back: 'I should be a sad man if you all came back without clearing up the geography of the West Rongbuk ...'[39]

Mallory was disappointed with the outcome and fell into one of his moods. He too was concerned about the deteriorating weather conditions. On 1 June he wrote to David Pye: 'The mountain has taken his toll among us; but lord, how much worse it might have been! ...David, it's an infernal mountain, cold and treacherous. Frankly, the game is not good enough: the risks of getting caught are too great; the margin of strength when men are at great heights is too small. Perhaps it's mere folly to go up again. But how can I be out of the hunt?'[40]

With the monsoon imminent and weather conditions deteriorating by the day, Longstaff wrote in his diary: 'Everest a snow peak. Will take 3–5 days' sun to clear. Impossible now.'[41] Despite the poor forecast, Mallory set off on 5 June with Somervell, Crawford, Wakefield and 14 Sherpas. By the time they reached Camp III, some 45 centimetres (18 inches) of snow had fallen. It was a bad omen.

On the morning of 7 June, Wakefield stayed back while the rest of the party left for the North Col, wading through waist-deep snow. It was exhausting work and they changed leaders constantly as they forced a path through the new snow. They took a short break at 1.30 p.m., about 200 metres (600 feet) below the col; Somervell was leading with Mallory, Crawford and a Sherpa on the first rope. The other Sherpas followed, also roped together.

They had taken barely a dozen paces before they heard a rumble: 'We were startled by an ominous sound, sharp, arresting, violent, and yet somehow soft like an explosion of untamped gunpowder ... And then I began to move slowly downwards, inevitably carried on the whole moving surface by a force I was utterly powerless to resist ... For a second or two I seemed hardly to be in danger as I went quietly sliding down with the snow. Then the rope at my waist tightened and held me back. A wave of snow came over me. I suppose that the matter was settled ... I thrust out my arms above my head and actually went through some sort of motions of swimming on my back ... My arms were free; my legs were near the surface. After a brief struggle, I was standing again, surprised and breathless, in the motionless snow.'[42]

Mallory was able to see Somervell, Crawford and a porter close by, and below him were four Sherpas; but of the other nine men there was no sign. As they struggled down the col, it became clear what had happened: the men on the last two ropes had been swept over an ice cliff into a crevasse and tonnes of snow had poured on top of them. The shocked survivors wrestled with the loose snow in a desperate attempt to find their buried colleagues and managed to reach two of them alive – one had been buried for 40 minutes before being rescued.

However, seven porters died in the catastrophe and it was the wish of the surviving Sherpas that their friends should remain buried. The climbers withdrew from the mountain and a memorial cairn was built at Camp III in memory of those who had lost their lives.

The climbers were traumatized by the event and Mallory, as the climbing leader, blamed himself for making an attempt in dangerous snow conditions.

He wrote to Ruth: 'The consequences of my mistake are so terrible; it seems almost impossible to believe that it has happened for ever & that I can do nothing to make it good. There is no obligation I have so much wanted to honour as that of taking care of these men; they are children where mountain dangers are concerned & they do so much for us: and now through my fault seven of them have been killed.'[43]

The others too were shocked by events. Somervell later wrote: 'I remember well the thought gnawing at my brain. "Only Sherpas and Bhotias killed – why, oh why could not one of us Britishers have shared their fate?" I would gladly at that moment have been lying there dead in the snow, if only to give those fine chaps who had survived the feeling that we had indeed shared their loss, as we had indeed shared the risk.'[44]

Charlie Bruce also regretted his decision to allow the final assault on the mountain. He was well aware of the risks of climbing as the monsoon approached, especially as the climbers were in poor physical condition. In his final expedition report he noted: 'Strutt is a first class mountaineer in judgement and I wish to goodness he had command of the last party which went up.'[45]

From Base Camp, Bruce ordered a retreat from the mountain. Everest had beaten the climbers a second time. In the aftermath of any disaster, especially where there is loss of life, come the inevitable recriminations.

It was a demoralized party that struggled back to England on 16 July, and the very next day the climbers were asked to report to the Everest Committee. Many of the men also talked to Hinks in private, speaking more openly than at the committee hearing. Hinks subsequently wrote to Norman Collie, the president of the Alpine Club: 'The returning people at present are disposed to say nasty things about Howard-Bury last year and Mallory this year. Wakefield was a complete failure. I think they are all cross and jumpy like the people who came back last year and they want handling carefully.'[46]

Hinks's assessment was probably accurate, and many of the climbers, in private, were very critical of Mallory: 'The people who have come back think Mallory's judgement in purely Alpine matters was bad and much inferior to Norton of whom everyone speaks very highly. They evidently had sharp disagreements about the proper way to ascend the North Col, Finch going a different way from Mallory.'[47]

To his credit, Mallory took responsibility for the accident. He wrote to Younghusband: 'I'm very much to blame for this terrible accident, and I'm very sorry. I want you to believe that it was not the result of any spirit of recklessness or any carelessness of coolies lives. If I had known more about snow conditions here, the accident would not have happened, and so one may say it was due to ignorance ... I am particularly sorry for the loss of these men. They had done remarkably well.'[48]

Mallory received a generous reply from the chairman of the Everest Committee: 'However much you may blame yourself, I certainly am not one to blame you, for I have done precisely the same thing in the Himalaya, and only the purest luck can have saved me and my party from disaster .... But anyhow we do recognise that you performed a magnificent feat in beating all previous records by such a big amount as 2200 feet – and that in itself made the expedition worthwhile.'[49]

Collie, however, did not share Younghusband's admiration of Mallory, and he was much more critical: 'To *traverse* snow slopes is always dangerous and the best way is always to go *straight up*. It looks as if they zig-zaged [sic] up. Evidently Mt Everest is not a mountain to be monkeyed with, and it will need very experienced mountaineers ... it is a mercy that the accident wasn't the end of the whole party.'[50]

Tom Longstaff was not a climber, but well understood the risks. He wrote to Alexander Wollaston with an unusually frank assessment of the team: 'Mallory is a very good stout hearted baby, but quite unfit to be placed in charge of anything, including himself. Somervell is the most urbanely conceited youth I have ever struck – and quite the toughest ... Wakefield could not face the altitude at all – rather worse than I was, and is ignorant of the arts of mountaineering. Norton was a huge success in every direction. Fine eye for the country. Sound climber. Bird man. Plants. Always on for any job and always did the job well. He got Morshead down alive ... We so dreaded Finch that we were relieved to find his manners very passable: his temper agreeable: his mountain knowledge not overrated.'[51] On the accident he added: 'Mallory cannot even observe the conditions in front of him. To attempt such a passage in the Himalaya after new snow is idiotic.

What the hell did they think they could do *on Everest* in such conditions even if they did get up to the North Col. Route above is slabbly with strata the wrong way, and most dangerous after new snow.'[52]

The Everest Committee, and especially Hinks, also came under criticism from Longstaff. He believed that Bruce had been forced into allowing a summit attempt at almost any price, and in doing so had overlooked the dangerous conditions.

Strutt did his best to console Mallory in a letter: 'I am awfully sorry for you, and I know well how much you are feeling this disaster ..... I will add, if you will allow me, that after the great fall of fresh snow, seventeen persons on the North Col was fifteen too many, even after *two* days' perfect weather. I don't think these are criticisms; the man on the spot must be the sole judge, and he gets the reward or pays the penalty.'[53]

Mallory's old climbing friend Geoffrey Young was also supportive and told him (incorrectly, as it turned out) not to think '... that anyone has ever thought of placing any responsibility for the accident on you or the mountaineers ... You made all the allowance for the safety of your party that your experience suggested ...'[54]

Despite the loss of life on the North Col and the recriminations among the returning group, the Everest Committee was determined to try again. The deaths of the Sherpas apart, much of the 1922 expedition had been a great success. A new altitude record had been set and much had been learnt about the physiology of climbers at altitude and the value of oxygen. Bruce's organization had been outstanding and he was keen not to lose the sense of momentum and the goodwill that had been generated with the Tibetans. It was agreed that there was insufficient time to mount an expedition the following year, so all energies were directed towards an attempt in 1924.

Meanwhile, on his way home, Howard Somervell stopped off at the Neyyoor Mission in Travencore to visit a friend. He was so moved by the work that was being done there that he decided to give up a prestigious position he had been offered at University College Hospital in London, and instead he went to work in India as a missionary doctor.

Mallory, too, found himself at a crossroads in life. He had a wife and three young children to support, but no job, so he decided to earn some money by giving public lectures about the Everest expeditions. At the beginning of 1923 he went on a lecture tour of the United States, travelling from Washington DC to Chicago and from Philadelphia to Boston. The tour was a mixed success: at times the lectures were well attended and he overcame his nervousness about talking to a large audience. The *New York Tribune* commented approvingly: 'He described the perils of the climb in simple language, and kept his personal part in the expedition very much in the background.'[55]

It was during this tour that a journalist asked Mallory why he wanted to climb Mount Everest, and he uttered those famous words, 'Because it's there.' Far from being a clever and enigmatic reply, it was most likely a tired and irritable retort to a question he had been asked a thousand times before. It has, nevertheless, found its place in history as an immortal phrase.

Unfortunately, the lecture tour was not a financial success, but Mallory's luck did change for the better on his return to England. Hinks had recommended him for the position of assistant secretary and lecturer of the Board of Extra-Mural Studies at Cambridge. Influential friends had written in support of his application and he was given the job.

Meanwhile, there were several changes in the Everest Committee; Farrar resigned and Bruce took over from Younghusband as chairman. The next job was to select the climbers for the new expedition.

CHAPTER SEVEN

'A Dismal World of Snow and Vanishing Hopes'

'I look back on tremendous efforts & exhaustion
& dismal looking out of a tent door on to a
dismal world of snow and vanishing hopes – &
yet, & yet, & yet there have been a good many
things to set on the other side.'

George Mallory's last letter to his wife, 27 May 1924

The first task for the new Everest Committee was to clear up some outstanding financial irregularities. First, there was the matter of £717 18s 11d in cheques and cash, with which the committee's cashier, C.E. Thompson, had absconded. The treasurer, Edward Somers-Cocks, took some responsibility for mismanaging committee affairs and he offered to pay £350 if the matter were dropped – which it was.

There was also an outstanding bill for £360 16s 1d from the Indian High Commissioner for the use of army mules during the 1921 expedition; these were the animals that had proved totally inadequate to carry the team's equipment through the forests of Sikkim. Rather than pay the debt, the committee sent a letter of complaint to the Viceroy of India, and left it at that.

Just as the committee members thought they were out of the woods financially, the Alliance Bank in Simla was declared bankrupt and they lost another £700. At about the same time, the committee found that the German rights to the 1922 Everest film had inadvertently been sold twice, and that they were about to face court action. The film was not a financial success and the modest £500 profit made from distribution now had to be held over, pending legal action from the Germans.

In this unsettled atmosphere the next job was to select the members for the new expedition. General Bruce was the universal choice to continue as leader, but, not for the first time, there were concerns expressed over his health. Like the other prospective climbers, Bruce was required to have a medical, which revealed that he had high blood pressure, a dilated heart and an irregular pulse. None the less, he was passed fit.

F.E. Larkins, one of the examining doctors, wrote to Bruce's own physician, Claude Wilson, to say that he was unhappy about passing Bruce. Wilson, on the other hand, was worried about the consequences if Bruce did *not* go on the expedition: 'I don't want him frightened and I don't want him turned down, and though I know there is a risk, I am willing to take full responsibility for letting him go, assuming that he keeps feeling as well as he is now.'[1] Larkins was not prepared to share the risk: '[I] cannot possibly let the Committee take him on without expressing a pretty strong warning. ... If he gets apoplexy out there, they have only themselves to kick.'[2] A compromise was eventually struck, which allowed Bruce to stay as leader, provided that he was re-examined by a doctor before he went beyond Darjeeling.

The selection committee then turned their attention to choosing the climbers and the climbing leader, who would also be Bruce's deputy. Mallory was on the selection committee, as he was the only person who had been on both previous expeditions to Everest. He seemed to be the obvious choice as climbing leader, yet he was ambivalent about going to Everest again and he did no more than put a question mark against his own name. The reasons for his equivocation are complex. He had never particularly liked Tibet and he feared the power the mountain might exert over him. He was also in the process of moving his family to Cambridge and he was looking forward to starting his new job. In truth, he had never been very good at making important decisions concerning his own life, and he was usually content to allow others to make the running.

Despite Mallory's obvious attributes, the selectors had to question his suitability. He had been reckless on the North Col in 1922 and he was well known for his chronic absent-mindedness. In the end, Edward Norton was asked to be climbing leader, and he proved to be a popular choice. However, the committee still wanted Mallory on the team, for in the public's eyes he embodied the challenge of Everest. Mallory thought it unlikely that his new employers at Cambridge would release him, but when the committee finalized the names of the team, Hinks wrote to the university, asking them to release Mallory for the expedition.

Indecisive as ever, Mallory wrote to his wife: '... I don't think they will hear of me going. It will be a big sacrifice for me either way. It is wretched not to be able to talk to you about this, darling. You must tell me if you can't bear the idea of me going again, and that will settle it anyway.'[3] To his great surprise, the university agreed to release him for six months on half pay. Once again, others had made an important life-decision on his behalf.

Mallory, still torn over the decision, could not bring himself to run against the consensus. He wrote to his father: '... it would look rather grim to see others, without me, engaged in conquering the summit ... I only hope this is a right decision. ... It has been a fearful tug.'[4] He was more honest about his fears with his friend Geoffrey Keynes, who later wrote: 'Shortly before starting he said to me that what he would have to face would be more like war than adventure, and that he did not believe he would return alive. He knew that no one would criticise him if he refused to go, but he felt it a compulsion.'[5]

Meanwhile, Mallory found a large house in Herschel Road, Cambridge, and his family moved in on 28 October 1923. At last, he was reunited with Ruth and the children, but their last few months together were frantic. The house was big and urgently needed decoration.

This was a difficult period in Mallory's nine-year marriage. He had been away from his wife for much of that time, either at war, up Everest or on lecture tours, leaving Ruth to raise three young children alone. Their only means of communication during his absences was by post, and they wrote literally thousands of letters to each other. Now Mallory was leaving again, for what his wife hoped was the last time.

The tensions of his imminent departure were fuelled by money problems.

Their old house in Godalming had not been sold and their new house in Cambridge needed constant attention and was proving very expensive to heat. Now their bank had warned them that they were overdrawn. Ruth even considered taking in lodgers to help pay the bills. She wrote to her husband on 3 March, a few days after he sailed from Liverpool: '... I do miss you a lot. I think I want your companionship even more than I used to. I know I have been rather often cross and not nice, and I'm very sorry ... I was unhappy at getting so little of you. I know it's pretty stupid to spoil the times I do have for those when I don't.'[6]

On his voyage out to India, Mallory had time to reflect on their relationship: 'I fear I don't make you very happy. Life has too often been a burden to you lately and it is horrid when we can't get more time & talk together. Of course we have both had too much to do ... Somehow or another we must continue to manage differently; to have some first charge upon available time for our life together.'[7]

In addition to Bruce, Norton and Mallory, the other members of the 1924 team included Howard Somervell, John Noel and Geoffrey Bruce from the 1922 expedition. Four NCOs from the 2nd/6th Gurkha Rifles again joined the party; Hurke, Shamsher, Tejbir and Umar. New climbing members included Noel Odell, the doctor-climber Bentley Beetham and Richard Graham. Two non-climbing members had specific duties; Major R.W.G. Hingston, an Irish, RAF surgeon, was the expedition doctor and naturalist, and E.O. Shebbeare of the Bengal Forest Department assisted Geoffrey Bruce in organizing the expedition transport.

Richard Graham was a strict Quaker and had been a conscientious objector during World War I. His selection caused immediate controversy among some members of the team. Somervell wrote from India threatening to resign his membership of the Alpine Club if Graham did not stay on the team. Mallory also supported him, but the dispute became so vitriolic that Graham eventually withdrew, not wanting the conflict to weaken the expedition rapport. His position was taken by John de Vere Hazard, a strange man whose behaviour was later to make the committee regret their choice.

Missing from the list of climbers was George Finch, who had continued to irritate the Everest Committee with his lecturing activities. During the summer of 1923, and without referring the matter to the committee, Finch had lectured on the Continent about the 1922 expedition, only to receive an invoice from the committee for 50 per cent of his earnings. Finch refused to hand over so much. In retaliation, the committee instructed him not to make Everest the principal topic of his lectures – and they even tried to copyright the name of Mount Everest in order to limit his activities.

Now that Percy Farrar was no longer a member of the committee, Finch had lost his greatest supporter and he knew that his days were numbered. He continued to work on his beloved oxygen apparatus, but he was not invited on the 1924 expedition. Instead, Odell assumed responsibility for oxygen equipment, as well as replacing the much-maligned A.M. Heron as the expedition geologist.

John Noel returned on the 1924 expedition as photographer, and in one single act he managed to solve the financial problems of the committee. Despite the fact that the 1922 expedition film had been only a limited success, Noel offered to buy all the photographic rights of the new expedition for the huge sum of £8000, made payable to the committee *before* departure. This offer saved the expedition an additional £2000, which they had allocated to photography.

Noel raised the money for the photographic rights by forming a company called Explorer Film Ltd, and invited Francis Younghusband to be company chairman. The funds were raised from the general public in anticipation of a share of the distribution profits. Even the Aga Khan was persuaded to invest in the film company. The resourceful Captain Noel had processed all his negative film in a special dark-room tent at Base Camp two years previously, heating the tent with a yak-dung stove. This time he built a special processing laboratory in Darjeeling. The exposed film from Everest was sent back to India by relays of horsemen and the processing of film and lantern slides kept two assistants busy seven days a week for four months.

The last member to join the team was Andrew Irvine, known as 'Sandy' because of his blond hair. He was a surprising addition because of his youth and relative lack of experience. Born on 8 April 1902, the third of William and Lilian Irvine's five children, he was brought up in a comfortable, middle-class home in Birkenhead.

His education followed a traditional pattern: preparatory school,

Shrewsbury public school, then Oxford. His acceptance at the last was something of a struggle as he initially failed the entrance examination. Finally, after attending a 'crammer', he was accepted at Merton College to study engineering, more for his skills as an oarsman, one suspects, than for his intellectual ability. He represented the university twice in the Oxford and Cambridge Boat Race, his team winning convincingly in the second year.

Irvine's selection came about through a chance meeting with Noel Odell in Spitsbergen in the summer of 1923, when the young undergraduate was taking part in an Arctic expedition. Irvine impressed Odell with his strength, endurance and good humour. When a place arose on the Everest climbing team later that year, Odell had no hesitation in recommending the young man to the committee.

Some members considered Irvine too young and lacking in mountaineering experience. There was some justification in this: he was 12 years younger than the average age of the expedition and had climbed no higher than 1830 metres (6000 feet). Odell, however, knew that he had grit. On one occasion, he and Irvine had skied 20 kilometres (12 miles) across a glacier and climbed more than 900 metres (3000 feet) to make the first ascent of a mountain, which is still called Irvinefjellet.

Irvine's biggest contribution to the expedition was his engineering skill. From a very early age, he built toys and experimented in a small storeroom at home. When he was 17, his father bought a new Essex motor car and Irvine set about drilling out all the rivets and replacing them with bolts. When finished, he shook it vigorously and declared he had eliminated the 'nocks'.[8] The vehicle subsequently served the family well for over 10 years.

On the Everest expedition, Irvine soon earned a reputation for being able to fix almost anything mechanical. With the unexpected departure of Finch from the party, Odell found the responsibility of maintaining the oxygen apparatus a little daunting – he was a geologist by training, not an engineer. By recommending that Irvine join the team, he could share the burden of the maintenance work. It was a wise decision, and Irvine worked constantly on the equipment throughout the expedition. *En route* to Everest, he wrote in his diary: 'Found all but one of the oxygen frames had been more or less damaged in transit, so spent afternoon and evening repairing them with copper rivet and wire. Also made tin lampshades to replace the cardboard ones which continually caught fire.'[9]

Mallory wrote to Ruth about his first impressions of Irvine: '... sensible & not highly strung he'll be one to depend on, for everything perhaps except conversation'.[10] Somervell was also impressed when he first met him in Darjeeling: 'Irvine, our blue-eyed boy from Oxford, is much younger than any of us, and is really a very good sort; neither bumptious by virtue of his 'blue', nor squashed by the age of the rest of us. Mild but strong, full of common sense, good at gadgets (none of the oxygen apparatus would have worked were it not for him ...) If ever a primus-stove goes wrong, it goes straight to Irvine, whose tent is like a tinker's shop. He's thoroughly a man (or boy) of the world, yet with high ideals, and very decent with the porters.'[11]

The selection committee formally offered the final place on the team to Irvine on 24 October. Unlike Mallory, he did not prevaricate and accepted at once, unable to believe his good fortune. Odell later wrote of his apprentice: 'Though lacking in mountaineering experience it was felt that the natural aptitude he had already shown, together with his undoubted gifts of mechanical and general practicable ability, not to speak of temperamental suitability, fitted him for inclusion in the party ...'[12]

As with the previous Everest expeditions, the party converged on Darjeeling from different directions. Charlie Bruce and Edward Norton left England early and arrived in Bombay on 16 February. Mallory, Irvine, Hazard and Beetham sailed from Liverpool on 29 February on board the SS *California*. Although Mallory did not share a cabin with Irvine as he had hoped, they did take their meals together and their friendship flourished during the voyage out to India. Since his lectures in England in 1923, Mallory was something of a minor celebrity and people questioned him during the voyage about the new expedition, or asked to have their picture taken with him.

Odell made his way from the Persian oilfields, Hingston from his RAF posting in Mesopotamia, and Somervell from Travancore in southern India where he was working as a mission doctor. The assorted members were instructed to meet at the Mount Everest Hotel in Darjeeling during the third week of March.

The expedition departed for Tibet on 25 March 1924, taking the usual route north through the Himalayas, through the Serpo La to Kampa Dzong, and then west towards Tingri Dzong. Within two weeks, illness began to weaken the team. Beetham came down with a bad case of dysentery, from which he never made a full recovery. Mallory had abdominal pains, thought to be appendicitis, but he recovered once Somervell made ready with his surgical tools.

Of greatest concern was the health of Charlie Bruce. He had gone on a tiger shoot before the expedition began and had 'bagged' more than intended when he unknowingly contracted malaria. On 7 April he celebrated his fifty-eighth birthday in usual ebullient manner, with a bottle of the finest rum sent out by his brother for the occasion. He felt poorly the next day and made a delayed start, but he later collapsed with a fever.

The next day he had a second attack, and after some discussion it was agreed that he should give up the leadership and return to India under the medical care of Hingston. Norton was appointed in his place, and he selected Mallory as climbing leader. Mallory, understandably, was thrilled with the new arrangement. During the month-long trek to Base Camp, the friendship between Mallory and Irvine continued to flourish, and it is clear from their writings that they spent a lot of time together.

Throughout the expedition, Irvine suffered from sunburn because of his pale skin. He first wrote about the problem on 11 April: 'My face is very sore from wind and sun, also my nails and surrounding skin are splitting, and my nose is peeling badly.'[13] He was never to get any respite from the sun for the rest of his time in Tibet. Despite his discomfort, however, he continued to spend every spare moment mending equipment: whatever needed fixing was passed to Sandy. On the day he first mentioned his sunburn, he wrote: 'I spent all afternoon trying to make the blow-lamp work, with complete failure ... I then resorted to a primus for heating my soldering iron. I mended Mallory's bed, Beetham's camera, Odell's camera tripod and sealed up a full tin of paraffin and tore my wind-proof trousers.'[14]

Unfortunately, serious problems soon became apparent with the oxygen apparatus. When the cylinders reached Calcutta, several were found to be empty and others were only half-full; the problem was traced to leaking valves. The cylinders were re-filled before leaving India, but when the expedition reached Shekar Dzong, a third were found to be empty again. Irvine re-built and improved on the original design, making them 2 kilograms (5 lb) lighter in the process.

Unfortunately, no comparable improvements had been made in the climbers' clothing since 1922, despite George Finch's innovative attempts to develop a down-filled jacket for high-altitude climbing. In fact, the clothing and equipment on the 1924 expedition were little different from those used in previous decades of Alpine climbing. Each expedition member had been given a £50 allowance and they all dressed in a similar fashion. Norton described his outfit thus: 'Personally I wore a thick woollen vest and drawers, a thick flannel shirt and two sweaters under a lightish knicker-bocker suit of windproof gaberdine …soft elastic Kashmir putties and a pair of boots of felt bound and soled with leather and lightly nailed …a very light pyjama suit of Messrs Burberry's 'Shackleton' windproof gaberdine … a pair of long fingerless woollen mitts inside a similar pair made of gaberdine … On my head I wore a fur-lined leather motor-cycling helmet, and my eyes and nose were protected by a pair of goggles of Crooke's glass, which were sewn into a leather mask … A huge woollen muffler completed my costume.'[15]

However, the expedition did make an effort with the food, and their order from the Army and Navy Co-operative Society included 60 tins of quail in *foie gras*, 300 1-lb (0.5 kilogram) Hunter Hams and four dozen bottles of Montebello 1915 champagne.[16]

As the expedition approached Rongbuk, various ideas began to emerge about how to tackle the mountain. Mallory consulted everyone and then formulated his plan. On 17 April he wrote to his wife: 'I've had a brain-wave – no other word will describe the process by which I arrived at another plan for climbing the mountain. … This plan has such great advantages over all others that Norton has taken it up at once & this evening we had another powwow & everyone has cordially approved.'[17]

Mallory proposed a classic siege attempt on the mountain. He was convinced that the only way to succeed on Everest was to construct a pyra-mid of camps and equipment up the mountain, with each camp supplying the one above it. The further up the mountain, the smaller and more basic the camps became, with the highest camp of all used as a springboard for the final assault on the summit.

He planned to make two early attempts on the mountain in case the monsoon arrived early. These would be mounted simultaneously, with one party using oxygen and the other without. Camp V would be established at around 7773 metres (25,500 feet), Camp VI at 8077 metres (26,500 feet), and Camp VII at 8321 metres (27,300 feet). On summit day, the oxygen group would start from Camp VI and the other group from Camp VII. The two teams would be able to support each other and could be expected to reach the summit at about the same time.

Mallory proposed that those from the high camp should climb without the 'English gas', and that he and Irvine would start from Camp VI with oxygen. The climbers were surprised that Mallory chose Irvine as a summit partner over the more experienced Odell. Norton was not happy with the choice, but he felt that there was little he could do, as he had effectively given Mallory *carte blanche* over the summit plan. Irvine, on the other hand, was delighted: 'I'm awfully glad that I'm with Mallory on the first lot, BUT I WISH EVER SO MUCH THAT IT WAS A NON-OXYGEN ATTEMPT [Irvine's emphasis].'[18]

The expedition reached Rongbuk on 28 April and Norton calculated that the first attempt could be made around 17 May. This was earlier than previous attempts, but memories of the early monsoon in 1922 now made Norton seize the earliest opportunity. The schedule seemed a good one, but made little allowance for the uncertainties of mountain weather. Another important lesson they had learnt from earlier climbs was not to allow the climbers and Sherpas to become exhausted early in the expedition. They therefore recruited 150 local porters to carry to the lower camps, thus saving the climbing Sherpas for later in the climb.

On 3 May, Mallory, Irvine, Odell, Hazard and 20 porters left Camp II on the East Rongbuk Glacier, intending to establish Camp III under the North Col. John Noel travelled with them, filming on the way. A second group of 20 porters followed a day later with more supplies. Unfortunately, a severe storm struck the mountain and the second team did not reach Camp III with the extra supplies.

Temperatures plunged to -45°C (-22°F) as arctic winds swept the glacier. The climbers struggled through blinding blizzards, and those stranded at

Camp III survived with only a blanket apiece and a handful of uncooked barley. When Geoffrey Bruce eventually broke through to Camp III with the much-needed supplies, he wrote: 'No one moved about the camp; it seemed utterly lifeless. The porters were wretched, and this terrible blizzard, coming immediately on top of their hardships of a few days ago, completely damped their spirits and energy. Many of them became so apathetic that they would not even attempt to cook for themselves . . .'[19]

The following day Mallory rose at 6.30 a.m. to go down to Camp II, as Irvine recalled: 'Energetic beggar. I feebly asked if I could be of any help, without the slightest intention of moving from my warm sleeping-bag. He gallantly refused my offer, so I went to sleep again until about 9 a.m.'[20] Bruce also stayed up at Camp III, but the conditions did not improve: 'As evening came on, the wind blew still harder in tremendous gusts from every direction. All the tents were again filled with snow with all the consequent discomfort. The cold was intense, and the thermometer fell to 39° below freezing point.'[21]

Operations ground to a halt and Norton ordered a wholesale retreat until the conditions improved. By 12 May, everyone was back at Base Camp, but the expedition had paid a heavy price. Those porters who were not sick or injured were hopelessly demoralized. One Sherpa had a broken leg and several others had contracted pneumonia, but the most serious cases involved the Gurkha NCO Shamsher, who had developed a blood clot on the brain, and the cobbler Manbahadur, who had frostbitten feet up to the ankles. Neither man could get the major surgery their conditions required to save their lives and both were buried on the outskirts of Base Camp. It was an inauspicious start to the third Everest expedition.

On 15 May the abbot of Rongbuk met with the party and gave both the climbers and the Sherpas his blessing. But the expedition could do nothing but wait for the weather to improve. They were grounded at Base Camp for a week, and Noel, who was sharing a tent with Mallory, commented that he was restless, highly strung and very impatient at the enforced delay.

Mallory was not the only member of the party to be frustrated with the weather conditions. Norton, too, was becoming very worried and he was haunted by the possibility that the monsoon might come early. Fortunately, soon after the Lama's visit, the weather improved and Norton grasped the opportunity to make new plans for the summit.

Work began on restocking the camps and a new summit date of 29 May was set. Mallory and Norton, followed by Odell and the Sherpa Lhakpa, began to fix ropes up the North Col, which had changed from previous years. They wanted to avoid the disastrous route of 1922, so they laid a more direct course, which included an ice chimney 60 metres (200 feet) high. This they protected with hollow wooden stakes and fixed ropes. Norton wanted to return from the col as quickly as possible, and they began their descent at 3.45 p.m. He later wrote: '... the less said about the descent the better. We took the 1922 route and, going very fast, had a series of slips and tumbles into crevasses, for which there could be no explanation but sheer carelessness.'[22]

Not for the first time, the North Col was their undoing, and Mallory had fallen into a crevasse. He wrote to Ruth: 'Meanwhile, I, below, finding the best way down, had walked into an obvious crevasse ... the snow gave way, and in I went with the snow tumbling all round me, down luckily only about ten feet before I fetched up half-blind and breathless to find myself precariously supported only by my ice-axe, somehow caught across the crevasse and still held in my right hand – and below was a very unpleasant black hole.'[23] He shouted for assistance, but nobody heard him. He realized he would have to rescue himself and managed to cut a hole through the side of the crevasse and squeeze through, only to find himself on the wrong side. By the time he returned to Camp III, he was exhausted.

The next morning, Somervell, Irvine and Hazard climbed the col with 12 Sherpas and established Camp IV, but heavy snow made the ascent difficult. The plan was for Somervell and Irvine to return to Camp III, leaving Hazard and the Sherpas to set things up. It continued to snow throughout the night and for most of the next day.

The morning of 23 May dawned bright and clear as Bruce and Odell, together with 17 porters, set out for the North Col, hoping to push on to Camp IV and possibly Camp V the following day. They were just part way up when the weather deteriorated, and they could only watch as Hazard and a group of Sherpas began to descend through another heavy snowfall. Hazard had decided to abandon Camp IV in the deteriorating weather, but four

Sherpas were frightened by the steepness of the route on the North Col and had refused to leave the camp.

It was a nightmare scenario for Norton and he was furious with Hazard for abandoning the Sherpas. He now had four terrified men stranded at the top of the North Col with little food and the possibly of frostbite. Any attempt to rescue them could trigger an avalanche in the heavy snow. Most of the climbers at Camp III were unfit to mount a rescue, as many were suffering from a variety of illnesses, ranging from bad throats to diarrhoea (Irvine tried to cure his attack with lead and opium). As the weather continued to deteriorate, Norton feared this must be the onset of an early monsoon, and all his hopes for a successful summit attempt were dashed. His priority now was to develop a rescue plan.

The next morning dawned bright and fine, and despite the occasional deep patches of snow, Norton, Mallory and Somervell, the most experienced and well-acclimatized climbers, trekked back up the col to rescue the stranded Sherpas. Everything went well until the three climbers got close to the ledge at the top of the col. To reach the ledge required a careful traverse close to the top of the col in snow that was clearly ready to avalanche. Somervell insisted on taking the risk and leading, securely belayed by Norton and Mallory. Just 9 metres (30 feet) from where the four frightened men were waiting, Somervell ran out of rope. There was no alternative but for the four stranded Sherpas to make their way unassisted, one at a time, to where Somervell was waiting for them.

The first man made his tentative way to the rope and then on to the anchor point. The second man waited patiently until the first had reached safety, before he too began to move along the rope. For some inexplicable reason the last two men decided to move down together.

The inevitable happened. The unstable snow gave way and they began to slide towards the ice cliff 60 metres (200 feet) below. Incredibly, the two Sherpas came to a halt in the loose snow after just a few metres. Somervell untied himself, drove his ice-axe deeply into the snow, passed a rope around the shaft and lowered himself carefully until he could grasp the nearest man, pulling him to safety. He lowered himself a second time and repeated the manoeuvre.

It took until 7.30 p.m. for the three climbers and four Sherpas to return to Camp III, still in shock. The next day, 25 May, the expedition abandoned the camp at the head of the East Rongbuk in another retreat from the mountain. For the second time in less than a fortnight, the expedition was disheartened and discouraged.

What Norton did not realize was that the weather on Everest that spring was very unusual; it was caused by weather patterns coming in from Afghanistan, and not by an early monsoon coming up from the Indian subcontinent. Had he known, he could have held back at Base Camp, waiting for a pre-monsoon period of good weather. Instead, the expedition had retreated twice from the mountain under the onslaught of appalling weather, and they now waited exhausted and debilitated at Base Camp for new instructions.

Norton could do one of two things: he could abandon the expedition, or he could come up with one final plan that made the most of what little remaining strengths they had left. He called the climbers together at Camp I to discuss the options. It was agreed that they could mount one final, lightweight assault on the mountain, with six climbers supported by the few remaining fit Sherpas moving up to the North Col together.

Miraculously, the sky cleared and fine weather returned. In order to lighten loads, even the use of oxygen was abandoned. It was decided that Mallory and Geoffrey Bruce, who had spent the least amount of time at altitude and were therefore probably the fittest climbers, would make the first attempt. Behind them, Somervell and Norton were ready as another strong pair. Odell and Irvine stayed at the camp on the North Col to support the climbers; Noel, who was filming, remained with them. Hazard stayed at Camp III.

Noel observed that Mallory looked unwell and exhausted, and thought he kept going on nervous energy alone, his strength having been sapped by the dreadful conditions. Before he left Camp I, Mallory wrote his final letter to his wife on 27 May: 'Dear Girl, this has been a bad time altogether – I look back on tremendous efforts & exhaustion & dismal looking out of a tent door on to a dismal world of snow and vanishing hopes – & yet, & yet, & yet there have been a good many things to set on the other side ... The only chance now is to get fit and go for a simpler, quicker plan ... But I am quite doubtful if I shall be fit enough ... Darling, I wish you the best I can – that your anxiety will be at an end before you get this – with the best news which will also be the quickest. It is 50 to 1 against us but we'll have a whack yet & do ourselves proud. Great love to you. Ever your loving, George.[24]

On 30 May the team was assembled at Advanced Base Camp, ready for the first ascent. Mallory and Bruce climbed the col the next day and spent the night at Camp IV. On 1 June the climbers went up to the ridge, followed by eight Sherpas carrying their supplies. It was bright but cold, and a vicious north west wind slowed their progress. At 7625 metres (25,000 feet) half the porters dropped their loads and descended, exhausted by the harsh conditions. Meanwhile, Camp V was established another 90 metres (300 feet) up the mountain. Mallory, Bruce and the remaining Sherpas settled down for the night.

That same day Norton, Somervell and six Sherpas climbed to the North Col. The next day they pushed on up the North Ridge as planned, from Camp IV to Camp V. Beyond the col, they were hit by the full force of the wind. Norton later wrote: 'The wind, even at this early hour, took our breath away like a plunge into icy waters of a mountain lake, and in a minute or two our well protected hands lost all sensation as they grasped the frozen rocks to steady us ... Though it seemed to cut clean through our windproof clothes, it yet had so solid a push to it that the laden porters often staggered in their steps.'[25]

Halfway between the two camps, Norton met Mallory's group coming down, exhausted after a sleepless night's battering in the freezing wind. Norton continued up, and by 1 p.m. his group reached Camp V. That afternoon, a rock dislodged from the higher of the two tents, rolled down and struck two porters in the lower tent. One man had a gashed head and returned to Base Camp the next day; the other Sherpa, Semchumbi, had a badly cut knee, but gamely agreed to continue.

To their surprise, the wind dropped the next day and the weather improved. The climbers decided to move up the mountain. Unfortunately, Somervell was developing a sore throat from breathing the cold air, and Semchumbi could not continue with his injured knee. At 1.30 p.m. Norton called a halt and established Camp VI. They had reached an altitude of 8170 metres (26,800 feet).

The next day they decided to make a summit attempt and started early at 6.40 a.m. – even though neither man was fit. Somervell's throat was still painful and Norton was shivering violently, as he recalled: 'The day was fine and nearly windless – a perfect day for our task – yet it was bitterly cold, and I remember shivering so violently as I sat in the sun during one of our numerous halts, dressed in all the clothes I have described, that I suspected the approach of malaria and took my pulse. I was surprised to find it only about sixty-four, which is some twenty above my normally very slow pulse.'[26]

An hour later, the two climbers reached the Yellow Band, but the altitude was slowing their progress and both men found themselves gasping in the thin air. Somervell's raw throat was also causing him breathing difficulties and he was racked with bouts of coughing. Norton, meanwhile, had taken off his dark glasses in order to see better on the dark rock, and now his eyes were inflamed and he was having difficulty seeing.

Despite these problems, the two men climbed beyond the Yellow Band and began to cross the North Face, keeping 150–180 metres (500–600 feet) below the North East Ridge. By midday they were close to the great gully, which runs down from the summit pyramid. Somervell's throat was getting worse and his coughing exhausted him; he could go no further.

Norton continued alone and later wrote: '... there was a lot of powdery snow which concealed the precarious footholds. The whole face of the mountain was composed of slabs like the tiles of the roof, and all sloped at much the same angle as tiles. I had twice to retrace my steps and follow a different band of strata; the couloir itself was filled with powdery snow into which I sank to the knee or even the waist ...'[27] It was now 1 p.m. and Norton realized that he had to return if he was going to make it safely back to Camp VI.

Despite his obvious disappointment, Norton established a new altitude record of 8573 metres (28,126 feet), which was to remain unchallenged for almost 30 years. (Five days later, Odell estimated that Mallory and Irvine reached an altitude of 8610 metres (28,250 feet), but this record has never been confirmed.)

It took Norton an hour on the treacherous ground to return to his companion. Reunited, they roped together and began their descent at 2 p.m. Somervell dropped his ice-axe, which went tumbling down the

North Face. When the two climbers reached Camp VI, they collapsed their tent and covered it with stones to stop it blowing away; they then continued down the mountain. They arrived at Camp V as night began to fall, but decided to continue down to the North Col. Once on safer ground, they unroped and continued separately. Norton descended quickly down a large snow patch below Camp V without any problems, and he expected his colleague to follow quickly.

Unfortunately, Somervell, now alone on the mountain in the growing gloom, had developed an obstruction in his throat and was beginning to suffocate: 'Somewhere about 25,000 feet high, when darkness was gathering, I had one of my fits of coughing and dislodged something in my throat which stuck so that I could not breathe neither in nor out.'[28] The inner lining of his throat had become frostbitten and a section had become loose, blocking his windpipe and thus preventing him from breathing.

'I could not, of course, make a sign to Norton, or stop him, for the rope was off now; so I sat in the snow to die whilst he walked on, little knowing that his companion was awaiting the end only a few yards behind him. I made one or two last attempts to breathe, but nothing happened. Finally, I pressed my chest with both hands, gave one last almighty push – and the obstruction came up. What a relief! Coughing up a little blood, I once more breathed really freely – more freely than I had done for some days. Though the pain was intense, yet I was a new man ...'[29] It was a lucky escape for Howard Somervell, who was seconds away from suffocation; he had coughed up the frostbitten mucus lining of his larynx.

Reunited, the two climbers made their way back down the mountain in the growing darkness. Norton began to shout for support. Soon, Mallory and Odell located the two exhausted climbers and helped them back to Camp IV, where Irvine was busy preparing soup and tea. During the night, Norton was stricken with a blinding pain in his eyes. He had developed opthalmia (snow-blindness), which was to affect him for the next 60 hours.

With Norton and Somervell safely down the mountain, Norton's hasty plan for a quick and lightweight assault on the mountain was complete. Yet the fine weather continued and the Sherpas had made good use of it to re-supply the high camps with food and oxygen. Even while Norton was still on the mountain, Mallory had begun to develop the idea of one last attempt on the summit before the heavy snowfall of the summer monsoon would make the mountain too dangerous because of avalanche risk.

Mallory still wanted the relatively inexperienced Sandy Irvine to accompany him. Norton was not against the attempt, but he thought Irvine an unwise choice and advised Mallory to climb with Odell, who was now well acclimatized. Mallory was adamant that Irvine should be his partner, and Norton – still snow-blind and in great discomfort – decided not to overrule the man he had appointed as climbing leader. Noel recalled Norton's concern: ' "There is no doubt Mallory knows he is leading a forlorn hope." I had the opportunity of observing Mallory closely … and I formed the positive opinion that physically he had become an unfit man.'[30]

Mallory's insistence on taking the inexperienced Irvine has puzzled climbers and mountaineering historians ever since. Some see it as a fulfilment of Mallory's romanticized view of conquering Everest, with himself playing the ageing Sir Galahad in his final bid for the Holy Grail of the summit, accompanied by the athletic, 22-year-old Irvine, who seemed to embody everything that Mallory had been in his youth.

Others have hinted at a deeper, more romantic attraction between the two men. They point to their growing friendship since the voyage out from Liverpool, and to Mallory's student friendships with known homosexuals at Cambridge, which implies, they claim, a certain sexual ambiguity in Mallory. There have also been unsubstantiated rumours that Mallory had a homosexual relationship during his visit to Canada in 1923. There seems, however, little evidence for these claims. Duncan Grant, a close friend of Mallory's, was emphatic that he was not bisexual. Nor is there any evidence that Irvine had anything other than heterosexual inclinations – by all accounts, he had always taken a very healthy interest in the opposite sex before coming out to Asia.

In fact, given the two options open to him – Irvine or Odell – Mallory's choice makes logical sense. Irvine was young, fit and an expert at fixing the notoriously fickle oxygen apparatus. Mallory, on the other hand, was hopelessly impractical. Although he would have preferred to climb without oxygen, he was convinced by now that it was the key to reading the summit. Although Odell was nominally in charge of the equipment, it was Irvine who showed the mechanical proficiency to keep it working.

Mallory wrote to his wife on 24 April, explaining his preference: 'It was obvious that either Irvine or Odell should come with me in the first gas party. Odell is in charge of the gas, but Irvine has been the principal engineer at work on the apparatus – what was provided was full of leaks and faults and he has practically invented a new instrument ... so Irvine will come with me. He will be an extraordinarily stout companion, very capable with the gas and with the cooking apparatus; the only doubt is to what extent his lack of mountaineering experience will be a handicap; I hope the ground will be sufficiently easy.'[31]

Clearly, Mallory was aware of Irvine's climbing limitations, but his decision to take the younger climber was made after considerable reflection. This would also be a last-ditch attempt on the summit, so Mallory might have preferred a climbing companion who would not question his decisions on the mountain. On previous climbs, Mallory had sometimes shown a determination that bordered on recklessness. Reaching the summit of Everest had now become an all-consuming passion for him. Noel even claimed that Mallory was mentally ill in his determination to reach the summit. On this attempt, Irvine was unlikely to question his mentor when it came to important decisions on the mountain, leaving Mallory free to go 'all out' for the top.

There are also good reasons why Mallory did not want to climb with the older man. Odell had been slow to adjust to altitude during the expedition, and it was only after Mallory's disappearance that he showed how superbly acclimatized he had since become. Odell also had a reputation for being slow to start in the mornings. After climbing in Spitsbergen together, Tom Longstaff wrote that Odell was a notoriously slow starter, only at his best after 12 hours. This would not have endeared him to Mallory, who was always impatient to get going and who knew that an early start on summit day was essential. Nevertheless, Odell must have been very disappointed to be excluded from this final attempt on the summit.

Meanwhile, Irvine, although fit and well acclimatized, was still suffering from sunburn. On 3 June he wrote: 'A most unpleasant night when everything on earth seemed to rub against my face, and each time it was touched bits of burnt and dry skin came off, which made me nearly scream with pain.'[32] There was no respite from the discomfort and on 5 June, he wrote his last few lines in his diary: ' … it has been very trying for everyone with a freezing air temperature and a temperature of 120 in the sun, and terribly strong reflection off the snow. My face is perfect agony. Have prepared two oxygen apparatus for our start tomorrow morning.'[33]

Wearing an oxygen mask for the next three days must have been almost unbearably painful for Irvine, yet he never had any doubts about accompanying his friend and mentor on their last climb together.

On the morning of 6 June, Mallory and Irvine enjoyed 'a choice fry of sardines' for breakfast, strapped on their double oxygen cylinders and prepared to leave for Camp V with eight Sherpas. Before they left, Odell grabbed his camera and took the last picture of these two climbers. It was a quiet departure with a portentous air about it. By 5 p.m., four of the Sherpas had returned with a message from Mallory that they had arrived safely at Camp V. The scribbled note added: 'There is no wind here and things look hopeful.'[34]

The next day the two men and the four remaining Sherpas climbed to Camp VI, a solitary two-man tent clinging precariously at 8168 metres (26,800 feet) on the North Face. After dumping their loads, the four Sherpas returned to Camp V, where they met Odell, who had climbed up from Camp IV in support of the two climbers. Sherpa Lakpa told Odell that the two climbers were fit and well and settled into the camp. He brought two messages written by Mallory – one for Noel Odell and the other for John Noel. They read:

Dear Odell,
We're awfully sorry to have left things in such a mess – our Unna cooker rolled down the slope at the last moment. Be sure of getting back to IV tomorrow in time to evacuate before dark as I hope to. In the tent I must have left a compass – for the Lord's sake rescue it; we are without. To here on 90 atmospheres for the two days – so we'll probably go on two cylinders – but it's a bloody load for climbing. Perfect weather for the job.

Yours ever,
G. Mallory[35]*

Dear Noel,

We'll probably start early tomorrow (8th) in order to have clear weather. It won't be too early to start looking for us either crossing the rock band or going up skyline at 8.00 p.m. [He meant 8.00 a.m.]

Yours ever,

G. Mallory[36][†]

The two men slept at Camp VI on their final night. Everything was working in their favour: they were well supplied, they had sufficient oxygen and the weather was promising. The sky was clear, the wind had dropped and it was not particularly cold: perfect conditions for a summit attempt.

The following morning, 8 June, the two climbers set off. Nobody can be sure what time they left that morning, but Mallory was well known for his early starts and it is inconceivable that the men overslept at that altitude, where any sleep at all is considered a blessing. He would probably have tried to leave by 6 a.m., although this would have entailed rising at 4 a.m. in order to dress, eat and squeeze tired feet into frozen leather boots. But when Odell climbed to Camp VI later that morning, the tent was in a shambles,

---

* These notes are the last known to have been written by Mallory and they contain important evidence to help us piece together the last few hours of his life. Mallory mentions the loss of the cooker; this means that he and Irvine would not have had a hot breakfast in the morning, or the ability to melt snow, which might have led to serious dehydration later in the day. Forgetful as ever, Mallory left his magnetic compass at Camp IV; this might have hindered his movement on the mountain in bad visibility. He also refers to the oxygen cylinders containing 90 atmospheres; when full, the cylinders contained 120 atmospheres, suggesting that Mallory and Irvine had used three-quarters of a tank each on their two-day climb from Camp IV to VI. This rate led Mallory to believe that they could reach the summit on just two cylinders.

† Mallory's note to John Noel refers to his plans for filming, as Noel would be watching their progress with a powerful telephoto lens. To reach the skyline on the ridge by 8 a.m. (the reference to 8 p.m. is a slip) would mean that the two climbers would have to leave camp very early, probably at daybreak around 6 a.m. Clearly, Mallory intended an early start, although other evidence suggests that this might not have been the case. The reference to crossing the rock band suggests that Mallory had still not decided that evening whether to go for the ridge route (which would be his natural preference) or to try the traverse under the ridge, pioneered by Norton. We know from Noel's last sighting that Mallory finally chose the ridge route.

suggesting that their departure might not have gone smoothly that morning.

Meanwhile, further down the mountain, Odell also rose at 6 a.m. He climbed from Camp V up to the high camp to support the summit bid, taking food with him in case the other climbers had run short. The sky was clear, but by 8 a.m., clouds had rolled in from the west and these prevented him from being able to see the North East Ridge, which runs up to the summit. However, the mist was thin and the brightness of the sky suggested that the higher parts of the mountain might still be in sunlight: '.... one could see a certain luminosity that might mean comparatively clear conditions about its upper half. This appearance so impressed me that I had no qualms for Mallory and Irvine's progress upward from Camp VI and I hoped that by this time they would be well on their way up the final pyramid of the summit.'[37]

The weather continued fair: the wind was light with occasional snow flurries and Odell busied himself looking for fossils. When he reached an altitude of about 7925 metres (26,000 feet), he came to a small crag, which he decided to climb rather than circumvent. He looked at his watch and saw it was 12.50 p.m. Before him, the mist cleared to reveal the whole of the peak, and Odell saw Mallory and Irvine on the ridge. It is a sighting that has intrigued historians ever since and come under great scrutiny. Odell subsequently changed his story under intense questioning, but his original version is arguably the most reliable:

'There was a sudden clearing of the atmosphere, and the entire summit ridge and final peak of Everest were unveiled. My eyes became fixed on one tiny black spot silhouetted on a small snow-crest beneath a rock-step in the ridge; the black spot moved. Another black spot became apparent and moved up the snow to join the other on the crest. The first then approached the great rock-step and shortly emerged at the top; the second did likewise. Then the whole fascinating vision vanished, enveloped in cloud once more.

'There was but one explanation. It was Mallory and his companion moving, as I could see even at that great distance, with considerable alacrity, realising doubtless that they had none too many hours of daylight to reach the summit from their present position and return to Camp VI by nightfall. The place on the ridge referred to is the prominent rock-step at a very short distance from the base of the final pyramid, and it is remarkable that they were so late in reaching this place. According to Mallory's schedule, they should have reached it several hours earlier if they had started from the high camp as anticipated.'[38] The clouds rolled in and the two climbers were never seen again. Odell estimated their height at 8610 metres (28,250 feet) and said *both* men were moving strongly up towards the summit.

Odell's sighting has intrigued and frustrated historians ever since. Under intense questioning over the years, he has diluted his original observations with various qualifications. Yet his original report is quite clear: 'the *entire* summit ridge and final peak of Everest' was visible, he was adamant that he could see clearly 'even at that great distance', and he saw distinct movements of two individuals against snow cover over a period of several minutes.

Some writers have dismissed Odell's sightings as nothing more than an illusion or possibly birds flying among the rocks. Yet the man was an experienced geologist, trained to making careful observations in the mountains. He was also well acclimatized and had perfect eyesight (he did not require prescription spectacles until late in life). The fact that the two black objects were silhouetted against snow also suggests that he could see clearly.

If Odell's sighting is accepted as valid, it raises the question of where exactly the two climbers were on the ridge at 12.50 p.m. Were they moving around the First Step? If so, they were very late to make the summit. Were they at the Second Step? This is unlikely as no climber could negotiate this formidable obstacle so quickly. Or had they climbed even higher up the ridge to the Third Step, as Audrey Salkeld argues in her book (see page 221). If so, they were even higher than Odell's estimate, and had less than 150 metres (500 feet) further to climb up to the summit.

After his last fleeting glimpse of the two climbers, Odell carried on up the mountain and arrived at Camp VI at 2 p.m. It was beginning to snow and a bitter wind had picked up. The inside of the tent was shambolic, as Mallory had warned in his note, with food and oxygen equipment scattered around in a mess that was typical of him.

Odell also examined the oxygen equipment spread around the camp. There were cylinders and parts of a regulator inside the tent, but the aluminium carrying frames were left outside. Irvine might have been working on a faulty system, thus delaying their departure. If the equipment needed repair, however, the cylinders and frame would most likely have been kept together inside the tent.

An alternative explanation is that Mallory took the cylinders inside for the night so that they could use the oxygen for sleeping; if so, the frame would have been unnecessary and would only have taken up precious space in the tiny tent. Using oxygen for sleeping has great benefits, but it would obviously cut down on what was available for the summit attempt. However, a stash of oxygen from the 1922 expedition was not far away, and it is possible that Mallory recovered these spare cylinders and was able to use them to supplement his and Irvine's meagre supply.

Odell also found that Mallory had left his signalling flares in the tent, (possibly to lighten his load). At the time, he did not realize that Mallory had also left his torch and lantern behind. (A later expedition in 1933 found these essential bits of equipment in the tent.)

During the afternoon, the weather began to deteriorate: the wind rose, it began to snow and visibility became poor. Odell stayed in the tent for over an hour, waiting for the squall to pass. Thinking that Mallory and Irvine might have decided to retreat in the poor conditions, he then climbed 60 metres (200 feet) above the camp and began to shout and yodel for the two climbers. There was no reply. He waited, but eventually returned to the camp. The blizzard lasted two hours, then the sun came out, the wind dropped, and the light snow covering began to melt. Odell looked closely up at the ridge but saw nothing more of the two climbers.

Mallory's instructions had been clear: Odell was to return to Camp IV for the night and await their return from the mountain. Odell therefore closed up the small tent at 4.30 p.m. and made a rapid descent down to the North Col, periodically turning around to scan the upper slopes for any sign of the missing climbers. At Camp IV he met up with Hazard and related everything that had happened. At this early stage Odell was not unduly concerned about the climbers. In fact, the speculation was more about how high they had reached, rather than any doubts about their safety.

The two men kept a watch on the ridge all night in the hope of seeing something from the missing climbers, but because Mallory had left both his torch and his flares at Camp VI, he had no means of signalling to those keeping vigil. In the morning Odell left with two Sherpas for the higher camps. They spent the night at Camp V and then climbed on to Camp VI the following day, using oxygen. The camp was exactly as he had left it and there was no sign of Mallory or Irvine.

Odell continued up beyond the high camp in the hope that he might see some evidence of what had happened to the two men, but over 50 hours had passed and there was no sign. After two hours, he gave up the search and made preparations to inform the rest of the party of the tragedy. He placed two sleeping-bags on the snow in the shape of a 'T' – this was the pre-arranged signal for Hazard at Camp IV, informing him of a fruitless search.

Odell then collected Mallory's prismatic compass and Irvine's modified oxygen apparatus, closed up the tent at Camp VI, and headed back down the mountain one last time. Meanwhile, Norton, Bruce, Noel and Hingston were anxiously waiting at Camp III for news of the climbers. When Odell arrived at the North Col, he laboriously prepared another signal for those waiting at Advanced Base Camp – this time six blankets were used to create the shape of a cross against the white snow.

The other climbers down at Camp III saw the signal and knew there was no hope. John Noel recalled: 'Captain Norton was standing beside me. He was snow-blind and his eyes were covered in bandages. I had my camera automatically focused on filming the Sherpas high above us on the North Col. At the same time I was free to look through my powered telescope. Then, what we all feared took place. I perceived the Sherpas place blankets, and their own bodies, in the snow in the shape of a cross. I couldn't believe it. I placed my eyes repeatedly back to the telescope in the hope that the signal would change ... but it didn't. Of course, Norton, who was blind, was relying on me for informing him.... But I simply hadn't the heart to tell him. "What does it say?" he kept asking. The Sherpas eventually told him it was a cross, and they were dead.'[39]

Momentarily, Norton was tempted to send a small party up the main Rongbuk Glacier to the base of the mountain, in case the missing climbers had fallen down the North Face, but he soon realized the pointlessness of the exercise. There was now little chance of finding any signs of the lost climbers, and none of the climbers were in any condition to return to the mountain. The 1924 expedition was over.

Norton recalled: 'We were a sad little party; from the first we accepted the loss of our comrades in that great rational spirit which all our generation had learnt in the Great War, and there was never any tendency to a morbid harping on the irrevocable. But the tragedy was very near; our friends' vacant tents and vacant places at table were a constant reminder to us of what the atmosphere of the camp would have been had things gone differently ... the sense of loss was acute and personal, and until the day of our departure a cloud hung over the Base Camp.'[40]

Sir Francis Younghusband wrote of the climbers: 'Where and when they died we do not know. But there in the arms of Mount Everest they lie for ever – lie 10,000 feet above where any man has lain in death before. Everest indeed conquered their bodies. But their spirit is undying. No man onward from now will ever climb a Himalayan Peak and not think of Mallory and Irvine.'[41]

CHAPTER EIGHT

'A Mountain of Beautiful Remembrance'

'While there are hearts to quicken still at tales of heroism, merciless Everest — terrible to us — will remain for them a mountain of beautiful remembrance.'

Obituary to George Mallory by Geoffrey Winthrop Young

R uth Mallory was in Cambridge when she received a letter from her husband, written on 24 April 1924: 'The telegram announcing our success if we succeed, will precede this letter, I suppose: but it will mention no names. How you will hope that I was one of the conquerors! And I don't think you'll be disappointed. Ever your loving, George.'[1]

A telegram *was* sent from Tibet, but it was not what Mallory had predicted. Three days after the two climbers were last seen, Norton sent a runner from Base Camp to Phari Dzong with a coded message. It read 'OBTERRAS LONDON — MALLORY IRVINE NOVE REMAINDER ALCEDO — NORTON RONGBUK.'[2]

Hinks received the telegram at the RGS on the morning of 19 June. Once decoded, it explained that Mallory and Irvine had died making a final summit attempt, but the rest of the expedition was safe at Base Camp. Unfortunately, the press got wind of the news before Hinks informed the relatives of the two climbers. The first that Ruth Mallory knew of her husband's death was when a journalist appeared on the doorstep, asking for her reaction. Stunned at the revelation and the way in which it was delivered, she went for a long walk with close friends.[3]

The next day the Everest Committee issued an official press release and sent a telegram back to the expedition in Tibet: 'COMMITTEE WARMLY CONGRATULATES WHOLE PARTY HEROIC ACHIEVEMENTS PUBLISHED TODAY ESPECIALLY APPRECIATE CONSUMMATE LEADERSHIP. ALL DEEPLY MOVED BY GLORIOUS DEATH LOST CLIMBERS NEAR SUMMIT. BEST WISHES SPEEDY RESTORATION EVERYONE HEALTH. COLLIE.'[4] Douglas Freshfield (a previous president of the Alpine Club) took exception to what he thought was the inappropriate, almost celebratory wording of the cable. Although Norman Collie, the then president of the Alpine Club, had signed it, Freshfield suspected that it had been drafted by Hinks, and he wrote and complained to him that '..."congratulations" was the word [that] stuck in some people's throats.'[5]

That Saturday, Arthur Benson, Mallory's former tutor at Cambridge, read about the deaths in his newspaper and saw nothing to celebrate in the 'glorious death' of his old student: 'This entirely knocked me out. It is so utterly tragic. I think people have a right to risk their lives – but this is his *third* expedition, and he had a wife and two [sic] children ...'[6]

The news rocked the country, and throughout the rest of June and into July private consolations and public tributes poured in, including a message of condolence from King George V. At Charterhouse, headmaster Frank Fletcher remembered his former colleague: 'With us he has left special memories of a dear friend, memories of clean strength and glorious endurance and high adventure, and a love of beauty and beautiful things, which is one form of the love of God.'[7]

No climbers, before or since, have been so honoured in death. On 17 October a memorial service was held in St Paul's Cathedral, attended by relatives, friends and dignitaries, including the King, the Prince of Wales, the dukes of York and Connaught, Prince Arthur of Connaught, and members of the Royal Geographical Society and the Alpine Club. In his tribute to Irvine the Bishop of Chester recalled 'his brilliant, his amazing, his premature achievements as a climber, [how he] would laugh as he set himself the humblest tasks, or use the splendour of his giant great strength to bear the burdens of other men'.[8]

That evening, the RGS and the AC filled the Royal Albert Hall with a joint meeting, at which Norton spoke of Mallory: 'A fire burnt in him, and it made him one of the two most formidable antagonists Everest has ever had. ... His death leaves us the poorer by a loyal friend, a great mountaineer, and a gallant gentleman.'[9]

In private tribute, Mallory's old friend Geoffrey Keynes wrote to Ruth: 'I knew long ago that this was going to happen, but that doesn't make the fact any easier to bear.... You are the only person who could possibly know how much I loved George, and so I feel that I know something of what you have got to bear.'[10] A week later, Geoffrey Winthrop Young wrote: 'I was in France, and until we knew more I could not write. And I can't really now: it is a long numbness of pain, and yet but a shadow of yours, for indeed one cannot think of you separately. An unspeakable pride in that magnificent courage and endurance, that joyous and supreme triumph of a human spirit over all circumstances, all mortal resistance; and the loss unutterable ...'[11]

Ruth wrote back to Young: 'I don't think I do feel that his death makes me the least more proud of him. It is his life that I loved and love. I know so absolutely that he could not have failed in courage or self-sacrifice. Whether he got to the top of the mountain or did not, whether he lived or died, makes no difference to my admiration for him. I think I have got the pain separate. There is so much of it, and it will go on so long. ... Oh Geoffrey, if only it hadn't happened! It so easily might not have.'[12]

William and Lilian Irvine, too, were devastated. While Sandy Irvine had some inkling of the risks involved in making a summit attempt, his parents probably did not, and the news of his death came as a terrible blow. Every night until the day she died Irvine's mother lit a candle and placed it in the front porch of her house in the forlorn hope that it had all been a dreadful mistake and one day her son would return home to that welcoming light.

The climbers still in Tibet also had to come to terms with their shock. Three days after the tragedy, Somervell wrote from Base Camp, still uncertain about what had happened: 'No news. It is ominous. A few people have filtered back to the Base, very pessimistic. It is very disappointing to think that Mallory and Irvine may have failed – but they may never come back. They may be dead. My friend and fellow-climber, Mallory, one in spirit with me – dead? – I can hardly believe it.'[13] As time passed, he tried to rationalize the deaths and put them in perspective: 'There were only two possibilities – accident or benightment. It is terrible. But there are few better deaths than to die in high endeavour, and Everest is the finest cenotaph in the world to a couple of the best of men.'[14] Before they left Base Camp, the climbers built a memorial cairn 4 metres (15 feet) high to those who had lost their lives on the three Everest expeditions to date: Dr Kellas in 1921, seven Sherpas in 1922, and Shamsher, Manbahadur, Mallory and Irvine in 1924.

Norton wrote to the secretary of the Alpine Club: 'I feel the loss of Mallory and Irvine very much. Mallory and I shared a tent off and on for days and weeks; he was more than my right hand for all matters pertaining to the mountain and simply backed me up through thick and thin. Young Irvine was a real winner. I wish one could know whether they succeeded or not before the end.'[15]

Inevitably, there was great debate among the climbers over how Mallory and Irvine had met their deaths. Odell was alone in believing they had died from exhaustion and exposure on the mountain, having reached the summit and returned in darkness. The others thought that Mallory and Irvine had simply fallen to their deaths, probably during their descent; Norton in particular could not imagine Mallory giving up through exhaustion.

When Norton wrote to Hinks about the accident, he was careful not to place blame on either the climbers or their equipment: 'I have little doubt in my own mind that the party was roped – one or other slipped and pulled the other down. I was near the ground where they were last seen myself, and it is a dangerous place – every single stone slopes outwards and with a powdering of new snow such as occurred and while they were up there, it can become very nasty.... I don't think we need blame the [oxygen] apparatus.'[16]

Hinks, however, had never approved of using oxygen, and he wanted to hold an inquiry when the expedition returned to London to determine whether malfunctioning of the equipment was in any way to blame for the deaths of the two climbers. However, with no concrete evidence of the circumstances, it was difficult for the Everest Committee to come to any conclusions, or to make a case of negligence against the manufacturers of the apparatus. The company also pointed out that Irvine had modified the equipment, and they alleged that he had used low-pressure tubing in a high-pressure part of the system, which could have resulted in leakage. Consequently, the committee dropped the idea of taking legal action.

Inevitably, speculation was also rife among the climbers and the Everest Committee over whether the two climbers succeeded in reaching the summit. Odell had no doubts: '... I think myself that there is a strong probability that Mallory and Irvine succeeded,'[17] and his conviction remained unshaken until his death at the age of 99. Charlie Bruce too felt sure they were successful and he wrote to Hinks: 'I think that [Odell] gives a very reasonable opinion that the top was reached and that Mallory and Irvine were over taken on their way back: probably by dark.'[18]

Tom Longstaff shared Bruce's belief: 'Mallory wrote in the last letter I got from him: "We are going to sail to the top this time and God with us – or stamp to the top with our teeth in the wind." I would not quote an idle boast, but this wasn't – they got there all right.... . It is obvious to any climber that they got up... now they'll never grow old and I am very sure they would not change places with any of us.'[19]

Mallory's old friends also voiced their conviction that the two climbers made it to the top. Geoffrey Young was adamant: '... my own impression [is] that the accident occurred on the descent (as most do) and that if that is so, the peak was first climbed, because Mallory was Mallory.'[20] David Pye and Lady O'Malley were similarly convinced, as was John Noel, although for different reasons.

Others were less sure. Douglas Freshfield thought the plan of sending just two climbers to the summit without any back-up was appropriate only on shorter climbs, and was 'wholly unsuitable, if not suicidal in the case of great ascents'.[21] Norton was not convinced either: 'It remains a case of "not proven", and that is all that can be said about it.'[22] Both men infuriated the 'summit supporters'. Young wrote angrily to Freshfield, challenging the motivation of those who doubted that Mallory and Irvine had reached the top: 'Of course there must always be an inclination in such an open question for those who hope to return to the attack to think the summit still unclimbed.'[23]

Whether the two climbers were successful or not also had important financial implications. Under the terms of the contract with *The Times*, an additional £1000 would be paid to the committee if the summit were reached. The Everest story had generated huge public interest and the newspaper was quite prepared to pay the 'summit bonus' if there was a definitive ruling on the issue, but the committee was not prepared to be conclusive. Hinks wrote to *The Times*: 'We all hope that they reached the top and like to think of them resting there rather than at the head of the main Rongbuk Glacier after a fall, but there does not seem to be any possibility of a definite conclusion, and I think that you will agree the Committee can hardly be in a position to make any positive statement.'[24]

John Noel was consistently adamant that Mallory and Irvine succeeded in reaching the summit, but he was always somewhat mysterious about the reason for his certainty. Shortly before his death in 1989, he related an extraordinary tale. Several days after Mallory and Irvine had died, Noel visited the monastery in Rongbuk, taking with him a personal article belonging to Andrew Irvine. He was shown into a dark cell where a monk concentrated on the article and by the power of his mind, was able to project an image on to a blank wall, rather like a film projector. In fact, Noel claimed it looked very much like a faded black and white film.

'There, quite clearly, were Mallory and Irvine with their backs to the summit, which was a small distance above them. ... They were coming down. Mallory, just below the final pyramid, fell into a crevasse and died. Irvine continued down as best he could and fell, due to exhaustion, and died. ...

'Comparing it with my film, I recognized that the crevasse was between the Yellow Band and the final pyramid. That's where Mallory is, with Andy Irvine further down. In all events, it still doesn't prove that they climbed it, as they were coming down, though the summit looked very close. Then, of course, this was a vision shared by the monk and myself, not what you would call scientific. ... Who is going to believe it?'[25]

Within a few years of the climbers' deaths, more psychically generated stories began to circulate about what happened to Mallory and Irvine. In many ways this was not surprising because the story of their defeat was well known, and spiritualism was an extremely popular entertainment in Edwardian England.

One such story involves an Austrian climber called Frido Kordon. After attending a séance conducted by his son in 1926, Kordon claimed that Mallory and Irvine succeeded in reaching the summit at 5 p.m. but that Irvine collapsed and died soon after. Mallory buried his body, marking it with a stone cairn. Soon after beginning his descent, Mallory also fell and was killed.

Other stories of a similar nature circulated widely, but one of them takes on an eerie significance in view of details that came to light only years later. John Noel was approached by a man called Williamson, who reported psychic contact with Andrew Irvine. It was apparently revealed to him that both climbers reached the summit late in the day. During their unroped descent, Mallory slipped to his death, leaving Irvine, cold and exhausted, to continue down the mountain alone. The young climber was overcome with tiredness and sat down on a slab to rest, placing his ice-axe beside him. Huddled up and shaking in the intense cold, an image of Mallory appeared before him, saying: 'Come on, old chap, it's time for us to be going on.' The story struck Odell as quite plausible, as it explained how Irvine's ice-axe came to be lying on a slab just below the ridge (see the report of the 1933 expedition, page 147–9).

Biographer Audrey Salkeld also recounts the story of how Mallory's wife made contact with her dead husband.[26] Some time after his death, Ruth received a letter from Will Arnold Forster, a close family friend. Forster had known Mallory for many years and was convinced that he had made contact with him through a 'table-turning' session. When the table moved and spelt out the letters 'G·E·O', Will asked: 'Is that you, George?' 'Y·E·S' came the reply. He then asked where he was when his soul passed on to the next life. 'T·H·E·T·O·P.'

'George,' he enquired, 'is there anything I should tell the Everest Committee?' Back came the enigmatic reply: 'O·R·G·A·N·I·C E·X·H·A·U·S·T·I·O·N.'

When Ruth heard about the contact, she travelled down to Cornwall to stay with Forster and his wife, and together they tried to communicate with Mallory a second time.

'Do you know who is here?' Will asked. 'R·U·T·H' was spelt out. Ruth asked several questions of George – whether he knew when she was thinking about him and if he knew what she and the children were doing – and his positive answers gave her great consolation.

'And are you active and busy?' she asked of him. 'Y·E·S' came back the reply.

After the tragic events of 1924, the Dalai Lama refused visas to anyone wanting to climb the mountain. Major Frederick Bailey, who was now responsible for British relations with Tibet, had dealt with many diplomatic incidents in his time, including the furore over Heron's geological excavations in 1921 and the deaths of seven Sherpas in 1922. Now a new row was brewing. John Noel's film of the expedition had been released and the Tibetans objected to certain sequences in it, claiming that they were misleading. They also disliked their monks being used to dance and play music before showings of the film in British cinemas and disapproved of their religious traditions being reduced to a music-hall act. So they made an official complaint to the British.

Even though Bailey was an experienced explorer, he was concerned about the effect the Everest expeditions had on the fragile Tibetan culture and economy, and his worst fears were realized with this latest altercation. He wrote to Hinks on 1 January 1925: 'There is no doubt that no one in Tibet welcomes these expeditions and permission is only obtained out of friendliness to us, and that will cease to weigh sufficiently with the Tibetans if the actions of the expedition hurt their religious and other feelings.'[27] Bailey fully supported the Dalai Lama's decision to issue no more visas, and it was not until after his retirement in the late 1920s that there was any chance of another attempt on the summit.

On 19 March 1931 a new Mount Everest Committee was founded with Sir William Goodenough as president: Tom Longstaff and Francis Young-husband represented the RGS, and J.J. Withers and Norman Collie the Alpine Club. Despite representations to the Tibetan government, permission to mount a new expedition was still not forthcoming. However, rumours began to circulate that American or German expeditions might apply for permission, and this threat to national pride galvanized the authorities into putting pressure on the Tibetans to authorize a British expedition. Eventually, the Dalai Lama granted 'reluctant permission in deference to the wishes of the British government in order that the friendly relations may not be ruptured'.[28]

Responsibility for organizing the new expedition fell to Hugh Ruttledge, an ex-commissioner from the Indian Civil Service. He had experience of trekking in the Himalayas, but had no pretensions to being a mountaineer. He did, however, have a very strong team of experienced climbers, including Frank Smythe, Eric Shipton, Colin Crawford, Percy Wyn Harris, Lawrence Wager, T.E. Brocklebank, E. St J. Birnie, Dr. W. McLean, E.O. Shebbeare and Jack Longland. The clothing and equipment, however, showed little improvement over what was used in 1924.

The expedition went out to Tibet in early 1933, leaving Darjeeling at the end of February and arriving at Rongbuk on 16 April. They reached the North Col by 13 May and Camp V was established on 22 May at 7830 metres (25,690 feet). After a period of bad weather, they managed to put in Camp VI on 29 May at 8350 metres (27,400 feet). The site was in a precarious position on a tiny ledge less than 1 metre (3 feet) wide, which sloped away from the mountain. In fact, a quarter of the tent hung down over the North Face. Despite their inevitable discomfort, Wager and Wyn Harris settled down for the night, and Longland returned to the lower camp with the Sherpas.

As he began his descent, a great storm swept the mountain. Within minutes, visibility dropped to a few yards and Longland and his porters found themselves struggling for survival. Out of the gloom appeared a small patch of green: it was the 1924 Camp VI where Mallory and Irvine spent their last night. The men searched the tent and found the lever-torch and a folding candle lantern that Mallory had left behind before starting the summit attempt nine years previously. The torch was still in perfect working order.

Despite the appalling conditions, Longland and his Sherpas succeeded in reaching the lower camp. After a sleepless night at Camp VI, Wager and Wyn Harris set out for the summit. They climbed diagonally towards the North East Ridge and an hour later they stumbled upon an ice-axe leaning against an outcrop of rock.

It was an astonishing find. The axe was lying 18 metres (60 feet) below the ridge crest and 225 metres (750 feet) from the First Step. It was in good condition and still had the Swiss manufacturer's name engraved on it. The axe could only be from the 1924 expedition, when all the climbers used axes of that make. It must have belonged to either Mallory or Irvine because the other climbers that went high that year traversed the North Face and did not climb to the ridge. Unknown to Wager and Wyn Harris, the markings on the wooden shaft of the axe were identical to those used by Irvine to mark all his equipment.

The question the climbers asked themselves was how did the ice-axe come to be lying in that position? Did Irvine accidentally drop it, and did it then tumble down and come to rest 18 metres below? If so, the two climbers must have decided to continue with just one axe between them, which is not an unreasonable decision to make on a mountain which is mainly rocky. Or did the inexperienced Irvine pause for a rest, put the axe down and forget to pick it up when he continued? In that case he must have decided it was not worth the effort to return for it.

Or did the location of the axe mark the site of an accident and were their bodies lying somewhere down the fall line? If so, the climbers must have fallen during their *descent* because Noel Odell had seen the two men at 12.50 p.m. *higher* up the mountain, on their way to the summit. This was, perhaps, the simplest explanation: as the two climbers came down off the mountain, perhaps during the afternoon snowstorm, one of them slipped on the slabs. If it were Irvine, he dropped his axe and pulled Mallory down with him. If it were Mallory, Irvine might have put down his axe in order to grab the rope with both hands, but unable to hold the weight, he was pulled down after his companion.

Wager and Wyn Harris were understandably excited about their find, for this was the first piece of evidence about the fate that befell Mallory and Irvine, and it gave a hint as to where their bodies might be lying.

The climbers left the axe where it was and continued on their climb, but they found moving along the ridge difficult, so they dropped lower down and continued to work their way along the Yellow Band. They reached a point directly below the Second Step, and from what they could see, it appeared to be a formidable vertical wall. They were probably too far away and viewing the step from the wrong angle to make a proper assessment, but they judged the outcrop to be unclimbable. Their assessment contributed to the growing opinion that Mallory and Irvine probably could not have climbed this barrier either, and therefore did not reach the summit in 1924.

Wager and Wyn Harris continued their traverse above the Yellow Band in difficult conditions and succeeded in getting beyond the Norton Couloir, where they paused. It was 12.30 p.m. and they were just 300 metres (985 feet) below the summit at roughly the same altitude reached by Norton in 1924. The rocks, however, were covered with hard snow and it would have been dangerous to continue. On their descent, Wyn Harris retrieved Irvine's ice-axe, leaving his own in its place to mark the spot.

On 1 June Shipton and Smythe made a second summit attempt; although Smythe continued alone beyond the First Step, he did not get any further than Wager and Wyn Harris. With the monsoon close, the expedition abandoned any hope of getting higher. Many of the climbers were in poor shape: Birnie had severe frostbite, McLean had pneumonia and Shipton had lost his ability to speak coherently. Smythe called their retreat 'a descent of broken men'.

In terms of climbing ability and experience, the 1933 expedition was one of the strongest ever mounted on Everest. Despite not reaching the summit, they had recovered Irvine's ice-axe and Wager and Wyn Harris were able to make a close assessment of the Second Step.

The failure of the British expeditions to reach the summit in the 1920s and 1930s created a mystique about the mountain, and the stories of climbers battling against extreme conditions created widespread publicity. The Tibetans continued to exert strict control over access to Everest, but unofficial expeditions inevitably tried their luck on the mountain. Of all these unauthorized ventures, the most remarkable was made by Maurice Wilson in 1934.

Wilson was a Yorkshireman, born in Bradford in 1898. Like most young men of his generation, he joined the British Army on his eighteenth birthday and fought in France. He had a distinguished record in the infantry and was awarded the Military Cross during the third battle of Ypres, before being seriously wounded by machine-gun fire and subsequently invalided home.

After he was demobilized in 1919, Wilson was restless and began to drift; first to London, then to the USA and New Zealand. He eventually returned to England, still frustrated and unable to settle down. He was almost certainly close to a nervous breakdown, and became seriously ill with tuberculosis. Despite losing a great deal of weight, he refused medical assistance and over a period of two months, he claimed to have cured himself through a rigid regime of prayer and fasting. At last, he believed, he had found his true vocation in life and he resolved to teach his recuperative secret to others.

In 1932, while still convalescing in Germany, he caught sight of an old newspaper cutting about the 1924 attempt on Everest. Being convinced that fasting and divine faith were the secret to achieving whatever ambition you had in life, he decided to mount his own expedition to the mountain in order to publicize his curative regime. His plan was simple: he would fly to Everest, crash-land his aircraft on the East Rongbuk Glacier and then make his way to the summit on foot. He was convinced that his faith would see him to the top. But before he could achieve his goal, he had two further challenges: as he was neither a pilot nor a mountaineer, he would have to learn to be both.

He began with flying. Formal licensing had been introduced in Britain by the 1930s, so he was obliged to take instruction. He bought himself a three-year-old Gypsy Moth, which he renamed *Ever Wrest*, and took flying lessons at the London Aero Club. According to contemporary reports, he was not an accomplished pupil, and his flying lessons proved to be nerve-racking for his instructor and expensive for the pupil. He did, however, succeed in getting his private pilot's licence. He then went off to the Lake District and north Wales for five weeks of scrambling over rocks, and returned knowing even less about mountaineering than he did about flying.

By April 1933 he deemed himself ready, so he flew up to Bradford to see his parents before departing for Asia. Unfortunately, somewhere over the Yorkshire Moors he lost engine power and his subsequent crash-landing demolished a farmer's hedge and turned his aircraft upside-down. The repairs took three weeks, by which time he had attracted rather more publicity than he would have wished.

Inevitably, the Air Ministry got wind of his intentions and he was officially notified that under no circumstances was he to fly through Nepalese air space. Undeterred, he continued his preparations, and on Sunday 21 May he made his final preparations to leave Stag Lane Aerodrome in Enfield, north London.

Unfortunately, his notoriety had attracted both local residents and journalists. With minutes to go before take-off, the Air Ministry sent him a last-minute telegram, forbidding him under *any* circumstances from making his flight. He tore up the order and threw it away, but in the excitement of the moment, he became flustered and mistakenly took off downwind, only just managing to clear the end of the runway.

His extraordinary solo flight took him across Europe to Cairo, where he was denied permission to fly over Persia (now Iran). On arrival in Bahrain, he was refused fuel, but he persevered and reached India successfully. Here he was finally grounded when the authorities impounded his aircraft. He had succeeded in flying nearly 8000 kilometres (5000 miles), despite the best efforts of the British government to have him grounded *en route*.

Wilson sold his aircraft for £500 and made his way to Darjeeling. Here he applied for permission to go through Sikkim and Tibet on foot. Not surprisingly, the authorities denied him a visa. Undaunted, he assembled a team of three porters, all of whom had been on the 1933 British expedition, and set off for Tibet illegally. He took the precaution of travelling at night, disguised as a Tibetan monk, and reached the Rongbuk monastery in 25 days (10 days less than the British expedition had taken the previous year).

After a short rest, he set out alone and in good weather up the East Rongbuk Glacier, carrying a 20-kilogram (45-lb) rucksack. The twenty-first of April was his birthday and he wrote: '36 to-day. Wished myself many happy returns. Had hellish cold feet all night. Storm still raging ...'[29] The following day the weather continued to deteriorate and he reached a point just 5 kilometres (2 miles) short of Camp III. He recorded in his diary: 'No use going on. Eyes terrible & throat dry.... even [with] herculean effort, could not make Camp III in time, weather bad.'[30]

Wilson was now in a serious predicament: he was inexperienced, alone at high altitude, short of food, in great pain from his old war-wound and exhausted. By now, the temperature had fallen to -30°C (-22°F), yet somehow he summoned enough energy to gather his things and struggle back to the monastery. He had been alone on the glacier for nine days. Despite his ordeal, he wrote in his diary that night: 'I still know that I can do it.'[31]

Nearly three weeks passed before he was ready to make another attempt. This time he took two of his Sherpas, leaving Rongbuk on 12 May 1934. With the help of the porters, who knew the valley well, they reached Camp III in just three days. His strict fasting diet was soon thrown to the wind when the men discovered a food cache left over from the 1933 expedition; they dined on Fortnum and Mason's finest foods, including potted quail and Carlsbad plums, finished off with a large box of chocolates.

The men were confined to their tents for the next few days as fearsome winds blasted the glacier. By this time Wilson was suffering from altitude sickness. As the weather improved, he set off alone towards the North Col, sleeping out in the open on exposed ice-shelves, as best he could. After four days, he reached his final obstacle – a wall of ice 12 metres (40 feet) high, which had proved such a barrier to the British expedition the previous year. With no climbing support, no experience and no equipment, the ice chimney defeated him.

He staggered back to Camp III on 25 May, exhausted and beaten. He wrote in his diary 'Only one thing to do – no food, no water – get back.'[32] After two days of rest, he had recovered and did his best to persuade the Sherpas to accompany him to Camp V: 'This will be a last effort, and I feel successful ...'[33] His Sherpas refused to accompany him and on 29 May he set off alone. The last entry in his diary on 31 May 1934 read: 'Off again, gorgeous day.'[34]

The following year, Maurice Wilson's body was found by Eric Shipton's expedition. He was lying on his side alongside the remains of his tent. He had probably died from a combination of exposure and exhaustion. Among his effects, Shipton and Warren recovered his diary, which is now kept in the archives of the Alpine Club in London. The climbing party wrapped his remains in his tent and buried him by rolling the body into a crevasse on the East Rongbuk. But just as his body occasionally reappears from its interment in the ice (it was found by the Chinese in 1960, again in 1965 and several times since), so stories of a bizarre nature continue to resurface about the man.

Rumours began to circulate that Eric Shipton found a second, secret notebook in which Wilson kept a record of his sexual fantasies. Other rumours persist that when his body was found, he was wearing women's clothing and that Chinese climbers later found a woman's high-heeled shoe in a pre-war camp. It is a matter of record that at one time he ran a women's dress shop in Wellington, New Zealand, but rumours of fetishism remain unproven.

Maurice Wilson's determination and compulsive preoccupation with Everest is an indication of the power the mountain can exert over individuals. A maverick he certainly was, mentally unstable he might have been, but his extraordinary journey showed will-power and tenacity against almost insurmountable odds. Despite having no mountaineering experience, he succeeded in reaching an altitude of 6400 metres (21,000 feet) on a covert excursion across Tibet — a trek that would defeat all but the most determined adventurers today.

Perhaps his greatest achievement of all, though, was not in reaching the North Col unassisted, but in navigating his tiny Gypsy Moth biplane safely to northern India, despite the determination of His Majesty's government to prevent the journey.

In 1935 the expedition that found Maurice Wilson's body was led by Eric Shipton, and included Bill Tilman, Edwin Kempson, Edmund Wigram and the New Zealand climber L.V. Bryant. Among the Sherpas was the 20-year-old Tenzing Norgay. The primary intention that year was to explore the surroundings rather than concentrate on a summit attempt, and in two months the climbers succeeded in climbing 26 peaks in the Everest region.

British climbers returned again in 1936, this time led by Hugh Ruttledge. That year the weather conditions were unusual and the winds came from the east, bringing a great quantity of snow. The monsoon also came early, bringing further snow, and the mountain soon became dangerous, so the expedition returned early.

Two years later there was another attempt, led by Bill Tilman, but this was run on a very limited budget and equipment was pared down to the basic essentials. The expedition arrived on 6 April 1938 and conditions were perfect, which allowed them to set up the first three camps quickly. However, the weather changed for the worse and by mid-May, there were heavy falls of snow.

On 29 May, with the young Tenzing in the Sherpa party, the climbers reached 7450 metres (24,440 feet). Smythe and Shipton made a summit attempt on 8 June, but extreme cold and heavy snow forced them to retreat. Tilman and Peter Lloyd made a second attempt, which was also unsuccessful. The last hope of climbing Everest from the north had faded. Europe was once more bracing itself for war, and over a decade would pass before climbers would again stand on the flanks of the mountain and gaze up at the unclimbed summit.

World War II changed the political landscape of the region. After 1945, Tibet was closed to foreigners, but the southern approach to Everest opened through Nepal, and the British sent out a reconnaissance expedition in 1951. The return of the climbers rekindled Everest fever in post-war Britain and plans were made for an attempt on the summit in 1952.

The Swiss, however, took pole position from the British and obtained the only climbing permit from the Nepalese in 1952. In the spring Raymond Lambert and Tenzing Norgay climbed to the South East Ridge and set a new altitude record of 8600 metres (28,210 feet), but they failed to reached the summit. Their permit allowed them to climb at any time during 1951, so they returned in the autumn, but that attempt was also unsuccessful.

The British were allowed back to Everest in 1953, this time with an expedition led by John Hunt, which was well organized and planned to the last detail. The climbers also benefited from the experience of the Swiss in the previous year, and their equipment and understanding of high altitude were much improved as a result.

At 11.30 a.m. on the morning of 29 May the New Zealand climber Edmund Hillary and the Nepalese Sherpa Tenzing Norgay stood together on the summit of Everest. Hillary peered over towards the North Ridge where Mallory and Irvine would have approached the summit 29 years earlier. Instinctively, he looked for a sign of their passing, but saw nothing except snow, ice and bare rock.

It took several days for word of the summit success to reach London, but Britain was able to celebrate the good news on the morning of 2 June 1953, the day of the coronation of Princess Elizabeth.

When the Chinese Army marched into Tibet in 1950, the northern route to Everest was effectively blocked to Western climbers. However, this did not prevent the communist nations from continuing to climb this classical route to the summit.

In 1952 reports of a disastrous Russian attempt on the summit began to filter out from the Soviet Union, and stories appeared in European climbing journals and *The Times*. The Swiss had failed in their spring attempt on the Nepalese side, and the story from the Soviet Union was that Russian climbers had made an attempt in the autumn from the north, hoping to beat the British attempt planned for the following year. If successful, it would have been a tremendous propaganda coup for the Soviets at the height of the Cold War.

The Russian expedition apparently left Moscow on 16 October 1952, and after several unexpected delays, established Camp VII at an altitude of 8170 metres (26,800 feet). Disaster subsequently struck the party and six climbers, including the climbing leader Pawel Datschnolian: they simply disappeared and were never seen again, despite an extensive search. The expedition is reported to have returned very late in the year – on 27 December – when survival on the mountain would have been very tenuous.

The question still remains whether this attempt on the summit in the autumn of 1952 actually took place. All the evidence is circumstantial and the Soviet mountaineering authorities have vigorously denied that any attempt took place (although this is *exactly* what would be expected if the attempt had been a disaster).

Perhaps a more convincing reason to suppose that the attempt was fictitious is that after the Sino-Soviet split (which began in 1959), the Chinese made no attempt to embarrass the Russians by confirming the story. Given the tense relations between the two communist nations during the 1960s, it is unlikely that the Chinese would have missed the opportunity to capitalize on the disaster, especially after they succeeded in reaching the summit in 1960. It is most likely, therefore, that the 1952 Soviet attempt was the result of Cold War misinformation.

The Chinese had no history of serious, high-altitude mountaineering prior to 1955. Then, in a display of true socialist cooperation, the Russians began to help the Chinese, teaching them climbing techniques and supplying them with equipment. This collaboration culminated in joint reconnaissance expeditions of the northern route to Everest in 1958 and 1959. But before this partnership could mount a full summit bid, growing political differences between the two countries halted all cooperation.

Instead, China decided to go it alone, and in true Maoist style. The expedition was on a massive scale, involving 214 men and women, and a mix of Chinese and Tibetan climbers. On 19 March 1960 they established Base Camp at 5120 metres (16,800 feet) on the Rongbuk. They even built an 80-kilometre (50-mile) road through the mountains and over the Pang La, to give access to the glacier. The weather was poor and it took the expedition five weeks to reach the North Col. Climbing painfully slowly in worsening weather, the team took another six days to reach the Second Step, before retreating exhausted to Base Camp.

The expedition stumbled upon the body of Maurice Wilson above Advanced Base Camp (ABC). His body had been buried in a crevasse in 1935, but the movement of the glacier had worked the body back to the surface in the intervening years. The climbers also found pre-war oxygen equipment near Camp V at an altitude of 7788 metres (25,550 feet). The apparatus, probably used by Noel Odell in 1924, was taken back to Beijing, where it was found to be in perfect working condition.

With a weather forecast that promised a short break of fine weather before the imminent monsoon, a summit party of four climbers set out from their high camp at 8500 metres (27,900 feet) on 24 May: they were Chu Yin-hua, Liu Lien-man, Wang Fu-chou and Konbu (sometimes spelt Gonpa, a Tibetan climber). After several hours of climbing, they reached the Second Step, which had defeated their previous attempt several days earlier. Wager and Wyn Harris judged the obstacle in 1933 to be impossible to climb, and it is this feature that could have defeated Mallory and Irvine 36 years previously.

The Second Step is about 30 metres (100 feet) high, with an average slope of 60 to 70 degrees. The climbers were able to skirt around the base, but near the top of the step is a near-vertical face, which prevented further progress. Liu took the lead and made four determined attempts on the top section: each time he fell from the steep, rotten rock, exhausted. After his last try, he was so debilitated that he could barely stand.

A second climber, Chu Yin-hua, impatiently took over the lead and removed his heavy boots, crampons and thick woollen socks to try the rock section bare-footed. Again he fell — twice. By this time snow flurries began to fall, promising more bad weather. The climbers later wrote: 'What was to be done? Turn back like the British climbers had done before? No! Certainly not! The whole Chinese people and the Party were watching us.'[35]

In one final, drastic attempt, Liu Lien-man (now partially recovered from his previous attempts) made use of his training as a fireman and crouched down to allow Chu to stand on his shoulders. With a great effort, he was able to stand up and allow Chu to reach the top of the slab and haul himself to the top.

It took the four Chinese climbers five hours to ascend the Second Step, but there were more problems to come. Liu was so exhausted from his earlier efforts that he collapsed shortly after leaving the Second Step. Their oxygen supplies were also running low, and it was now 7 p.m. and dusk was beginning to fall. Amazingly, the climbers decided to have a political powwow at 8595 metres (28,200 feet) to decide what to do: 'The three Communist Party members ... and Konbu then held a brief Party group meeting. It was decided that the assault group should advance to the summit as quickly as possible and Liu Lien-man should remain where he was.'[36]

The climbers helped Liu to shelter under a small cliff and set off for the summit. Literally crawling on all fours in the final stage of the climb, the three remaining climbers reached the summit just before dawn. They had taken neither food nor liquid since leaving their camp 19 hours previously. They stayed on the summit for 15 minutes, leaving a small plaster bust of Mao Tse-tung and a Chinese flag as evidence of their achievement. They picked up nine pieces of rock to present to Mao on their return and began their descent. Collecting Liu on the way down, they discovered that he had saved his oxygen for their return.

The expedition leader, Shih Chan-chun, claimed that two of the successful summit party (Wang Fu-chou and Chu Yin-hua) had been climbing for only two years, and none of the Chinese had more than five years' experience. The climbers apparently used very little oxygen and Liu Lien-man had survived a night bivouac at over 8535 metres (28,000 feet) without it. The climbers did not return to their high camp until 4 p.m. that afternoon. It had taken them 19 hours to climb the mountain and nearly another 12 hours to descend.

Shih attributed their remarkable success to: '… the leadership of the Communist Party and the unrivalled superiority of the socialist system of our country – without all this, we, the ordinary workers, peasants and soldiers, could never have succeeded.'[37] Whatever their secret, their success on the mountain is an indication of just what can be achieved by climbers who are very determined, possibly even desperate, to succeed. But their climb was not without its tragic misfortune. The impatient Chu Yin-hua (who was only 22 years old at the time) lost several toes as a result of removing his boots at that altitude.

The extraordinary summit success of the Chinese inevitably raised deep scepticism in Western climbers, fuelled by the absence of a summit photograph (admittedly, difficult to achieve at night). However, the passing years have softened the views of the hard-liners and it is now accepted that the Chinese did, indeed, succeed in making the first *successful* summit attempt on Everest from the north.

Their experience in 1960 also offers further circumstantial evidence, which helps to clarify Mallory and Irvine's attempt. If the Chinese succeeded in scaling the Second Step and then reached the summit after 19 hours, could the more experienced Mallory not have succeeded too in making a late but successful bid for the summit?

The new decade plunged China into the Cultural Revolution and news reports from inside the country became more unreliable than ever. One story leaked out that an expedition in 1966 to the north side of Everest had been virtually wiped out, with only two climbers surviving from a party of 26. Then, in 1969, the New China News Agency claimed that three surveyors succeeded in reaching the summit independently of each other, apparently without oxygen or support facilities. These uncorroborated stories did little to convince China-watchers or international climbers that the country was capable of mounting a serious expedition to Everest.

However, in 1975 the Chinese mounted another determined attempt on the mountain. As in 1960, the expedition comprised a very large number of climbers — 410 in all — again led by Shih Chan-chun. The climbers established Base Camp in the middle of March, and by 4 May had succeeded in putting 37 men and seven women in high camp on the North Face at an altitude of over 8200 metres (26,900 feet).

Bad weather forced the climbers down the mountain, but on 27 May, nine climbers (eight Tibetan and one Chinese) succeeded in reaching the summit. Here, they planted a Chinese flag and a red-painted metal survey pole to make sure there was no misunderstanding about their success this time. This was the largest group to stand together on the summit, and the party included Phantog, the first woman to reach the summit from the north. (Junko Tabei, a member of a Japanese team on the south side, became the first woman to climb Everest just 11 days previously.) The Chinese/Tibetan team spent 70 minutes on the summit, making scientific observations and taking photographs.

Once again, the Chinese had a remarkable summit success, and this time they made absolutely certain there would be no doubting their achievement. The following September a British expedition found the survey pole partially buried in snow, its red paint stripped from the metal by the fearsome Everest winds.

Down at Base Camp, the Chinese team celebrated in typical Maoist style: '... with cheers of "Long live the great leader Chairman Mao!" and "Long live the great Communist Party of China!", and the beating of drums and gongs and the cracking of fireworks. Happy and excited, people hailed the great victory of Chairman Mao's proletarian revolutionary line, the fruitful achievements of the great Proletarian Cultural Revolution and the Movement to Criticize Lin Piao and Confucius and the tremendous success of conquering the summit of Qomolangma Feng [Everest].'[38]

The 1975 Chinese expedition carried an aluminium ladder up to the Second Step and secured it close into the corner of the upper part of the outcrop. Ever since, climbers going up to the summit have been able to use this aid and thus avoid having to climb the most difficult section of the ridge.

In 1979, the Chinese allowed the first expedition from a non-communist country since the Second World War to climb Everest from the north. During this Sino-Japanese reconnaissance, one of the most enigmatic and intriguing mysteries associated with Mallory and Irvine's disappearance came to light.

On 11 October 1979 Ryoten Yashimoro Hasegawa, the climbing leader of the Japanese team, was heading up towards the North Col with Wang Hong-bao, a Chinese climber. As the two men walked up the East Rongbuk Glacier towards Advanced Base Camp, Hasegawa casually asked Wang about the whereabouts of Maurice Wilson's body, which the Chinese had found in 1975: 'I asked Mr Wang if it was somewhere near here that the remains of the Englishman ... had been found.'[39]

To Hasegawa's amazement, Wang dismissed the story of Wilson's body with a wave of his hand and started to talk about a *second* body, which he claimed lay much higher up the mountain: 'Mr Wang had been a member of the [1975] Chinese attempt at the summit. On the way, at about 8150 metres [26,740 feet], he said he had seen the much older remains of an Englishman ... lying on his side as if asleep at the foot of a rock. The clothes were so old you could take a pinch and it would blow away. There was a hole in his cheek big enough to put your fingers in. I was really amazed. To have such old remains of an Englishman at that height, you immediately think of Mallory and Irvine. To climbers on Everest, the disaster of Mallory and Irvine is legendary. Everyone knows it.'[40]

Hasegawa's story was so incredible that he was challenged about its accuracy. People pointed out that he could not speak Chinese, nor Wang Japanese, so there was a strong possibility of misunderstanding. Others argued that Wang had stumbled across the body of a dead Russian climber from the 1950s or 1960s and had mis-identified the remains.

Hasegawa, however, remained convinced that Wang's sighting was accurate: 'It's true Mr Wang didn't understand Japanese and I didn't understand Chinese. But since our meeting in Beijing, at least a month had passed. We had been living together and walking in the mountains together. Also we talked about the thing we had in common – mountain climbing. If you use gestures and mime, you can communicate the gist of things. Also the Chinese and Japanese write using the same Chinese script. When Mr Wang was telling me these things, he wrote "8150 metres, Englishman, body" with his ice-axe in the snow.

'In the 1960s a large group of Russians made an attempt on Everest, and

Geoffrey Bruce is helped by a sherpa on his descent in 1922, having reached a
record altitude of 8320 metres (27,300 feet) on his first mountaineering
expedition. He was accompanied on the summit attempt by George Finch.

Opposite: The 1975 Chinese camp on the North Face at approximately 8150 metres (26,740 feet). By lining up the base of the summit pyramid with the snow triangle (above left of tent) an approximate position of the camp can be determined.

Left: Climbers tackle a section of the North Col in 1924. The route was protected with ropes attached to wooden stakes driven into the ice and the climbers used rope ladders on the steeper sections.

Below: Conrad Anker at the base of the Second Step, before making his historic free climb without the use of supplementary oxygen. The main Rongbuk Glacier is in the background, 3000 metres (10,000 feet) below.

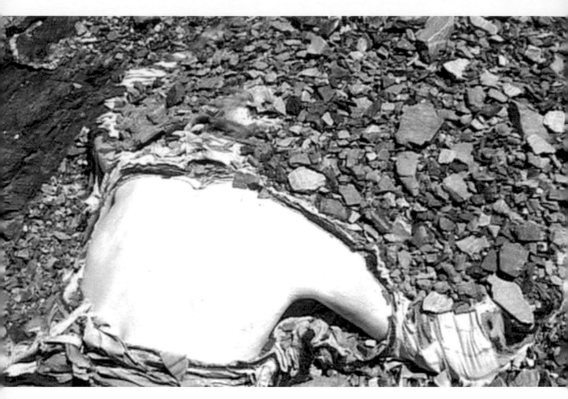

Above: Mallory's upper body, frozen into a self-arrest position, and mummified with the look of a marble statue. There is still a rope around his waist (bottom left).

Below: The green leather boot still on Mallory's right foot. His ankle was broken in two places just above the top of the boot.

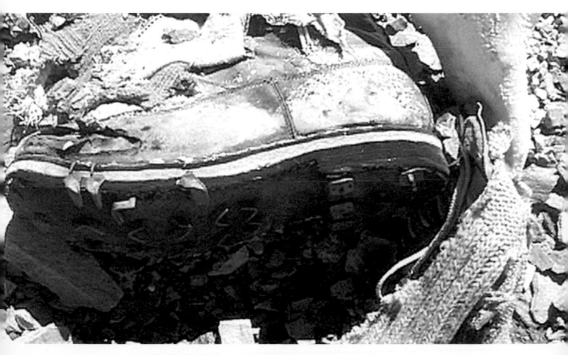

Above: The last picture taken of Mallory and Irvine, leaving Camp IV on 6 June 1924.

Below: The North Ridge, seen from Odell's perspective when he last saw the two climbers. The narrow angle and foreshortening give a different perspective on the First and Second Steps.

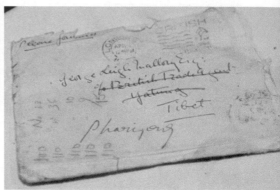

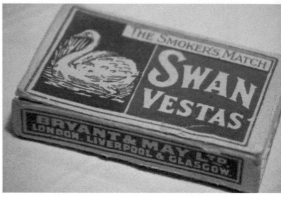

Artefacts recovered from
Mallory's body.

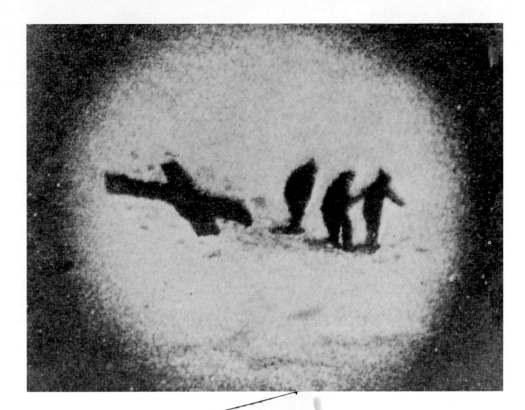

Above: Odell's signal, made from six blankets, indicating Mallory and Irvine had not returned from their summit attempt.

Left: The final note from George Mallory to John Noel, written on 7 June 1924 and sent down from Camp VI.

Above: Mallory's grave at 8170 metres (26,800 feet) on the North Face of Everest.

Below: The search party at prayer, 1 May 1999, having buried George Mallory. The Second Step (top centre) and the summit (top right) can be seen on the skyline.

apparently there was a serious accident. Consequently, people sometimes ask me whether the remains could be of a Russian, not an Englishman.... But I don't think so because Chinese climbers from the '50s and '60s learned from the Russian mountaineers about climbing as a sport. This means that the Chinese, including Mr Wang, knew the Russians well. So when Mr Wang explained about the age of the clothing and the deterioration of the body, putting it all together, there is no reason for them to have mistaken a Russian for an Englishman.'[41]

Hasegawa assumed that he would talk again to Wang about his discovery. However, the very next day, an avalanche struck a six-man party (which included both Hasegawa and Wang). Three Chinese climbers, including Wang, were swept to their deaths down a crevasse. Hasegawa was also carried away, but he was able to arrest himself with his ice-axe on the very edge of the crevasse, and survived with five broken ribs.

Everest guards her secrets well.

CHAPTER NINE

'A Mandatory Group Meeting'

'Let's all get together down here for Snickers
and tea. We need to have a mandatory group
meeting, now!'

*Conrad Anker's radio message when he found
Mallory's body on the North Face*

We landed in Kathmandu two hours late, after technical problems in Abu Dhabi forced us to change planes. We therefore missed seeing the majestic Himalayan peaks on our approach. Nor did we see the brown pall of smog that now hangs over the city. Nepal's first tarmac road was built as recently as 1956, but now the capital is choked with vehicles pumping out exhaust fumes, which blanket the city in suffocating pollution.

Next to me on the aircraft was Graham Hoyland, the BBC assistant producer on the film. Within 30 minutes of clearing Customs, we were off to the hotel in a convoy of small trucks to meet up with the rest of the expedition team who had arrived from all around the world during the previous few days. Eric Simonson, the climbing leader, had flown in from Seattle via Los Angeles and Bangkok with most of the climbing team. Film cameraman Ned Johnston, an American living in Sarawak, had arrived from Singapore. Jyoti Rana, the sound recordist, lived in Kathmandu. Licsl Clark, the American co-producer, and Thom Pollard, our high-altitude cameraman, had both flown in from Boston. Finally, Jochen Hemmleb, the expedition researcher, had joined us from Frankfurt.

The climbing team was impressive, all professional climbers or mountain guides, and four had previously reached the summit of Everest. Eric Simonson (43) had been a professional mountain guide for 25 years and made the summit in 1991 on his third attempt. Both Dave Hahn (37) and Andy Politz (39) had been to Everest several times before and both reached the summit from the north in 1994 and 1991 respectively. Graham Hoyland (41) was the fourth member of the team who had reached the summit. The Sherpa team were equally strong – at least four had been to the summit, some more than once.

Conrad Anker (36) had never been higher than 7000 metres (23,000 feet), but he was one of America's most respected rock-climbers and was well known for climbing some of the world's most challenging mountains. He was determined to make a summit attempt on this, his first Everest expedition, but most of all he wanted to climb the Second Step without using the Chinese ladder.

The two youngest climbers, Jake Norton and Tap Richards (both 26), were also professional mountain guides. This was their first expedition to Everest too, although both had climbed the neighbouring 8163-metre (26,780-feet) Cho Oyu. The other member of the team was Lee Meyers, a specialist in emergency medicine. He was also an experienced climber, but his prime responsibility on this expedition was to keep an eye on the health and well-being of the rest of the team.

There was, however, little time for introductions. A fax had just come through from our German co-producers, ZDF, which threw the viability of the expedition into question. It was a short newspaper article from that day's edition of *Das Bild*, a popular German tabloid newspaper. Scribbled in English above it was a note from the head of cultural programmes at ZDF: 'What does this mean, Peter? Is it a problem for you?'

Rather than struggle with my schoolboy German, I asked Jochen to translate. As he read aloud, we both turned ashen. The cutting explained that a Japanese climbing team had just returned from an expedition to Mount Everest, where they had successfully recovered Mallory's camera from the 1924 expedition.

As the producer of the documentary, I had worked and planned for over a year to get a climbing and documentary team out to the Himalayas, and now it appeared that the Japanese had beaten us to it. How could this be? Only two weeks previously I had been in Tokyo to interview Yashimoro Hasegawa, one of Japan's best-known climbers, and he had said nothing about a Japanese attempt to find the camera. If the report was true, there was nothing to do but return home and try to explain away the huge cost already incurred in preparing to make the documentary.

The film had been over a year in the planning. The idea came originally from Graham Hoyland, an experienced climber and an assistant television producer based in Manchester. He had worked for the BBC for many years in radio, and had been to Everest twice before on television documentary teams. In 1993 he became the fifteenth Briton to reach the summit.

His film proposal was to climb the North Face in the spring of 1999, the seventy-fifth anniversary of Mallory and Irvine's deaths, look for their bodies and try to recover their cameras. Any reclaimed film could prove whether the climbers had succeeded in reaching the summit on 8 June 1924.

Graham also had family reasons for wanting to solve the mystery; he was the great nephew of Howard Somervell, Mallory's friend and climbing companion. During the late 1960s, then aged 12, he remembers his great-uncle telling him about the 1924 expedition. Somervell explained how Mallory had left his own camera back at Base Camp, so he lent him his to take with him on the final summit attempt. Ever since, Graham had dreamed of finding Somervell's camera.

It was an enticing proposal, but a little far-fetched. Why had the bodies not been found before? What new evidence would increase our chances of finding something? I was concerned over the ethics of searching for the remains of two famous climbers who had been dead for three-quarters of a century. Most of all, I had sleepless nights about the dangers of asking people to film at over 8000 metres (26,500 feet).

Despite the obvious risks and uncertainties, the project was an exciting one, with huge potential if we found new evidence. Graham sent me his background papers and it was clear that this was no wild goose chase, but an idea based on new research. Jochen Hemmleb, a student at Frankfurt University, had used geological mapping techniques to identify the location of the 1975 Chinese camp on the North Face, and had estimated the latitude and longitude coordinates of the camp to an accuracy of about 30 metres (100 feet). From here, Wang Hong-bao had taken a short walk and discovered the body of an 'English dead'; the location was well away from the normal route to the summit, which explained why the body had not been discovered before.

I decided to go ahead with the film. A detailed budget and proposal was produced, and after protracted negotiations, a consortium of other film companies agreed to share the cost. At the same time, we began to talk to professional mountain guides about organizing an expedition. Then, in November 1998, we learnt that an American team had begun to develop similar plans to search for Mallory and Irvine. It seemed foolish and potentially dangerous to have two teams on the mountain at the same time looking for the same thing.

We met up in Boston: myself from the BBC, Liesl Clark from NOVA and Eric Simonson and his partners from Expedition 8000. Simonson had provisionally assembled a strong climbing team, but his project was underfunded and could not proceed without a major sponsor. It made sense to combine forces in a single, joint expedition. The last thing that anybody wanted was a race to find the bodies.

The next two months were frenetic for everyone concerned: in the USA, the climbing team was confirmed, and equipment and oxygen supplies ordered; in the UK, a film crew had to be organized, equipment ordered, schedules prepared and budgets honed. We also contacted the families of the two dead climbers to get their support for the venture and their permission to take DNA samples from the bodies.

By the third week in March, everything was finalized, packed and on its way to Kathmandu. The climbing team arrived a few days early, which gave them time to check their equipment and buy last-minute provisions. Graham Hoyland and I were the last to arrive, on 22 March. The group was finally complete.

That first evening in the hotel in Kathmandu was spent trying frantically to track down the source of the story in *Das Bild*. Fortunately, Britain and Germany were several hours behind Nepal, so we were able to resolve the matter that evening.

The previous day the British *Mail on Sunday* newspaper had published an extensive article about Mallory and our expedition. *Das Bild* had written a short story based on this news feature, but had either completely misunderstood the story or had inaccurately translated it. Whatever the reason, the German article had confused Hasegawa's expedition in 1979 with our intentions in 1999 and had misreported the story. With a huge sigh of relief, we realized we were back on track.

The drive east, out of Kathmandu and then north up to the Tibetan border, was cathartic. Months of organizing and preparation were over and anything forgotten would have to stay behind. The route was beautiful, along tree-lined roads and past patchwork fields, with an ever-changing panorama of Himalayan peaks to the north. The hillsides were dotted with houses built of bricks made from the deep red soil of the Kathmandu Valley, creating a view that looked more like Tuscany than Nepal. As night fell, we stopped at a small guest-house in Barabhise.

The following morning we were up at 4.30 a.m. and the convoy arrived at the Tibetan border at 7 a.m. Seven tonnes of tents, food, fuel, film equipment and climbing gear – everything that the expedition needed for two months – was laboriously unloaded from our Nepalese vehicles on to four Chinese trucks for the journey through Tibet to Base Camp. The one consolation was that it was a lot easier than walking to the Rongbuk, as Mallory and Irvine had done 75 years previously.

We crossed the narrow Friendship Bridge, which represents no man's land between Tibet and Nepal. Although this is Tibet's most important land border with the outside world, the roads leading to it were in appalling condition. Our equipment went by truck, but passengers had to walk across the bridge, past green-uniformed, humourless Chinese guards, who scrutinized our progress across the bridge. It is always a nerve-racking experience going through Chinese Customs with film equipment. All our travel documents and equipment lists were in order, but Customs officers the world over can be unpredictable. As it happened, everything went smoothly, and we were through the formalities in less than 30 minutes, ably assisted by two representatives from the Chinese Mountaineering Association.

Zhangmu is a typical frontier town where you can buy anything from a new stereo radio for your truck to a woman for the night. The town marked the beginning of the long climb up on to the Tibetan plateau, and houses and shops sprawled along a 4-kilometre (2½-mile) road, which wound its way up the steep side of a mountain. Life here was full of the unexpected, and everyone soon learned to watch out for garbage casually being tossed out from upstairs windows into the street below – anything from empty beer bottles to what the Chinese euphemistically call 'night soil'.

For anyone going to high altitude, a slow adjustment is essential. At Everest Base Camp you breathe only half the oxygen that is available at sea level; at the summit, just one-third. The process of allowing your body time to adjust to low oxygen levels is therefore essential to surviving at high altitude. Although the physiological changes are still not fully understood, much progress has been made in the past 15 or so years.

You find yourself short of breath, your heart beats faster and you develop headaches. Within a couple of days your body begins to produce extra red blood cells to carry more oxygen. Small blood capillaries called mitochondria, which supply blood to your muscles, become bigger and more effective, and there are also changes in the flow of blood to your brain. These transformations to your body take place over several weeks as you move up to higher altitude.

There is, however, a limit to the *rate* at which the body responds to increasing altitude, and individuals vary in their speed of adaption. If acclimatization is rushed, you get altitude sickness, which can be fatal. Even though the overland distance from Kathmandu at 1370 metres (4500 feet) to Base Camp at 5200 metres (17,060 feet) is only about 400 kilometres (250 miles), you need at least a week for your body to adjust. The best way to cope is to take life slowly, exercise gently, and drink vast quantities of liquid – at least 4 litres (8 pints) a day. When the 1920s' expeditions travelled from Darjeeling, they walked 480 kilometres (300 miles) to the Rongbuk and took over a month. This allowed them plenty of time to acclimatize, and they were also very fit by the time they arrived.

On 25 March 1999 we started our journey into the Tibetan interior. The next stop was Nyalam, only 30 kilometres (19 miles) north of Zhangmu, but the route climbs 1400 metres (4600 feet) up the steep and rugged gorge of the Bhode Kosi River. The unmetalled road is carved into the sides of the deep ravine and the climbers called it Valium Valley, with good reason. Within a few kilometres, the muddy road gave way to 15 centimetres (6 inches) of snow, which the driver used to good effect to slide the rear of the bus around the tight hairpin bends, much to the consternation of the passengers. Hundreds of metres below us, the river boiled its way back to Nepal.

This section of the road is frequently blocked by snow and rock avalanches, but we had news that the road ahead was clear. The winter had been exceptionally dry and the snowfall light, so the avalanche risk was low. The drooping leaves on the stunted trees that cling precariously to the valley sides were also testament to the dry conditions, and the radio regularly brought news of forest fires burning in Nepal.

The Snow Land Hotel in Nyalam belongs to the mayor of the town, and is an example of how private ownership is beginning to sweep the most remote parts of China. We ate in the hotel restaurant across the road, where the food was excellent, but the rooms were basic and the place was soon nicknamed Rat City. Every night a healthy-looking rodent would gnaw at our rucksacks and shin up the thin curtains over our beds, making sleep difficult for the squeamish.

Two days at Nyalam gave the team an opportunity for light hiking at an altitude high enough for the acclimatization process to start. Everyone was experiencing similar symptoms: lethargy, loss of appetite and headaches. Some of the more energetic members of the team, Conrad Anker and Andy Politz especially, took off early and hiked across the mountains, 600 metres (2000 feet) above the town. The rest of us took the easy option and gently ambled along the main street and up to the top of a nearby hill.

The next stage saw us driving north in snow that had fallen overnight and now lay up to 30 centimetres (1 foot) deep. After two hours of grating gears and straining engine, we cut through the Himalayas proper as we crossed two high passes, the Lalung La at 5200 metres (17,060 feet) and the Yakruchong La at 5125 metres (16,810 feet). A brief stop allowed us to stretch our legs and sample the oxygen-depleted air at high altitude. For the first time, we began to realize what it would be like living in the rarefied atmosphere of Base Camp.

Once over the passes, the route turned east across the high Tibetan plateau, a dust-dry desert displaying every conceivable shade of brown. We were skirting the northern flanks of the Himalayas, which rose majestically to our right. To our left were the much lower brown hills of the Tibetan plateau. As we drove east, we frequently passed the stone ruins of old Buddhist monasteries, stolid silent witnesses to the brutal Chinese repression of Tibet's national religion.

John Noel's first impressions in 1913 are as appropriate today: 'There is in this terrible country, which its inhabitants think is the most beautiful in the world, an unforgettable fascination. Life in Tibet is life at its hardest, but the traveller always longs to get back to the wild grandeur of mountain and stretch of rocky plain.'[1]

This is a cold, dry and hostile environment, typically about 4300 metres (14,000 feet) above sea level. Yet somehow the Tibetans eke out a basic existence, close to the maximum altitude for permanent human settlement. Farmers grow potatoes and barley during the brief summer months, and goats and sheep scavenge for the scant spring grass. When Noel first explored Tibet, he thought this was the most desolate country in the world, yet despite the hardship and extreme poverty, the people always have a ready smile for visitors.

After several hours, we arrived at Tingri, 4350 metres (14,270 feet) above sea level. This was where the 1921 expedition set up Base Camp and where we experienced the same 50-kph (30-mph) dry and dusty winds that make life were so uncomfortable. In the 1920s Tingri was an important trading centre; today it is a desolate and isolated truckstop on the Friendship Highway – an impressive name given to a narrow road of crushed stones that links Lhasa with western Tibet.

Little has changed since Charles Howard-Bury wrote about the town in 1921: 'Tingri itself was situated on the side of a small hill in the middle of a great plain, from which, looking to the South, was visible the wonderful chain of snowy peaks, many of them over 25,000 feet in height, which extends Westwards from Mount Everest.'[2]

To the south we could see the snowy flat top of Cho Oyu, the world's sixth-highest peak, rising above beige-coloured hills. Further to the east was the Goddess Mother herself, flying her distinctive banner of cloud made from tiny ice crystals, which stretched for dozens of kilometres downwind and is a sure sign of strong winds near the summit.

We spent two more days acclimatizing in Tingri before leaving at dawn on 29 March for the last leg of our journey, a six-hour back-breaking drive over the Pang La, the 'Grassy Col', to Base Camp. We stopped for a short break at the pass, where the view is breathtaking. Everest was now only 65 kilometres (40 miles) away – the closest that Noel managed to get in 1913.

It was impossible to take your eyes off the mountain; there was no plume on the summit that day, not a cloud in the sky, nor even a breath of wind. Everybody was thinking the same; what a perfect day for the summit. We could also see that the North Face was practically clear of snow. Provided the weather did not change for the worse, when the climbers reached the search area in five or six weeks' time, there was a chance they would find something of the 1924 expedition.

We drove the last four hours along the road the Chinese built in 1960 to reach the Rongbuk. We felt like Lilliputians in a land of giants; the world was on a scale that many of us had never experienced before. Glacial moraine towered hundreds of metres above us, boulders the size of buses were perched precariously on rock towers, and dry river-beds more than a kilometre across hinted at the raging torrents that were unleashed on the region when the snow melted.

By early afternoon we passed the Rongbuk monastery, the highest religious building in the world. In 1921 hundreds of monks and nuns were in residence, but today there are only a few dozen, trying to rebuild the site as best they can. The Chinese are now allowing Buddhist monasteries to be renovated throughout Tibet – at least in the areas visited by tourists.

Our arriving so early in the season had been a risk, as avalanches could easily have kept us in Zhangmu. But the gamble had paid off and we were the first expedition on the mountain. The Sherpas had gone ahead and established our Base Camp on the eastern side of the valley at 5200 metres (17,060 feet), about 1.5 kilometres (1 mile) closer to the mountain than the British expeditions of the 1920s. It was a good position on a flat, stony outwash plain, with fresh water from a mountain stream close to hand.

Three big communal tents had been erected, together with many of the individual tents. All we had to do was unpack our personal equipment and collect as many rocks as we could carry to pin down our tents against the fierce Tibetan wind that blows down the valley most of the time. This would be our home for the next two months.

The Rongbuk, meaning 'valley of steep ravines', is a bleak place, even in good weather. Thousands of years ago the Rongbuk Glacier gouged the valley into a U-shape, but it is now a shadow of its former self, having retreated up the valley since the last ice age. Today, rubble ridges rise steeply on both sides from the rock-strewn valley floor and a kilometre (half a mile) south of the camp we could see the surface of the glacier itself, now completely covered with rock debris.

Beyond the glacier, though, was one of the wonders of the natural world: the North Face of Everest. In the clear, dry Himalayan air the mountain looked closer than 20 kilometres (12 miles) – a colossal granite fortress of rock and ice, challenging climbers to come and chance their luck on its slopes. When Mallory first arrived in the Rongbuk in 1921, he was equally impressed with scale of the mountain: 'The sight of it now banished every thought. We forgot the stony wastes and regrets for other beauties. We asked no questions and made no comment, but simply looked.'[3]

For us, too, the mountain banished every other thought. Every day that we spent at Base Camp, we looked constantly, trying to gauge the strength of the wind from the size of the cloud streaming from the summit and scrutinizing the upper slopes for any signs of new snow which could render our search impossible.

The weather dominates life on Everest. The early mornings started calm, but the wind usually filled in around 10 a.m. and would continue to blow strongly until late afternoon or evening. Fine glacial dust found its way into everything: eyes and ears, hair, clothes, books, radios, tape-recorders and cameras. The nights, especially when the moon was full, were spectacular, with the haunting spectre of Everest plainly visible to the south.

Once the expedition members had settled in, the routine of camp life quickly became established. Dawn in March comes before 6 o'clock, but the early mornings were cold, and few rose before 7.00 a.m. After breakfast, everyone went about their daily tasks, usually with an insulated mug in hand, trying to maintain their daily intake of liquid. The first few days were taken gently, and most people nursed high-altitude headaches. Even the gentlest exertion left us light-headed and gasping for breath.

The priority for the documentary team was to film interviews with the climbers before they left for Advanced Base Camp. Meanwhile, the climbers themselves spent their time preparing their equipment and training. The golden rule for successful acclimatization is to climb high and sleep low, and most days saw them setting off to climb the ridges that surrounded Base Camp.

One of the inevitable topics of conversation at Base Camp was whether Mallory and Irvine succeeded in 1924. Usually, the expedition split into the sceptics, led by Dave Hahn, and the romantics, who included Graham Hoyland. Those who had been up to the Second Step understood what a difficult obstacle it was to climb, even with the aluminium ladder, and they tended to doubt that the two climbers could have made it without the modern climbing aid. But those who believed Mallory succeeded kept coming back to his absolute determination to conquer the summit. There is no doubt that he had a serious attack of 'summit fever', but was it enough to get him to the top? The Chinese succeeded against the odds in 1960, so why, they argued, could Mallory not have done the same in 1924?

On 1 April the Sherpas held their puja, a time-honoured ceremony to placate the mountain gods. Two lamas came down from the Rongbuk monastery for the event, just as they did for the British expeditions in the 1920s. The Sherpas collected juniper wood to burn on the fire, and the small stone altar was decorated with long strings of Buddhist prayer flags that radiated from the shrine like a star.

Tsampa flour, beer and 'Everest Whiskey' was laid out to be blessed, along with the odd ice-axe for good measure. The monks chanted their prayers, played bells and hand drums, and asked for a safe passage on the mountain. Once the formalities were over, we tossed tsampa over each other and toasted everyone's safety and good luck in beer and whiskey.

The following day, Conrad, Tap, Jake and Thom set off for Camp II before the first yak team arrived at Base Camp. The yaks and their drivers are hired by most expeditions to take equipment and food up the East Rongbuk Glacier to Camp III. Even Base Camp is too high for Tibetan yaks to live there permanently, and they come from villages further down the valley to rendezvous with the climbing expeditions. When they arrived, the formalities of negotiation began: the yak herders complained that it was too early in the season, so the yaks were weak and must therefore carry smaller loads. Reaching agreement took hours, but eventually prices and numbers were clinched.

By midday, the loading began. Each yak had a barrel or bag on each side and each individual load had to be checked and weighed before being strapped to the animal. No combined load could be more than 50 kilograms (110 lb). In all, 42 yaks and six Sherpas headed up the East Rongbuk that day to establish Camp II, taking less than half the expedition's equipment. Three animals carried fodder, as there is no grazing at these altitudes.

To walk with the yaks from Base Camp was to follow in the very footsteps of Mallory and the other Everest pioneers. The journey began with a trek up a rough, narrow, boulder-strewn track to the east of the Central Rongbuk Glacier. On the left was the steep side of the valley, with huge boulders perched precariously on rock pinnacles and liable to avalanche at any time. It pays to choose the site of your rest break here with care.

After a time, Everest disappeared from view and in a couple of hours we turned left into the East Rongbuk Valley, the very place that Mallory missed during the 1921 reconnaissance. The East Rongbuk offers the key to Everest, but it is a deceptively small ravine which initially runs to the east, seemingly away from the mountain. Here, the narrow trail skirted the steep side of the valley, before running alongside the milk-white melt-water stream from the glacier. The fully loaded yaks found some of these sections difficult, but endless whistling and cajoling by the yak herders, occasionally supplemented with a well-aimed rock, kept the animals on the move.

Further up, beyond the site of Mallory's Camp I, the small valley turned south towards Everest, even though the great mountain still remained hidden behind the massive flank of Changtse. Here, rock and rubble gave way to the blue-white ice of the magnificent East Rongbuk Glacier, where huge ice pinnacles or *seracs* jutted out from the surface like giant shark fins; Mallory called this part of the glacier a 'Fairy Kingdom'. The movement and compression of the glacier created these spectacular sculptures as it slowly migrated down the valley, accompanied by a symphony of cracks and groans from the ever-moving ice.

After stopping overnight at Camp II, the climbers and Sherpas entered what the early Everest pioneers called the 'trough' – a route through the moraine rubble flanked on both sides by ice pinnacles. This marks the final section of the trek up to Advanced Base Camp (ABC), where Camp III is established below the imposing face of the North Col. The yaks returned to Base Camp and were loaded ready for a return trip. Meanwhile, the climbers and Sherpas began to check out the route up the col. This year the best course was further to the left than the route taken in previous years, making it steeper but more direct. There was very little snow on the col and most of the route was blue ice, making it a tough but safe climb up to Camp IV.

The tents at Camp III must be well anchored to withstand the gusts that roar off the North Col and flatten anything but the sturdiest of structures. It is also very cold at 6400 metres (21,000 feet) – not a comfortable place to stay for long. At this altitude, the body begins to deteriorate quickly and climbers need to return to a lower altitude after a week or so to recover.

Our expedition was still well ahead of the other teams, and took responsibility for putting in the ropes up the face of the North Col. From Camp III to the North Col takes between two and five hours, depending on your fitness and the conditions. Our climbers fixed over 900 metres (3000 feet) of rope on the col, which this year was steep and very icy in places. At the very top was a near-vertical ice wall, which was the final and exhausting section to complete before reaching the haven of Camp IV.

The wind on Everest generally blows from west to east, and the slopes up to the North Col are in the lee of the wind, causing snow to accumulate. This is generally not too much of a problem in the spring when there is little snow on the mountain, but it does make the North Col a dangerous place during the summer monsoon snowfall, as Mallory found to his cost in 1922.

By 11 April, after 10 days at high altitude, everyone was ready to return to Base Camp for a break. Only the indomitable Andy Politz stayed at ABC with the Sherpas, determined to continue putting in ropes and moving equipment and oxygen up to Camp IV.

That day, however, Graham Hoyland was taken ill at ABC. He had developed numbness on the left side of his face and down his left leg, caused by a mild stroke called a transient ischaemic attack. The disruption of blood to the brain results in the temporary numbness, but unless the patient gets to a lower altitude quickly, the condition can worsen, leading to giddiness, disorientation, paralysis and even blindness.

Graham came down quickly on oxygen, and together with Lee Meyers, our expedition doctor, we kept an all-night vigil over him in case of complications. For 30 years he had dreamed of searching for his great-uncle's camera. Now he was faced with a difficult choice: should he continue with the expedition but risk his condition deteriorating at high altitude, or should he abandon the quest and return to England?

Being told by the doctor that it would be dangerous to stay at high altitude, Graham decided to leave for Kathmandu the next day. It was a wise decision, but a devastating blow to someone who had waited so long to climb the North Face. It was also a salutary lesson for everyone else. Graham was an experienced climber who had been to 5800 metres (19,000 feet) at least 20 times before, and the medical condition developed with no warning. He knew that he had got off lightly, for if the symptoms had come on at a higher altitude, the outcome could have been much more serious.

The weather continued to be unseasonably warm, with little snow on the North Face. With confidence running high in the team, the climbers returned to Advanced Base Camp on 14 April. From ABC, they continued to supply Camp IV on the North Col. Here the climbers get their first close look at the broad sweep of the North Face. The North Col is like a giant saddle between Everest and Changtse. The shape of the mountain funnels the wind up and over the col, making the site even colder and windier than ABC. Being first on the mountain, the climbers had their choice of campsite, and they selected a position behind a huge wall of snow and ice, which gave them some respite from the relentless wind.

Over the next few days, the climbers began to work their way up the North Ridge towards the site of Camp V. The ridge is an exposed snow ramp, which is frequently a barrier to further progress up the mountain during strong winds. In the past, climbers have literally been blown 100 metres (300 feet) up the mountain during vicious gusts. Consequently, new ropes have to be fixed all the way up the mountain to give the climbers some security.

For the next few days, the weather was bright and dry, but the wind remained strong. The climbers and Sherpas continued to move equipment up to the col and everyone hoped the Sherpas would make it to Camp V by 16 April. That morning, eight of them left Camp IV early, hoping to complete fixing the ropes over the last 200 metres (660 feet) of the route. Once away from the protection of the ice wall, however, they were struck by powerful gusts of wind. They struggled to the top of the snow slope, but found it difficult even to stay upright. Having no death wish, the Sherpas turned back to Camp IV. To have established the route this far by mid-April was well ahead of schedule, and they were justified in feeling pleased with what they had achieved.

By now, several other expeditions had arrived at ABC. The first of these was the Ukrainian national team, which had experienced climbers but lacked Sherpa support. The Ukrainians already had Camp IV in place and there was much speculation about whether they had also made it to Camp V. Russell Brice, the New Zealand veteran climber, had also established his palatial camp at ABC; in addition there were Belgians, Swiss and a solo Chinese climber. By the end of the month, there would be nearly a dozen teams at ABC.

By 19 April the wind had moderated and Conrad Anker and the Sherpas put in Camp V at about 7800 metres (25,600 feet); the next day the Sherpas carried seven loads up to the camp and the springboard was finally in place. The climbers returned to Base Camp for a well-earned rest and to wait for the right weather conditions to allow them to start the search on the North Face.

On 24 and 25 April the team moved back up to ABC, and over the next few days, climbers and Sherpas continued to move loads up to Camp IV. Then, on 30 April, the team left the North Col for Camp V. The route up to the camp is not too steep, mainly snow to 7600 metres (25,000 feet) then a combination of snow and rock above; but it is an exhausting, relentless toil. The climbers are each in a world of their own – a world of laboured breathing, aching legs and the sound of their boots squeaking on the dry powdery snow.

The biggest problem, however, is wind, making it a laborious climb. Without using oxygen and moving steadily with a reasonable pack, the climbers took about seven hours to reach their goal. Eric Simonson found himself struggling at this altitude; unable to keep up with the rest of the team, he returned to ABC.

Camp V is neither a comfortable nor a popular site with climbers. In fact, the site is not really a proper camp in the way that ABC and the North Col are broad, flat areas where tents are grouped together. Instead, Camp V is a line of flat platforms for tents, cut into the rough scree and ice which slopes 20–30 degrees down towards the North Col. The biggest of these cleared ledges can accommodate up to four or five tents, but most barely have room for one or two, and the encampment stretches for up to 500 metres (1660 feet) along the North Ridge.

The site offers virtually no protection against the wind, and the tents must be well secured to anything available – rocks, pitons, oxygen bottles – then cargo nets and more ropes are securely fastened over the top. The wind can be deafening, making any proper rest near impossible during a storm. Climbers have been known to sleep with their ice-axes in case the tent is blown down the mountain and they need to self-arrest through the floor of the tent.

Above the camp, blue-black alpine choughs (*Pyrrhocorax graculus*) circled on the updrafts of air, conserving their energy in the thin, cold Himalayan atmosphere. It is astonishing that these small, acrobatic birds can survive at this altitude, but they have even been seen to fly over the summit. For the moment, however, spring brings a fresh batch of climbers to the mountain and the birds are content to scavenge for leftover food around the camp – and on the remains of climbers who had failed during previous expeditions.

At such high altitude, life is basic; the priorities are to force yourself to eat and drink as much as you can, and to stay warm. Going to the toilet is one of life's more challenging daily functions; if you are not wearing crampons, it is essential to clip on to a rope, otherwise you could find yourself sliding down the mountain in very embarrassing circumstances. Some of the climbers also began to breathe oxygen at night to help them sleep and keep warm. Despite the discomfort of wearing a mask all night, supplementary oxygen brings immediate relief to headaches and weary limbs.

On the evening of 30 April the wind dropped, it started to snow and the mountain disappeared from view behind a dark and ominous cloud. The climbers woke at 3 a.m. to make a decision on whether to start the search.

On schedule at 5 a.m. the radio crackled into life. Dave Hahn responded, and when asked how he had slept, said 'I didn't, but we're not here to sleep. We're here to climb.'[4] Despite a bad night on the mountain, the climbers were in good spirits and had decided to start the search.

Thom Pollard continued to film throughout the climb up to Camp V. Now, as the climbing team was leaving early in the morning to move up the mountain to begin the search, his oxygen apparatus developed a fault. He tried to keep up with the rest of the climbers, but without supplementary oxygen and with the extra weight of camera equipment, he found himself falling behind. Reluctantly, he decided to turn back. Meanwhile, the remaining five climbers – Conrad Anker, Jake Norton, Andy Politz, Tap Richards and Dave Hahn (now using the video camera) – continued up the North Ridge. It was very cold and windy and, for Conrad, the highest he had ever climbed.

The climbers made their way slowly up the North Ridge on a mixture of snow, rock and ice. Dave Hahn recalls: 'There was so little snow. I was continually marvelling at that, but also it made it tougher going. You really had to be careful about what you were putting your feet on.'[5] The climbers were following the same route used by Mallory and Irvine 75 years previously; to their right was the great North Face, which somewhere held the secret of what happened in June 1924.

Above Camp V, the North Ridge merges into the North Face, creating a 'wind shadow', which gives welcome protection to climbers. Consequently, the climb up from Camp V is often easier than lower down the mountain, despite the higher altitude. There was also fixed rope along the route. By now, most climbers were using oxygen, but, remarkably, both Conrad and Jake were climbing without.

At 10.00 a.m. the climbers arrived at the site of Camp VI at 8300 metres (27,230 feet), which the Sherpas had succeeded in putting in only a few days previously. The plan was to move out west across the North Face and locate the 1975 Chinese camp, then continue westwards at that altitude in search of the body found by Wang.

The climbers spread out, with Dave, Tap and Andy searching high on the North Face, and Jake and Conrad lower down. The rock on this part of the mountain is a series of overlapping slabs sloping at approximately 30 degrees; this, combined with patchy snow and ice, made the search a hazardous venture.

At 11.00 a.m. came a radio message. It was Jake Norton, who reported finding a distinctive blue oxygen bottle of the type the Chinese used in 1975; the climbers knew they were getting close. Next on the radio was Conrad, who had found a body, but from the clothing and equipment it was clearly recent, probably a Russian climber who had fallen from the ridge in 1997.

Conrad continued moving west and lower, looking at the terrain and using his experience to identify likely resting sites. Within minutes, he stumbled upon another body, very bleached, but on closer inspection it too had modern climbing gear. He was reading the mountain, trying to understand the micro-geography and assess where a body might come to rest if it fell from the ridge. Andy Politz radioed that he was searching too far west of the likely site, but Conrad was following his intuition, not the search plan.

Meanwhile, Tap Richards found a third body, which he thought might have lain there for about 20 years, probably from the 1975 Chinese expedition. We were not surprised at these discoveries and expected to find as many as a dozen bodies on this part of the North Face. The area here is not as steep as the Yellow Band higher up, and any climbers who fell from the North East Ridge would plunge down the steep section until they come to rest on flatter terrain at this level.

Conrad continued his search, and at 11.45 a.m. he noticed the remains of an old tent fluttering in the wind. As he moved in that direction, something else caught his eye: 'I looked over to my right and all of a sudden I saw a patch of white, that wasn't rock and wasn't snow. . . . I saw a hobnailed boot, old clothing that was all natural fibres, wool and cotton, and I knew right away this is what we're looking for.'[6] He was convinced that he had found Andrew Irvine, so he radioed for his team members to break off their own search to join him: 'Let's all get together down here for Snickers and tea.'[7] The climbers kept their radios inside their down-filled jackets to keep the batteries warm, so they often missed radio calls. Only Jake responded to the request, so Conrad tried again with a more authoritative message: 'We need to have a mandatory group meeting, now!'[8]

We knew that other climbing teams on the mountain were monitoring our radio communications and were concerned that they might release important news before us. So it was decided that if a body *were* found, the search team would go into radio silence. Conrad's call to the other climbers for 'a mandatory group meeting' was telling them that he had made an important find. Remarkably, it had taken only 90 minutes.

Standing alone on the North Face with the long-dead climber was a moving experience for Conrad Anker: 'I first saw a hobnailed boot. Then the natural fibres of his clothing were another clue. We didn't know it was George [Mallory] at first because all of the assumptions were that it was Sandy [Irvine's] body that was discovered by Wang.... I sat there, and there was a moment, just a brief moment in time, he and I were there together. He wasn't disturbed that I was there ... just to be there as a fellow climber. ... It was quite peaceful.'[9]

Jake Norton was close to Anker's position and moved down the mountain in response to the radio call: 'Conrad was sitting with a stunned look on his face .... I looked over, and sure enough, poking out of the gravel I could just see this white, yellowish porcelain-like body in a prone position. It looked like it was still trying to self-arrest .... As soon as I saw the hobnailed boots, I knew that it was the right body.'[10]

Dave Hahn was the last of the five climbers to arrive at the scene: 'There was no question that this body I was now looking at was different, very different ... there was something of history that you were looking at .... There was dignity to this figure, partly because of the age, partly because he had become in some senses part of the mountain .... We were all just stunned into silence for a while.'[11]

The body that Conrad found was lying face down on the scree slope. The clothing crumbled to the touch, just as Wang had told Hasegawa. The back of the body was exposed where the clothing had deteriorated in the sunlight; the exposed skin was bleached to the whiteness of a marble statue. There was a green leather hobnailed boot still on the right foot, and the tibia and fibula of the right leg were broken and angulated in a classic boot-top fracture. The left leg was crossed over the right in a resting position, suggesting that the climber was still conscious after coming to rest. The climber's right shoulder was broken and his forehead showed a serious, but probably not fatal, impact injury. He also had broken ribs from the fall and the skin on his chest was still discoloured black and blue from bruising. A climbing rope trailed from his waist and the end was broken, as if snapped.

The climber had clearly died from a fall, but the body was intact and not severely traumatized, so he could not have fallen far and certainly not from the ridge 300 metres (1000 feet) above. Conrad Anker had seen several bodies on the North Face, and it was obvious to him that this body was lying in a very different position: 'In relation to the other two bodies I'd seen who'd obviously gone for the big tumbles and had been contorted, [this body's position] led me to believe that he was still alive at the point when he came to rest. He was in an upward position, both arms up and his legs down. And his left leg crossed over his right leg, which was broken. That's sort of a natural thing when you're in pain, to put one limb over another to hold it.'[12]

The body was frozen into an ice-gravel scree and it was difficult to excavate at that altitude. Nor could the climbers use oxygen because the pack and mask made moving and talking difficult. Carefully, the climbers began to check the body, trying to disturb it as little as possible. 'At first, we definitely thought it was Irvine,' Jake Norton recalls. 'That's what we'd been prepared for. I even went as far as scratching out a little tombstone for Irvine saying 1902 to 1924. Then we started investigating the body. The clothes were pretty much in tatters, but we had to investigate everything. The clothing around his back was ripped off aside from his collars, and I noticed some tags there and I saw a name ... G.L. Mallory. My first reaction was, this is Irvine and he just borrowed Mallory's shirt, so we dismissed it as that because there was blond hair sticking out and we knew Mallory had black hair. We later discovered more name tags – it was indeed Mallory and the hair must have been bleached over 75 years of exposure.'[13]

Dave Hahn remembers a similar reaction: 'We all thought we were looking at Sandy Irvine and I didn't question it. Jake found this clothing label on the neck and he pulls this G. Mallory tag out. Our first thought was, "Interesting, Sandy Irvine wearing George Mallory's clothes." It took us a few minutes before it fully set in!'[14] Conrad Anker was overwhelmed with his discovery: 'To see him and his physique, he really lived for climbing. You looked at his strong arms and they were built for climbing. George had come to rest doing what he wanted to do.'[15]

More pieces of the jigsaw began to fall into place. There was no sight of his camera, but his glacier glasses were in his top pocket, and his knife, altimeter, a small pair of scissors and a box of Swan Vesta matches were also recovered. There were also various notes about equipment and stores and an unpaid bill dated 1924, all perfectly preserved in the cold, dry air.

Yet, most significantly, there was no sign of his oxygen apparatus. This suggests that Mallory had fallen during his *descent*. The rope around his waist also indicated that he was still roped to Irvine at the time of the accident. All this information would be analysed at a later date, but for the moment the climbers could only wonder in awe at their discovery.

Perhaps most moving of all were three letters from family and friends, recovered from the inside front pocket of his jacket. The envelopes still bore the stamps and postmarks that had carried them from England, through India and across Tibet.

After they finished their search, the climbers performed a committal service over the body. Mallory came from a long line of Church of England vicars, and had considered taking holy orders. There, high on the North Face of Everest, Andy Politz read from Psalm 103. When the service was over, the climbers buried the body of their hero under loose scree and returned to Camp V.

For much of that night, the climbers sat up talking about their extraordinary find. Inevitably, they debated whether Mallory and Irvine reached the summit in 1924. Dave Hahn later commented: 'There is a conceit as a climber, that climbers who've come before could not have been as proficient as we are [today]. You know that their gear wasn't as good – you know that limited them. But you're standing there looking at this man's body, you look at his arms. He's a climber. You could see the vitality in this figure. You could sense something of his determination. And I found myself coming away thinking, well maybe he did summit. The Second Step still looms. I don't know *how* he would have surmounted it, but I guess that's kind of the point. The guy obviously didn't let good sense get in the way of his determination. My mind has changed. He might have done it!'[16]

That night, there was a severe storm over the mountain, with peals of thunder echoing around the giant peaks and brilliant flashes of lightning. The wind blew strongly and it started to snow. It seemed as if Everest was angry at having its peace disturbed.

The climbers returned to Base Camp for a low-altitude rest, but the job was far from over. The artefacts had to be photographed and a full inventory made of what had been recovered. But most important of all was the preparation for the next attempt on the mountain. A search needed to be made for Irvine, and Conrad Anker still wanted to free-climb the Second Step *without* using the aluminium ladder, just as Mallory and Irvine would have climbed it in 1924. This would help us piece together Mallory and Irvine's final hours and give us important clues as to whether they could have surmounted this difficult obstacle.

By 14 May the search team was back at Camp V, but the unseasonably good weather had changed for the worse and heavy snow and wind had forced the climbers to bunker down in their tents. The wind rose to gale force, gusting to 100 kph (60 mph). Apart from the noise and cold, the climbers had the usual symptoms of poor sleep and lack of appetite. To add to their problems, they began to run short of food. The Sherpas Dawa Nuru and Ang Pasang were sent up from Camp IV to resupply the beleaguered climbers.

If the forecast improved as predicted, the team would move up to Camp VI on 17 May. Fortunately, the day dawned clear and the snowstorm stopped, but the winds were still blowing strongly at altitude. By 8.00 a.m. the climbers left Camp V, where they had been for three days, and made their way up to Camp VI. At 8300 metres (27,230 feet) this is the highest camp in the world, and from here, the climbers could turn around and see the whole length of the main Rongbuk Glacier stretching below them.

The new plan was to conduct a simultaneous summit and search attempt. Andy Politz, with Thom Pollard filming, would look for the body of Andrew Irvine. Meanwhile, Conrad Anker, Jake Norton, Tap Richards, Dave Hahn and two Sherpas would begin their summit attempt.

On this final leg of the expedition, there was one other piece of the mystery that the summit climbers might be able to clarify. During his summit attempt in 1991, Eric Simonson found two old oxygen bottles near the First Step, at an altitude of approximately 8500 metres (27,900 feet). Simonson could not remember their details, but they were almost certainly from a British pre-war expedition. If the bottles could be recovered, and they were found to be from the 1924 expedition, it would be another valuable clue about Mallory and Irvine's movements on 8 June.

The forecast was promising and the climbers rose at midnight to prepare for the summit. At this altitude, most climbers wake with a skull-splitting headache from dehydration and lack of oxygen. Lightweight stoves must be coaxed into life, and ice melted for a warm morning drink. The climbers massaged warmth back into their fingers and toes before putting on boots and mittens – not doing so runs the risk of frostbite later in the day.

It took the climbers over two hours that morning to prepare to face the mountain. They struggled into heavily padded one-piece down suits, which transformed them into a troupe of kaleidoscopic 'Michelin men'; this was followed by wind suits, insulated boots, neoprene gaiters and lightweight oxygen cylinders. Before they left, each climber ran through a mental check-list of essential equipment: goggles plus a spare, head torch with extra bulb and battery, radio, high-energy food, plastic bottles filled with warm liquid, plus a personal selection of lightweight climbing gear. This was all in stark contrast to Mallory and Irvine, 75 years before, who set off for the summit without the benefit of modern technology.

The team left their Camp VI a little after 2.00 a.m. and began to move across a mixed terrain of rocky slabs and patches of ice, making it difficult for the climbers to get into a regular rhythm. They tended to move at their own pace, intentionally spreading out along the fixed ropes for safety so that several climbers do not rely on the same section of rope or on the same untested anchor.

Soon they faced the Yellow Band, which involved a steep climb in the dark, with only the feeble light from their head torches to guide them. On most mountains, climbers stop to remove their crampons on rock; but on Everest, the transition from snow to rock and back is so frequent that crampons must be worn on the rocky sections, which increases the risk of a slip or a twisted ankle. Scrabbling up the steep sections in crampons grinds steel spikes into flaking rock and inevitably sends showers of small stones down on the climbers below. Everywhere the rock was fragmented and loose, and footholds and handholds frequently proved to be unreliable. From a distance, Everest looks like a giant monolith of granite; in reality, it is a crumbling ruin of rotten limestone.

The climbers were now moving into the 'Death Zone', an altitude so high and with so little oxygen in the atmosphere that the human body begins to deteriorate with remarkable speed; the climbers were literally dying with every passing hour. Even with supplementary oxygen, they knew they could survive at this height for only a couple of days. Altitude is an invisible killer.

As dawn came, they removed their head torches and looked out across a spectacular panorama. The elegant, pyramid-shaped peak of Pumori, the majestic Gyachung and dazzling, snow-covered Cho Oyu were now all *below* the altitude of the climbers. By 6.00 a.m. Dave Hahn radioed back to ABC to say that the climbing was slow but they were approaching the First Step, a rock buttress about 30 metres (100 feet) high, which the climbers could traverse to the right.

Beyond the First Step, the climbers moved on to an intimidating knife-edge ridge, with the Kangshung Face to their left and the North Face to their right. In places, the ridge was only about 30 centimetres (1 foot) wide, and on each side was a near-vertical wall of ice plunging 3000 metres (10,000 feet) down to the glaciers below. This is one of the most dangerous sections of the route to the summit when the wind is strong or the visibility poor. When the summit team moved along the crest, they were able to clip on to the tattered and fraying ropes that snaked along the ridge. With luck, they might hold a falling climber; in their day, Mallory and Irvine had no such back-up.

Within a couple of hours, the weather showed signs of improving. The large, lenticular cloud over the summit had gone and the sun was shining. By 8.40 a.m. the climbers reached the bottom of the Second Step and Conrad Anker prepared to make his historic attempt on this difficult section. He decided that rather than attempt the step head-on, it would be better to traverse around to the right and free-climb close to the Chinese ladder, even though this part of the cliff was still in the shadows.

At 9.30 a.m. Tap Richards came on the radio. With obvious dis-appointment in his voice, he announced that he, Jake Norton and the Sherpa Ang Pasang were going to turn back. The strain of spending four nights at high altitude had taken its toll and they felt they could not continue. Thirty minutes later, Dawa Nuru, the Sirdar, announced that he too would be returning. This left just Conrad Anker and Dave Hahn on the ridge.

Jake and Tap returned to Camp VI, but on the way they stopped at the First Step, where they found two old oxygen bottles exactly where

Simonson had left them eight years previously. They were identified as coming from the 1924 expedition and could only have been left there by Mallory and Irvine *en route* to the top. Another important piece of the jigsaw had slotted into place.

Meanwhile, Conrad Anker was making his attempt to free-climb the monumental Second Step. He first tried to climb a line of obvious weakness to the right of the ladder, but found the rock was loose and friable. It was an exposed section of the face and he judged it too risky, so he moved to a vertical crack just to the left of the Chinese ladder. It was a wide crack, too wide to jam a hand or foot into, but he was able to 'knee-bar' his way to the top. There he was able to insert a 75-mm (3-inch) 'friend', which gave him some protection in case he fell.

Unfortunately, at one point the ladder was in his way and he inadvertently stepped on one of the rungs. Purists will argue that by doing so, he broke his attempt to free-climb the Second Step. However, if the ladder had *not* been there, he might well have been able to find an edge to give him that support. Nevertheless, it was an extraordinary achievement: the first *confirmed* free-climb of the Second Step, without a backpack or oxygen. It also re-opened the debate about whether Mallory and Irvine had been able to ascend this obstacle in 1924.

Once Anker and Hahn moved beyond the Second Step, the summit pyramid was in full view for the first time, but there was still a long way to go. They crossed a long, gently rising scree terrace to the Third Step, which is an awkward outcrop on the ridge, but nothing like as demanding as the previous two, and it can either be climbed directly or traversed to the right in snow. Was this where Odell last saw Mallory and Irvine alive?

As Hahn and Anker approached the summit, Thom Pollard and Andy Politz were traversing the North Face below, searching for Irvine's body, but without success. This time they had with them a lightweight metal detector, and they returned to check whether they had missed anything on Mallory's body. As they ran the machine over the remnants of clothing, its distinctive high-pitched squeal disturbed the peace of the mountainside.

They were hoping that at last they might have found the elusive camera. Instead, Thom leant over the body and brought out Mallory's watch from the front right-hand pocket of his trousers. The glass face was missing and there were no broken shards of glass around, suggesting that the watch was broken when put away. The minute hand was also missing, but the hour hand pointed to just after two o'clock. Could this mark the time of the accident?

Up on the crest of the ridge, the weather conditions began to deteriorate for Anker and Hahn, just as they had for Mallory and Irvine. It began to snow hard and the going became much more difficult in near white-out conditions. The two climbers continued up the ridge and traversed the Third Step, but there was still some way to go in the crystal-clear air. Ahead of them was a steep ice-field subject to avalanches, a rock traverse and then a steep snow ramp leading up to the summit ridge.

The last 200 metres (660 feet) of their route was through deep snow, with huge, potentially dangerous cornices bulging out over the Kangshung Face to their left. A few more paces and they were on top of the world – a surprisingly small area no bigger than a billiard table, which sloped steeply away to the north and south. It was 2.50 p.m. and it had taken the two climbers two and a half hours since leaving Camp VI.

It was a remarkable achievement, particularly for Conrad Anker, who had been no higher than 7000 metres (23,000 feet) before coming out to Everest. Below them, the great Tibetan plateau stretched away to the north and the jungles of Nepal to the south; on a clear day, it is even possible to see the curvature of the Earth. But that afternoon Conrad was denied any such vista, for below him the clouds had rolled in and obscured the view.

Inevitably, with their oxygen running out, the two climbers had to turn around and begin their descent to Camp VI. The same question, however, was on everybody's mind: could Mallory and Irvine also have reached the summit 75 years before?

CHAPTER TEN

'Because Mallory was Mallory'

'The accident occurred on the descent (as most do) and ... if that is so, the peak was first climbed because Mallory was Mallory.'

Geoffrey Winthrop Young to Douglas Freshfield, August 1924

'What is the summing up of the whole thing?' asked Howard Somervell in 1924 as the expedition left Base Camp for home. 'Well, I think the mountain can be climbed – perhaps it has been. Above 28,000 feet there is a zone of about 200 feet of really badly loose rock, where, I believe, the disaster probably occurred. This is the chief danger, as the rock is both loose and steep ... .'[1]

Seventy-five years later, Jake Norton, now safely back from the expedition's historic discovery of Mallory's body and still visibly emotional about the experience, was even more emphatic: 'I know they could have made it, and I think they did, and I'll continue to believe that until there's conclusive proof otherwise.'[2]

Before the search expedition went out to Tibet, it was unlikely that we would find evidence showing that Mallory and Irvine did *not* reach the summit of Everest. There was, however, always the possibility that we could recover the small Kodak camera that Somervell lent to Mallory, and the slimmest of chances that the negative would prove that they did reach the summit. This is really the only evidence that will prove conclusively that they succeeded.

In the event, we did not find the camera, but the new evidence uncovered is just as exciting and it allows a new appraisal to be made about what happened to the two climbers on that fateful day on the North Face of Everest.

One of the enduring debates about Mallory and Irvine's last day on the mountain is about the *time* they left Camp VI. If that can be established, then their movements during much of the rest of the day can be predicated.

Today, climbers make a very early start, and Dave Hahn and Conrad Anker's summit bid on 17 May was typical. They retired to their tents around 4 p.m. on the previous afternoon and tried to get what rest they could. Fitful sleep is the most you can expect at that altitude, but they set their wristwatch alarms for midnight anyway. When they woke, they spent the next two hours eating what they could, melting water and trying to generate as much warmth in their feet before putting on their insulated double boots. They left their tent shortly after 2 a.m. and spent the next two hours climbing up through the Yellow Band before the first rays of dawn began to light their way.

The early expeditions made much later starts, which is one reason why their summit attempts consistently failed. On 3 June 1924, when Norton and Somervell made their unsuccessful bid, they left Camp VI at 6.40 a.m., which was a typical time for pre-war expeditions. Norton realized he was running out of time by 1 p.m., still 270 metres (900 feet) short of the summit. In 1922 Geoffrey Bruce and George Finch left camp for the summit at 6.30 a.m., and Mallory's attempt several days before did not see him on his way until 8 a.m. Even Wager and Wyn Harris in 1933 did not get away until 5.40 a.m., and, like Norton and Somervell, they turned back by 12.30 p.m., still hopelessly short of the summit.

Mallory was well known for his early starts and he would have wanted to get away promptly on 8 June. This was probably one reason why he did not choose Odell as his climbing partner: he had a reputation for being a slow starter. Mallory's last note to Noel was explicit: 'We'll probably start early tomorrow (8th) in order to have clear weather. It won't be too early to start looking for us either crossing the rock band or going up skyline at 8.00 p.m. [he meant 8.00 a.m.].'[3] We know, therefore, that it was Mallory's intention to make an early start that morning. When the 1933 expedition searched the 1924 Camp VI, they found a lever torch and folding candle. Even the chronically forgetful Mallory is unlikely to have left his camp in darkness without his torch; this suggests that the climbers did not leave before dawn (which is before 5 a.m. on Everest in early June).

A pre-dawn start was much too early, even for Mallory. It took the early mountaineers many hours to prepare for climbing, mainly because their leather mountain boots took for ever to unfreeze over their inefficient cookers before they could even get them on their feet. However, Mallory's Unna stove rolled down the mountain the previous evening, and without its meagre warmth, the climbers would probably have made an even slower start than they intended. Without the stove, the two climbers could not melt snow and ice for their water bottles either, so they must also have been dehydrated throughout their last day on the mountain.

Much has been made of the chaos left behind at Camp VI, where oxygen equipment was strewn inside their tent. Odell thought this might have indicated a last-minute hitch: 'Within were a rather mixed assortment of spare clothes, scraps of food, their two sleeping-bags, oxygen cylinders, and parts of apparatus; outside were more parts of the latter and of the Duralumin [light, strong aluminium alloy] carriers. It might be supposed that these were undoubted signs of reconstruction work and probably difficulties with the oxygen outfit ... The oxygen apparatus itself may have needed repair or readjustment either before or after they left Camp VI, and so have delayed them.'[4]

There are, however, alternative explanations. For example, Irvine might have worked on the equipment the previous afternoon and stopped when it got dark, leaving the unfinished work outside. Mallory was also well known for his untidiness, and the shambles in the tent was nothing unusual for him. The cylinders inside the tent might also been used by the climbers to breathe oxygen during the night. Odell's discovery is therefore inconclusive.

What seems most likely is that Mallory and Irvine did not leave Camp VI until 6 a.m. *at the earliest*, and it could even have been several hours later if they were delayed with their equipment. This would put Mallory and Irvine *at least* four hours behind Anker and Hahn, who left shortly after 2 a.m. on their summit day, and even as much as seven hours behind.

Mallory was known to be a 'ridge man', intuitively choosing routes along ridges in preference to traversing lower down a face. When he wrote his note to Noel the previous night, he was unsure which route he would take. But we know from Odell's last sighting that Mallory decided to follow his instinct and climb up to the North East Ridge that morning, in preference to a traverse of the North Face, which had defeated Norton and Somervell five days previously. Anker and Hahn followed the same route in 1999.

The next crucial piece of evidence about Mallory and Irvine's timing is Odell's reported sighting of them on the ridge at 12.50 p.m. Assuming that it was not a figment of his imagination, where exactly were they at the time? Once again, the 1999 summit bid helps us determine how far Mallory and Irvine might have climbed.

Both Hahn and Anker were experienced, young and fit climbers. Hahn had reached the summit of Everest in 1994, so he was familiar with the route and, unlike Mallory and Irvine, he *knew* the summit could be reached. The weather that morning was favourable, they were using the latest climbing gear and lightweight oxygen equipment, and they had the security of using fixed ropes most of the way to the top. Everything was working in their favour.

That morning, it took them two hours to climb up through the Yellow Band. Shortly after dawn, when they had been climbing for almost four hours, they were still short of the First Step. Such a time for the first stage of the route from Camp VI is typical for modern climbers; some have climbed it faster, many have been slower.

Taking Hahn and Anker's time as a reasonable average up to the First Step, and assuming that Mallory and Irvine left no earlier than 6 a.m., then the *earliest* time the two pre-war climbers could have reached the First Step would have been around 10 a.m.

There is more evidence that Mallory and Irvine reached that point after four hours' climbing. In 1991 Eric Simonson found two old oxygen bottles near the First Step, directly on the ridge route. Jake Norton and Tap Richards recovered these bottles after they turned back from the Second Step on 17 May, and they were positively identified as coming from the 1924 expedition. Mallory and Irvine were the only people who could have left them.

These bottles contained 535 litres of oxygen at a pressure of 120 atmospheres. On the climb from Camp IV to Camp V two days previously, Irvine set the apparatus to deliver 1.5 litres per minute. This gave almost four hours of oxygen from each cylinder. (The regulators could be set to deliver gas at a maximum rate of 2.2 litres per minute, it is unlikely that the two climbers would have used oxygen at this rate.) We also know, from his note to Odell, how much oxygen Mallory planned to use for the summit: '... we'll probably go on two cylinders – but it's a bloody load for climbing'.[5]

No climber carries unnecessary weight, and Mallory and Irvine would certainly have abandoned their first bottles as soon as they were empty, but obviously not before. So the discovery of oxygen cylinders dumped just before the First Step is further confirmation that they reached this position about four hours after they left Camp VI, some time between 10.00 a.m. and 1.30 p.m. (assuming they left no later than 9 a.m.).

Moving from the First to the Second Step is not technically difficult as the ridge ascends only 150 metres (500 feet) between the two, but the route runs along a daunting knife-edge between the Kangshung and North Faces. Hahn and Anker had the security of fixed ropes, albeit old and suspect, and it took them about two hours.

Mallory and Irvine would not have had the advantage of the ropes, so their passage to the Second Step must have taken at least as long, and possibly longer. This would put them at the base of the Second Step some time between 12.30 p.m. and 4.00 p.m. This raises the inevitable question of where Mallory and Irvine were seen at 12.50 p.m. by Noel Odell.

Odell's first impression was that the two climbers were moving up from the Second Step to the skyline, and this does fit the timing. His recollection was: '... the entire summit ridge and final peak of Everest were unveiled. My eyes became fixed on one tiny black spot silhouetted on a small snow-crest beneath a rock-step in the ridge; the black spot moved. Another black spot became apparent and moved up the snow to join the other on the crest. The first then approached the great rock-step and shortly emerged at the top; the second did likewise ...'[6] But Odell saw them for only a few minutes, and the climbers could not have scaled the Second Step in that time.

Alternatively, Mallory and Irvine might have been seen on either the First Step, or the so-called Third Step, just below the summit pyramid. The First Step also fits the timing if they left after 8.30 a.m., but the outcrop does not conform to Odell's description because it is too far away from the summit pyramid: 'The place on the ridge referred to is the prominent rock-step at a very short distance from the base of the final pyramid.'[7]

The alternative is that Odell saw the climbers on the Third Step, as suggested by Audrey Salkeld.[8] This part of the North East Ridge fits well with Odell's description, and Mallory and Irvine could have traversed the step in the time described by their companion. However, it took Hahn and Anker more than 10 hours to reach this position. If Mallory and Irvine were on the Third Step when Odell saw them at 12.50 p.m., they would have left their camp before 3 a.m., an impossibly early start for these climbers who had no means of lighting their way. Modern climbers have, on occasion, reached the Third Step in just seven hours, using the Chinese ladder. It is inconceivable, however, that Mallory and Irvine could have climbed an unknown route, without safety ropes *and* free-climbed the notoriously difficult Second Step this quickly.

When Odell saw the climbers on the ridge, he estimated that they were 244 metres (800 feet) below the summit. This puts them on the North East Ridge at an altitude of approximately 8600 metres (28,230 feet), which is 43 metres (140 feet) *below* the Second Step but more than 100 metres (330 feet) *above* the First Step.

The fact remains that Odell's sighting of Mallory and Irvine remains an eternal dilemma and none of the three steps fits the description and the time satisfactorily. Odell's position on a small crag between Camps V and VI at an altitude of 7925 metres (26,000 feet) gives a very oblique view of the North East Ridge (see photograph). The narrow angle of view and the effects of foreshortening would have made it difficult for Odell to judge distances. When Andy Politz climbed to Odell's position, he was able to distinguish the three steps as distinct features. It is possible, therefore, that the climbers were moving on snow somewhere between the First and Second Steps, or between the Second and Third Steps, but appeared to Odell to be much closer to the summit pyramid than they really were because of the optical effect of foreshortening in the clear air at high altitude.

The next puzzle is whether Mallory and Irvine were able to climb the Second Step. They must have been climbing for at least six hours before they reached this obstacle and would have used half the oxygen in their second and last cylinder. Odell reported cloud at this altitude at 12.50 p.m. By 2.00 p.m. it was snowing and the wind had increased. It would have been bitterly cold for Mallory and Irvine in these deteriorating conditions, but it would probably not have prevented them from tackling the Second Step, although the conditions might have slowed them.

In 1933 Wager and Wyn Harris were convinced that the Second Step was unassailable, and this has remained the perceived wisdom ever since. The Chinese ladder has made scaling the Second Step relatively straightforward since 1975, and nobody thereafter tried to free-climb the outcrop – until Anker.

However, the Chinese *did* climb the Second Step in 1960 before the ladder was there, using an unconventional but effective technique, when Liu Lien-man crouched down to allow Chu Yin-hua to stand on his shoulders and haul himself up. It took the Chinese five hours to get all four climbers to the top of the step, but they were not very experienced and none had the rock-climbing skills of George Mallory. The evidence from the Chinese 1960 expedition therefore suggests that the Second Step was climbable after all, albeit with difficulty.

Like the Chinese, Conrad Anker found that most of the Second Step was poor-quality rock, which broke away easily. Anker, who is a superbly skilled rock climber, took nearly an hour to climb the face. His final analysis was that Mallory and Irvine would have found the Second Step very difficult without modern equipment, but not impossible, and they could probably have climbed it in just over an hour.

If Mallory and Irvine reached the base of the Second Step between 12.30 and 4.00 p.m., and if Anker's estimate is accurate, the pre-war climbers could have reached the top of the Second Step some time between 2.00 and 5.30 p.m. This suggests that they climbed the Second Step during the storm, which lasted from 2.00 to 4.00 p.m.

Once past the Second Step, there is very little to prevent a fit, determined climber from reaching the summit, provided he or she still has the physical resources to continue climbing through heavy snow for several more hours. In 1960 Liu Lien-man, the Chinese climbing leader, was so exhausted that he could not continue beyond the top of the step, so he settled into a bivouac until his colleagues returned. The three other climbers continued and reached the summit just before dawn, 19 hours after leaving their high camp.

When Anker reached the top of the Second Step at 11.15 a.m., he commented that the summit pyramid looked tantalizingly close, but he knew it was deceptive because foreshortening gives a false perspective in the clear air. It took him another three and a half hours to reach the summit at 2.50 p.m. – a total of 12½ hours using oxygen. If Mallory and Irvine had succeeded in scaling the Second Step, they would have taken longer than Anker and Hahn to reach the summit, as they would have been climbing without oxygen by this stage. It would have been an immense struggle, but with the peak looking so close, Mallory would certainly have been tempted to go for the top.

Physically, neither man was in good health. Norton was convinced that Mallory was unfit, and Irvine was suffering agony from severe sunburn. Nor did they have the means to melt water that morning, so they would have been severely dehydrated. In addition, their second and last oxygen cylinder was about to run out. However, the mountain has been climbed successfully in similar circumstances when the 1960 Chinese team had nothing to eat or drink during the 31½ hours it took them to reach the summit *and* return to their high camp. Nor did they use much oxygen.

Like the Chinese (but for different reasons) Mallory had the unrelenting drive to conquer Everest and he was well known for his determination to reach the summit. John Noel always claimed that Mallory's obsession with Everest amounted to mental illness and that he thought of little else, day or night. The challenge consumed Mallory, and it is this exceptional state of mind that can ultimately carry a climber far beyond the normal limits of human resource and endurance to overcome fatigue and lack of oxygen. Such relentless tenacity in a climber should never be underestimated; in Mallory's case, it could have taken him to the summit.

Mallory knew that the 1924 expedition would be his last chance to climb the mountain that had consumed so much of his life. It troubled him that he had achieved so little in his life; he felt his war years were unremarkable, his time at Charterhouse frustrating and his career undistinguished. This was in stark contrast to his companions such as Somervell and Norton, who were eminent in their chosen professions. With his one great achievement in life only a few hours' climbing away, Mallory would have found it difficult to turn back. Without doubt, he had an extreme case of 'summit fever'. Mallory also had a reputation for being a fearless, maverick climber, sometimes bordering on reckless.

It is difficult to imagine Mallory and Irvine climbing for longer than the 19 hours taken by the Chinese in 1960, so if they did succeed in reaching the summit, it most probably took them *less* time than the Chinese, but somewhat *longer* than Hahn and Anker. Although Hahn and Anker did not make a particularly rapid ascent, they did so with modern, lightweight equipment, and with plenty of oxygen. So it is reasonable to suppose that *if* Mallory and Irvine reached the summit, it would have taken them between 13 and 18 hours. If they left their high camp sometime between 6 a.m. and 9 a.m., then the *earliest* they could have reached the summit would be 7 p.m., and the *latest* would be 3 a.m. the following morning (assuming they left at 9 a.m. and took 18 hours).

Ironically, if Mallory had been carrying a camera, as everybody supposed, it would almost certainly have been too dark for him to take a picture, so the only absolute proof of his success might not exist.

If Mallory and Irvine were still on or near the summit after nightfall, then Mallory must have known that their chances of returning safely to Camp VI were slim. An unplanned bivouac at that altitude, even in modern thermal clothing, is a serious situation for climbers to find themselves in.

In 1960 Liu Lien-man survived a night at 8690 metres (28,500 feet), but he had the advantage of wearing modern, post-war clothing. Today, there is significant improvement even on the 1960s' equipment. Hahn and Anker wore micro-porous underwear, fleeces and one-piece down suits, which provided 7.5–10 centimetres (3–4 inches) of modern, high-tech thermal layering. Even wearing the latest hi-tech clothing, an unplanned bivouac at night at these altitudes is likely to result in frostbite.

When Mallory's body was found, he was wearing seven or eight layers of clothing, which amounted to a thickness of no more than 6 millimetres (¼ inch). On the outside, he was dressed in a windproof 'Shackleton' jacket of tightly woven cotton; under that was a woollen cardigan; his underclothes included layers of thin cotton and silk. On the night that he died, the chill wind must have knifed through his inadequate clothing. Neither climber could have survived for long on the mountain, even if they hadn't fallen.

Mallory's body was found at 8170 metres (26,800 feet), below the First Step. Odell had previously seen the climbers approximately 435 metres

(1430 feet) higher than Mallory's final resting-place, which suggests that he was descending when he fell. We know he had abandoned his first bottle of oxygen some time during the morning's ascent, but he was not wearing his second bottle either, which is further proof that he was descending. He probably used up his second cylinder shortly after 2 p.m., so he must have fallen some time after that.

At this altitude, the body becomes frozen within a few hours of death and the injuries sustained during the fall are preserved and still very clear, even after 75 years. Apart from the obvious features, such as bone fractures and surface bruising, internal injuries could be detected on his body. This evidence allows us to reconstruct the last few hours of George Mallory's life, and, by association, also gain an insight into what happened to Andrew Irvine.

Mallory was lying on his front, facing uphill and with arms outstretched as if trying to stop himself sliding down the hillside. It was a position quite unlike the other bodies in the area. If a climber falls on rough terrain, he usually dies quickly and the body comes to rest in a random fashion. Mallory's position was much more composed and the body showed relatively few external signs of trauma. His position indicated that he was sliding out of control down an icy slope and trying desperately to slow himself using his bare hands; it is possible his gloves were ripped off during his attempt at self-arrest. This suggests that he was still alive when he came to rest on the snow slope, and actively struggling to stop himself sliding further down the mountain.

The North Face at this point slopes gently down from south to north at an angle of about 20 or 30 degrees, but below is a much steeper section. This is why Mallory's body, and those of many other climbers there, came to rest in this area. Not more than 20 metres (66 feet) behind him a steep cliff drops away and anybody going beyond that would continue to fall 3000 metres (10,000 feet) down the North Face to the main Rongbuk Glacier below.

Over the years, small stones and scree had slipped down the mountain and partially buried the body. The whole mass – body, aggregate and ice – were frozen together and Mallory had, in effect, become part of the mountainside. Every year, the North Face experiences avalanches, which must have slid over the body, leaving it undisturbed for the most part. During the summer monsoon, the body would be covered with deep snow for at least four or five months and would often have remained completely covered all year round. For this reason, as well as the intense cold and extreme dryness, the body and clothing have remained well preserved.

Much of the clothing remained on the top part of the body, except for the back, where his shoulders and middle back were exposed. This is the part of the body most exposed to sunlight, and during those brief periods when it was uncovered, intense high-altitude ultraviolet light and gamma rays would have caused the natural fibres to deteriorate.

Above the waist, his body was remarkably well preserved, bleached white and with the look of marble. All the climbers from the search expedition remarked on the impressive physical appearance of the man. Time had not diminished the muscular physique, and his arms and shoulders showed what a powerful climber he must have been. The backs of his hands were dark brown, probably sunburnt *before* he died.

Below the waist the body was more disfigured. Birds, probably alpine choughs, had scavenged around the buttocks. On his right foot he still wore his green leather hobnailed boot; the lower right leg had sustained a boot-top fracture of the tibia and fibula above the ankle, which is a common climbing break. His left leg was not injured and was crossed over his broken leg in a position that suggests he moved to make himself more comfortable – another indication that he was still conscious when he came to rest.

Mallory had also sustained an injury to his forehead, just above the left eye, and this had exposed part of the brain. It was a serious wound which would undoubtedly have caused severe concussion, but as most critical brain function is located at the back of the head, the injury might not have been instantly fatal. However, Mallory might have been only partially conscious after the fall and probably died from shock and hypothermia within a short time. His eyes were closed as if at peace.

The rope around his waist indicated that he must have been roped to Irvine when he fell. The cotton rope, probably made by Beales, was about 8–10 millimetres (⅜ inch) in diameter. It showed a clean break rather than abrasion. This type of rope had a very low breaking strain and would probably not have held the weight of a falling man, especially if the strain were taken around a sharp piece of rock and the rope was jerked tight as Mallory fell.

The rope was tied with a bowline knot to make a loop around his waist, and the loop had caused severe crushing of the ribs and burning to the skin; the indentations of the rope could still be seen on the surface of the skin around his chest. This suggests that Irvine had tried hard to belay Mallory as he fell, and had briefly held him before the rope broke. The chest was bruised down the *left* side, and this damage is consistent with a fall to the left, *away* from the mountain as he was descending the North Face.

The other artefacts found on the body probably add little to the evidence, unless detailed forensic analysis eventually reveals some hidden information. Mallory's altimeter was specially made for the Everest expedition and the dial could register altitudes up to 30,000 feet (9144 metres), but it was broken, so it tells us nothing about the maximum height they achieved. His watch was also broken; the hour hand pointed to shortly after two, but the glass face was missing and it was probably shattered before the accident. Even if the watch marked the time of the fall, there is no way of knowing whether it was two in the afternoon, or two the following morning. Either time is a possibility. Conversely, it could have run down and stopped at any time during the climb, or even frozen to a standstill.

More inconclusive evidence involves a photograph of Ruth, which Mallory planned to leave on the summit, according to family legend. Some writers suggest that as it was not on his body, he must have left it on the summit. But Mallory was so untidy that he more likely mislaid it before reaching Everest.

From the evidence on Mallory's body, we can attempt to reconstruct the last few hours of his life. We know he fell during his descent and that his glacier glasses were still in his pocket, which suggests that he and Irvine were returning in the evening or even at night. (It is possible that these were spare glasses, but knowing Mallory, it is unlikely he was organized enough to carry two pairs.) We know the climbers were roped together, and therefore both still alive at the time of the accident. Being roped suggests that they were moving over difficult terrain, descending in poor visibility or at night, or any combination of these conditions. Mallory had also forgotten his compass.

Given the men's inevitable state of exhaustion and that Mallory was by far the more experienced climber, it is likely that he was leading. Except for the rope burns, the trauma to his body was not severe, suggesting that he had not fallen far, and certainly not from the ridge which was more than 300 metres (1000 feet) above his resting position. It is more likely that they had come down from the North East Ridge on to the North Face and were moving through the Yellow Band, which can be treacherous underfoot. This is the very place where Howard Somervell guessed they had fallen: 'This is the chief danger, as the rock is both loose and steep ...[9]

Mountaineers in the 1920s used a classic technique in Alpine climbing, where the lead climber holds a coil of the rope in the *uphill* hand and as he passes small outcrops of rock, he drops the rope over them on his uphill side. This is a safety measure so that if either climber should fall, the loops over the rocks will help the partner to arrest the other climber.

As Mallory fell, the rope would have begun to uncoil, giving Irvine time to put a turn around a nearby boulder or brace himself before taking the strain. But Mallory had fallen too far and gained momentum, so when the rope came under tension, it snapped. The bruising on his left side but lack of severe trauma to the body generally is consistent with a fall of about 10 metres (33 feet), perhaps over the edge of a low cliff, followed by a slide down a snow slope of another 100 or 150 metres (300–500 feet). There are many small cliffs of this size above the snow slope where Mallory is now lying. He could have sustained the injuries to his forehead and right leg during the fall, or he could have encountered boulders as he slid down the snow slope. The blood on Mallory's jacket and the climbing rope suggest that he also sustained cuts and abrasions.

It has always been assumed that it was the inexperienced Irvine who fell, but this new evidence suggests otherwise, and gives a scenario where Irvine found himself alive but alone on the mountain. The young climber would have been in shock, possibly in poor visibility or even at night. He must have tried to find Mallory, but it would have been too dangerous to follow him straight down, so he probably moved slowly in case he met with the same fate, carefully zigzagging down the mountainside.

Irvine would have searched for his companion, calling for him by name and not knowing whether he was still alive. But Mallory had fallen and slid some distance and there was little chance of finding him, especially in poor conditions or in darkness. There is no evidence of any assistance having been given to the injured climber, so we can assume that Irvine did not find his companion's body.

One of two things then happened to Irvine. Perhaps he also fell and died during the search, but this seems unlikely. Wang Hong-bao told Ryoten Yashimoro Hasegawa that he found '... the much older remains of an Englishman ... lying on his side as if asleep at the foot of a rock'.[10] It is more likely that bad weather or nightfall forced Irvine to stop his search and rest. If he had fallen asleep, dressed as he was, he could not have survived the night. Somewhere on the mountain lies the body of Sandy Irvine, probably further to the east and closer to the Chinese camp than Mallory.

The time of the accident is crucial to determining whether or not the two climbers succeeded in reaching the summit. We know they were high on the North Ridge at 12.50 p.m.; if the broken watch marks the time of the accident, they must have turned around shortly after being seen by Odell, possibly when the storm came through at 2 p.m. This would be a logical time for them to turn back, and they would have been coming down during the storm. This could explain why Odell and the others, who were watching the mountain carefully, did not see them. It is possible that Mallory removed his glacier goggles during the storm in order to see better. However, the evidence for this scenario is flawed because the watch was almost certainly broken *before* the accident as it was in his pocket.

After 4 p.m. the mountain was bathed in sunshine and both Odell and those further down were keeping a close watch on the ridge and North Face. They would almost certainly have seen the climbers descending in those conditions and Mallory would certainly have been wearing his glasses in the bright sun.

Odell returned from Camp VI to Camp IV that afternoon, arriving at 6.45 p.m. Throughout his descent, he kept a close watch for the missing climbers. The night was fine with a pale moonlight, and this allowed Odell and Hazard to keep watch on the upper slopes from the North Col. However, if Mallory or Irvine were still alive at this time, neither man had the means to signal to their companions down the mountain.

If the climbers *had* succeeded in reaching the summit, the earliest they could have done so was 7 p.m., just as the sun was setting. Their return would be in darkness and without torches, with only a pale moon to light their way. It would have taken them at least four hours to reach the position of the accident, probably longer. If they had summitted later than midnight, their accident would have occurred after dawn and Mallory would have been wearing his goggles. So if they did reach the summit on 8 June 1924, we can refine the time further to between 7 p.m. and midnight.

The mystery of Mallory and Irvine therefore lives on. There is much to tantalize but still insufficient to enlighten; perhaps this will always remain the case. If Irvine's body is found in the future, it will add more clues to this enduring enigma and we might come a little closer to knowing what happened that day. With no conclusive proof for or against, the case must remain unproven.

And what of the elusive camera? Mallory is unlikely to have trusted himself with it on such an important climb and probably gave it to his companion. The camera, if found, will be with Irvine – faithful and dependable, even in death. But if they summitted at night, there will be no photographic record of their achievement.

Whether they reached the summit or not, George Mallory and Sandy Irvine set the world an example. Their determination, bravery and heroism inspired generations of climbers to face the challenge of a mountain, to hold ambitions dear, to work together and to persevere until the summit is reached. Their story, their aspiration and their energy is an example to us all. In death, as in life, they remain together on the mountain; they are in every sense, *the* men of Everest.

Geoffrey Winthrop Young, Mallory's mentor and friend, never had any doubt about what happened to the climbers:' ... after nearly twenty years' knowledge of Mallory as a mountaineer, I can say that difficult as it would have been for any mountaineer to turn back with the only difficulty past – to Mallory it would have been an impossibility ... Odell's opinion further confirms ... my impression that ... the accident occurred on the descent (as most do) and that if that is so, the peak was first climbed because Mallory was Mallory.'[11]

APPENDIX I

Glossary

Acclimatization the adaptation of the body to high altitude.

Alp a summer pasture above a valley but below the snowline.

Alpine Club the world's first climbing club, founded in London in 1857.

Alpine Journal the journal of the Alpine Club, published since 1863.

Alpine style a lightweight ascent of a high mountain, climbed as you would an Alpine peak.

Anchor a permanent or semi-permanent fixture to a rock or snow, to which fixed ropes are attached.

Arête a sharp, angular rock or ice ridge.

Belay to rope on to an anchor to safeguard another climber.

Bergschrund a crevasse between the head of a glacier and the mountain.

Bivouac a temporary open camp on a mountain without proper tents.

Buttress a large bulge of rock projecting from a mountainside.

Camp in high-altitude climbing, a tent or group of tents used as a staging post to climb a high peak.

Chimney a wide crack in rock, or sometimes ice, often used as a route up a rock face or pitch.

Cirque a French term for a corrie.

Col a dip or 'saddle' in a ridge, usually linking two peaks.

Cornice an overhanging ledge of snow.

Corrie a Scottish term for a circular hollow or basin in a mountainside.

Couloir a gully running down a mountain face.

Crack a fissure in rock too small to be a chimney.

Crampons a spiked metal attachment, strapped to a boot and used for climbing on snow and ice.

Crevasse an ice crack in the surface of a glacier, which can be very wide and deep, sometimes covered with snow and often a considerable hazard.

Cwm a Welsh word meaning 'cirque' or 'corrie'.

Dzong a Tibetan fort.

Exposure medical condition in which the body loses heat and develops hypothermia; open position on a mountain where a slip would have serious consequences.

Fixed ropes ropes anchored to rock or ice for the duration of an ascent, which climbers can clip on to for safety in difficult or dangerous sections.

Free climbing climbing without artificial aids, such as fixed ropes.

Friend a modern climbing device that is inserted into a crack; a rope is then attached to the friend, giving the climber protection.

Frostbite the freezing, usually of extremities such as fingers and toes; extreme cases may require amputation.

Gaiters outer casing of canvas or nylon to stop snow entering boots.

Glacier a river of ice which flows down a valley, fed by seasonal snow.

Glacier glasses very dark sunglasses used in extremely bright conditions, such as those found on a glacier or at high altitude.

Gully a wide fissure on the side of a mountain.

Harness nylon or canvas webbing that goes around a climber's body, to which a rope can be attached.

High-altitude boots usually 'double-boots', having a soft, warm inner casing inside a tough outer boot, made of plastic, sometimes leather or man-made fibre.

Himalayan style an ascent in which a series of camps is established on a high mountain; each is supplied progressively, eventually allowing a summit attempt to be made from the top camp.

Ice-axe a wooden, metal or fibreglass shaft with a spike at one end and a pick-shaped head at the other, essential for climbing on snow and ice.

Icefall an unstable and dangerous area of crevasses and pinnacles on a glacier.

La a Tibetan pass or col.

Lead climber an experienced climber who leads a group along a route.

Line the optimum route followed by a climber.

Moraine a ridge of stone and rock deposited at the edges and snout of a glacier.

Mountain sickness illness caused by rarefied air at high altitude; symptoms include headache, dizziness, lethargy and loss of appetite.

Nails as attached to the soles of pre-war climbing boots they helped grip on snow and ice in lieu of crampons.

Névé an accumulation of snow above the bergschrund.

Oedema a serious form of mountain sickness in which fluid accumulates in the lungs (pulmonary oedema) or the brain (cerebral oedema); either condition can quickly become fatal.

Overhang a rock or ice face that leans beyond the vertical.

Oxygen equipment Cylinder(s), regulator and face mask mounted on a pack frame, used to supply oxygen to a climber at high altitude.

Pack frame lightweight metal frame attached to shoulder straps.

Pass the easiest route over a mountain ridge between two valleys.

Peak a mountain summit.

Pillar a rock column jutting out from a mountainside.

Pitch the distance between two anchors; a short section of a climb.

Porter a person, usually local, employed to carry a load; on Everest, porters may be Sherpas, Bhotias or Tamangs.

Rib a small ridge on a mountainside.

Ridge a crest between two mountain peaks.

Scree loose stones on a slope.

Seige style see Himalayan style.

Serac a pinnacle of ice.

Sherpas nepalese mountain people, but originally from Tibet, frequently employed as porters.

Sirdar head Sherpa.

Slab a flat expanse of rock, often tilted at an angle.

Snow-blindness temporary but painful blindness caused by bright glare from a glacier or snowfield.

Snow line the lower level of permanent snow.

Solo climbing climbing completely alone.

Spindrift powder snow blown by the wind; can cause an avalanche.

Steps footholds cut into ice with an ice-axe or kicked into snow.

Theodolite precision instrument used by surveyors to measure angles, which are then used to create maps.

TIA Transient Ischaemic Attack, a temporary stroke brought on by exposure to high altitude.

Traverse to move more or less horizontally across a mountain; to climb up one side of a peak and down the other.

Tsampa finely ground barley flour, commonly found in Nepal and Tibet.

Unprotected climb a climb without safety aids (e.g. fixed ropes) to protect the climber from a serious accident or fall.

Wall a steep face of ice or rock.

White-out severe snowstorm in which it is impossible to tell where sky meets land.

APPENDIX II

People

Antonio de Andrade head of the Jesuit mission to the Mogul court in India who first visited Tibet in 1603.

Conrad Anker climber on the 1999 expedition who discovered Mallory's body and free-climbed the Second Step.

(Colonel) Eric Bailey British frontier officer who realized that Kintup's early report about Tibet was accurate.

(Major) Frederick Bailey British political officer in Sikkim who blocked expeditions to Everest between 1925 and 1932.

Bentley Beetham Lakeland schoolmaster and member of the 1924 Everest expedition.

Charles Bell British political officer in Sikkim until 1921, who assisted the early Everest expeditions.

Arthur Benson Mallory's tutor at Magdalene College, Cambridge.

E. St J. Birnic member of the 1933 Everest expedition.

Dr Karl Blodig distinguished Austrian mountaineer who climbed with Mallory in Wales.

Pierre Bouguer French scientist who developed early theories about the formation of mountains.

T.E. Brocklebank member of the 1933 Everest expedition.

Rupert Brooke gifted young poet and university friend of Mallory's; died of blood poisoning in France in April 1915.

(General) Charles Bruce affectionately known as Charlie or 'Bruiser'; leader of 1922 and 1924 Everest expeditions.

(Captain) Geoffrey Bruce member of the 1922 and 1924 expeditions and nephew of General Bruce.

L.V. Bryant New Zealand climber on the 1935 expedition.

Guy Bullock schoolfriend of Mallory and member of the Winchester Ice Club; joined the 1921 Everest expedition.

(Lance-naik) Tejbir Bura soldier in the 6th Gurkhas and member of the 1922 expedition.

(Colonel) S.G. Burrard surveyor with the Grand Trigonometrical Survey.

Simon Bussy friend of Mallory living in the south of France; a painter and a friend of the artist Pierre Auguste Renoir.

Chu Yin-hua member of the successful 1960 Chinese summit attempt.

Liesl Clark American television co-producer on the 1999 expedition.

John Collie one-time president of the Alpine Club.

William Conway famous English explorer of the Himalayas.

Colin Crawford member of the 1924 and 1933 Everest expeditions.

(Lord) George Curzon Viceroy of India 1898–1905.

Charles Darwin university friend of Mallory, whose grandfather wrote *On the Origin of Species*.

Pawel Datschnolian leader of what was rumoured to be an unsuccessful Soviet attempt on the north side of Everest in 1952.

Maurice Von Déchy pioneering Austrian climber of the Himalayas.

Clinton Dent climber who speculated as early as 1885 that Everest could be climbed.

Ippolito Desideri young Jesuit priest who travelled to Tibet in 1712.

Professor G. Dreyer scientist at Oxford University who developed early oxygen systems.

Oscar Eckenstein pioneer Himalayan climber.

(Sir) George Everest Surveyor General of India.

(Sir) Percy Farrar experienced Alpine climber and president of the Alpine Club.

George Finch talented climber and photographer, and member of the 1922 Everest expedition.

Peter Firstbrook producer of the BBC documentary *Lost on Everest*.

Frank Fletcher Mallory's headmaster at Charterhouse.

Will Arnold Forster a close family friend of the Mallorys; claims to have made psychic contact with George.

William Freshfield one-time president of both the Royal Geographical Society and the Alpine Club.

Harry Garret friend of George Mallory, who was shot through the head in Turkey during World War I.

Harry Gibson schoolfriend of Mallory and member of the Winchester Ice Club.

(Sir) George Goldie president of the Royal Geographical Society in the early 1900s.

(Sir) William Goodenough president of the new Mount Everest Committee, founded in 1931.

Alan Goodfellow friend of George Mallory who trained as a pilot during World War I.

Richard Graham a strict Quaker and conscientious objector during World War I; withdrew from the 1924 expedition.

W.W. Graham pioneer English climber; explored the Kangchenjunga region in 1882.

Robert Graves friend of George Mallory; served with the Welch Fusiliers during World War I.

Dave Hahn climber and video cameraman on the 1999 expedition.

Percy Wyn Harris climber on 1933 and 1936 expeditions; with Wager, found Irvine's ice-axe in 1933.

Ryoten Yashimoro Hasegawa climbing leader of 1979 Japanese team; told of the 'English dead' found at 8150 metres (26,740 feet) by Wang Hong-bao.

John de Vere Hazard member of the 1924 Everest expedition.

Hyder Young Hearsey Anglo-Indian cartographer who travelled widely through Tibet with Moorcroft.

Jochen Hemmleb expedition researcher on the 1999 expedition.

Michael Hennessy assistant to the Surveyor General of India, given joint credit for the 'discovery' of Mount Everest.

Dr A.M. Heron   geologist on the 1921 reconnaissance expedition to Everest.

(Sir) Edmund Hillary made first confirmed ascent of Everest in 1953 with Sherpa Tenzing Norgay.

Dr R.W.G. Hingston an RAF surgeon and doctor on the 1924 Everest expedition.

Arthur Hinks joint secretary to the Mount Everest Expedition throughout the 1920s and 1930s.

(Lieutenant Colonel) Charles Howard-Bury leader of the 1921 reconnaissance expedition to Everest.

Graham Hoyland Howard Somervell's great nephew and a climber on the 1999 expedition.

Baron Humboldt famous German explorer who encouraged the Schlagintweit brothers to visit India.

John Hunt expedition leader of the successful British attempt on Everest in 1953.

Andrew Comyn 'Sandy' Irvine member of the 1924 Everest expedition and Mallory's partner on the final attempt.

Graham Irving schoolmaster at Winchester and experienced climber who introduced Mallory to climbing.

Ned Johnstone cinematographer on the 1999 expedition.

Humphry Owen Jones friend of Mallory; died in a climbing accident in the Alps.

Dr Alexander Kellas high-altitude physiologist on the 1921 expedition; died in Tibet before reaching Everest.

Edwin Kempson climber on the 1935 expedition.

Geoffrey Keynes university friend of Mallory and brother of Maynard.

(Lord) Maynard Keynes economist and university friend of Mallory.

Kintup pundit, code-named K-P, travelled north into Tibet to discover the course of the Tsangpo River.

Konbu Tibetan climber on the successful 1960 Chinese summit attempt.

Frido Kordon Austrian climber who attended a séance in 1926 at which it was claimed that Mallory and Irvine reached the summit at 5 p.m.

Raymond Lambert Swiss climber who set a new record on Everest of 8600 metres (28,210 feet) in 1952.

William Lampton British Army Officer who began the Grand Trigonometrical Survey of India in 1802.

Dr F.E. Larkins a doctor on the medical board of the 1924 Everest expedition.

Liu Lien-man climbing leader of the 1960 Chinese summit attempt.

Peter Lloyd climber on the 1938 Everest expedition.

Jack Longland member of the 1933 Everest expedition.

Dr Tom Longstaff doctor on 1922 Everest expedition.

W. McLean member of the 1933 Everest expedition.

Ruth Mallory Mallory's wife, née Turner.

Manbahadur a cobbler on the 1924 expedition; developed frostbite and died at Base Camp.

Lee Meyers a specialist in emergency medicine and doctor on the 1999 expedition.

Lord Minto succeeded Curzon as Viceroy of India in 1905; also a member of the Alpine Club.

Thomas G. Montgomerie surveyor in the Great Trigonometric Survey of India, charged with training agents to infiltrate Tibet.

William Moorcroft eccentric English vet and explorer who made the first of his expeditions to Tibet in 1812.

Edmund Morgan friend of Mallory from Winchester; later became a bishop.

John Morley British Secretary of State for India; blocked plans for Everest expedition on diplomatic grounds.

(Captain) John Morris Gurkha officer and member of the 1924 Everest expedition.

(Major) Henry T. Morshead surveyor and member of 1921 and 1922 Everest expeditions.

Arnold Mumm offered to fund an Everest expedition to mark the fiftieth anniversary of the Alpine Club.

Albert Mummery late nineteenth-century British climbing pioneer.

(Captain) John Noel film-maker and member of 1922 and 1924 Everest expeditions.

(Major) Edward Norton member of the 1922 expedition and a popular choice as climbing leader in 1924.

Jake Norton climber on the 1999 expedition.

Dr Noel Odell geologist and member of the 1924 Everest expedition.

Odoric 14th-century Franciscan friar; possibly the first European to visit Tibet.

Phantog the first woman to summit from the north, in 1975.

Andy Politz climber on the 1999 expedition.

Thom Pollard high-altitude cameraman on the 1999 expedition.

Hugh Rose Pope friend of Mallory; died in a climbing accident in France.

David Pye student friend from Cambridge and Mallory's first biographer.

Harold Raeburn climbing leader of the 1921 reconnaissance expedition to Everest.

Hari Ram a pundit, code-named M-H; explored the high mountain massifs around Everest.

Jyoti Rana sound recordist on the 1999 expedition.

Cecil Rawlings young army officer reported seeing Everest from about 110 kilometres (70 miles) away in 1903.

Tap Richards climber on the 1999 expedition.

David Robertson Mallory's son-in-law and author of his second biography.

Donald Robertson climbing friend of Mallory who died in a climbing accident in Wales.

Hugh Ruttledge climbing leader of 1933 and 1936 Everest expeditions.

Cottie Sanders a female climbing friend of Mallory; later married and became Lady O'Malley.

Jack Sanders friend of Mallory; died in April 1915 in the first German gas attack of the war.

Adolf, Hermann and **Robert Schlagintweit** three Bavarian brothers who travelled extensively in Tibet in the 1850s.

Shamsher Gurkha NCO Sherpa; developed a blood clot and died at Base Camp on the 1924 expedition.

E.O. Shebbeare member of the 1924 and 1933 Everest expeditions.

Shih Chan-chun expedition leader of the successful 1960 and 1975 Chinese ascents.

A.E. Shipley zoologist and university friend of Mallory.

Eric Shipton climber on 1933, 1936 and 1938 expeditions and climbing leader in 1935.

Radhanath Sikdhar worked for the Grand Trigonometrical Survey of India; reputed to be the first to 'discover' Mount Everest.

Eric Simonson 1999 expedition leader.

Dolpa Singh pundit and cousin of Nain Singh.

Kinshen Singh pundit and nephew of Nain Singh; code-name A-K.

Mani Singh pundit and cousin of Nain Singh; code-name G-M.

Naatha Singh Nepalese surveyor; worked for the Survey of India and mapped peaks around Everest in 1907.

Nain Singh chief pundit, code-name No.1; travelled to Lhasa in 1866.

Frank Smythe member of the 1933, 1936 and 1938 Everest expeditions.

Dr T. Howard Somervell a doctor and climber on the 1922 and 1924 expeditions.

(Lieutenant Colonel) Edward Strutt climbing leader of the 1924 Everest expedition.

Junko Tabei member of the 1975 Japanese team and the first woman to climb Everest.

Tenzing Norgay Sherpa on 1935, 1938 and 1952 Everest expeditions; first confirmed ascent in 1953 with Edmund Hillary.

H.W. 'Bill' Tilman climber on the 1935 expedition and leader in 1938.

George Trevelyan friend of George Mallory; attached to the British Ambulance Unit in Italy during World War I.

Hugh Thackeray Turner widowed architect and Ruth Mallory's father.

Harry Tyndale schoolfriend of Mallory; member of the Winchester Ice Club.

Lawrence Wager climber on 1933 expedition; he and Percy Wyn Harris found Irvine's ice axe.

Dr Arthur Wakefield Lakeland climber and doctor; member of the 1924 Everest expedition.

Wang Fu-chou member of the successful 1960 Chinese summit attempt.

Wang Hong-bao Chinese climber (also spelt Wang Cow Pa, Wang Hung-bao or Wang Hong Bao) who discovered the 'English dead' at 8150 metres (26,740 feet) on Everest in 1975.

Andrew Waugh Surveyor General of India.

(Major) Edward Wheeler surveyor on the Survey of India; member of the 1921 reconnaissance expedition to Everest.

J. Claude White young army officer who took the first photograph of Everest in 1904.

Edmund Wigram climber on the 1935 expedition.

Dr Claude Wilson General Bruce's personal physician.

Hugh Wilson friend of George Mallory; killed at Hébuterne during World War I.

Maurice Wilson eccentric Englishman who flew solo to India and attempted to climb Everest alone in 1934.

(Sir) J.J. Withers represented the Alpine Club on the new Mount Everest Committee, founded in 1931.

Dr Alexander Wollaston doctor on the 1921 reconnaissance expedition to Everest.

Geoffrey Winthrop Young friend and mentor of Mallory and experienced Alpine climber.

Hilton Young friend of George Mallory; sent to Serbia with a Naval mission during World War I.

(Sir) Francis Younghusband famous soldier-explorer and one-time president of the Royal Geographical Society.

Notes

CHAPTER ONE

1　Young, Geoffrey Winthrop, *On High Hills: Memories of the Alps*, Methuen, London, 1927, p. 169.
2　Ibid., p. 170.
3　Ibid., p. 178.
4　Ibid., p. 179.
5　Letter from Mallory to his mother , August 1909, quoted in Robertson, David, *George Mallory*, Faber & Faber, London, 1969, pp 56–7
6　Letter from C.G. Bruce to A.R. Hinks, 4 July 1922, RGS Archives, EE 18/1.
7　Blodig, Karl. 1912. 'Ostertage in North Wales', *Climber's Club Journal*.
8　Karl Blodig, quoted in Pye, David, *George Leigh Mallory, a Memoir*, Oxford University Press/Humphrey Milford, Oxford, 1927, p. 42.
9　Cottie Sanders, quoted in Pye, op. cit., pp 42–3.
10　Avie Mallory, quoted in Robertson, op. cit., p. 17
11　Pye, op. cit., 1927, p. 6.
12　Letter from Mallory to his mother, 22 September 1900, quoted in Robertson, op. cit., p. 19.
13　Letter from Mallory to his mother, August 1904, quoted in Green, Dudley, *Mallory of Everest*, John Donald, Burnley, 1991, p. 19.
14　'In memoriam – George Herbert Leigh Mallory', *Alpine Journal*, Vol. XXXVI, No. 229, Nov. 1924, p. 383.
15　Irving, R.L.G., 'Five Years with Recruits', *Alpine Journal*, Vol. XXIV, No. 183, February 1909, pp 367–8.
16　Ibid., p. 453.
17　Recollections from Harold Porter, quoted in Green, op. cit., p. 21.
18　Lubbock, Percy (ed.), *The Diary of Arthur Christopher Benson*, Hutchinson, London, 1926, pp 126–7.
19　Cottie Sanders (Lady O'Malley) quoted in Robertson, op. cit., p. 37
20　Mallory, George, *Boswell the Biographer*, Smith, Elder & Co, London, 1912.
21　Letter from Mallory to Edmund Morgan, 1907, quoted in Green, op. cit., p. 34.
22　Letter from Mallory to Arthur Benson, quoted in Green, ibid., p. 35.

CHAPTER TWO

1　Cottie Sanders quoted in Robertson, David, *George Mallory*, Faber & Faber, London, 1969, p. 58.
2　Ibid., p. 59.
3　Letter from Mallory to Geoffrey Young, 30 December 1909, Alpine Club Archives.
4　Letter from Mallory to his mother, 25 September 1910, quoted in Robertson, op. cit., p. 65.

5 A schoolboy's recollection, quoted in Green, Dudley, *Mallory of Everest*, John Donald, Burnley, 1991, p. 46.
6 Cottie Sanders quoted in Robertson, op. cit., pp 68–9.
7 Tyndale, H.E.G., *Mountain Paths*, Eyre & Spottiswoode, London, 1948, p. 68.
8 Mallory, quoted in Robertson, op. cit., p. 86.
9 Letter to Mallory from his publisher, quoted in Robertson, op. cit., p. 87.
10 Letter from Rosamund Wills to Lady O'Malley, May 1914, quoted in Pye, David, *George Leigh Mallory, a Memoir*, Oxford University Press/Humphrey Milford, Oxford, 1927, p. 71.
11 Letter from Mallory to A.C. Benson, 25 April 1915, quoted in Pye, op. cit., p. 23.
12 Letter from Mallory to his wife, 15 August 1916, Magdalene College Archive.
13 Letter from Ruth Mallory to her husband, 28 September 1916, Magdalene College Archive.
14 Robertson, op. cit., p. 121.
15 Letter from Mallory to his father, 14 October 1918, Magdalene College Archive.
16 Letter from Mallory to his wife, 12 November 1918, Magdalene College Archive.
17 Robertson, op. cit., p. 129.
18 Geoffrey Young, quoted in Robertson op. cit., p. 143.
19 Noel, J.B.L., *Geographical Journal*, Vol. 53, 1919.
20 Letter from Percy Farrar to Mallory, 22 January 1921, quoted in Robertson, op. cit., p. 148.

CHAPTER THREE
1 Quoted in Wilford, J.N., *The Mapmakers*, Junction Press, London, 1981, p. 165.
2 Ibid.

CHAPTER FOUR
1 Wessels, C., *Early Jesuit Travellers in Central Asia*, Martinus Nijhoff, The Hague, 1924.
2 Ibid.
3 Desideri, Ippolito, *An Account of Tibet: The Travels of Ippolito Desideri of Pistoia, S.J., 1712–1727*, F. de Filippi (ed.), Routledge, London, 1937.
4 Moorcroft, William, and Trebeck, George, *Travels in the Himalayan Provinces of Hindustan and the Punjab and in Ladakh and Kashmir, in Peshawar, Kabul, Kunduz and Bokhara*, 2 vols, 1837, reprint, Oxford University Press, Karachi, 1979.
5 Allen, Charles, *A Mountain in Tibet*, André Deutsch, London, 1982.
6 Ibid.
7 Wilford, J.N., *The Mapmakers*, Junction Press, London, p. 169, 1981.
8 Hopkirk, Peter, *Trespassers on the Roof of the World*, John Murray, London, 1982.
9 Younghusband, Francis E., *Everest, the Challenge*, Nelson and Sons, London, 1936, p. 4.
10 Dent, C.T., *Above the Snowline*, Longmans, Green & Co., London, 1885.
11 Letter from Curzon to Freshfield, 1905, Alpine Club Archives, Minute Book 9.
12 Ibid.
13 Letter from Goldie to *The Times*, 18 March 1907.
14 Noel, J.B.L., *Through Tibet to Everest*, Edward Arnold, London, 1927, pp 30–1.
15 Ibid., p. 56.
16 Ibid., p. 62.

CHAPTER FIVE

1 John Noel's address to the Royal Geographical Society.
2 *The Times*, 1 June 1920.
3 The *Observer*, 6 June 1920.
4 The *Evening News*, 1 August 1920.
5 Quoted in Unsworth, Walt, *Everest*, Allen Lane, London, 1991, p. 31.
6 Mount Everest Committee Minute Book, Item 24.
7 Letter from Farrar to Hinks, RGS Archives, EE 12/1.
8 Letter from Mallory to David Pye, quoted in Pye, David, *George Leigh Mallory, a Memoir*, Oxford University Press/Humphrey Milford, Oxford, 1927, p. 105.
9 Letter from Mallory to his sister Avie, quoted in Pye, op. cit., p. 106.
10 Younghusband, Francis, E., *The Epic of Mount Everest*, Edward Arnold, p. 28, 1926.
11 Letter from Mallory to Geoffrey Young, 21 February 1921, quoted in Pye, op. cit., p. 106.
12 Letter from Mallory to his wife, 24 May 1921, Magdalene College Archive.
13 Letter from Howard-Bury to Hinks, RGS Archives, EE 13/1.
14 Ibid.
15 Letter from Mallory to Hinks, ibid., EE 3/4.
16 Ibid.
17 Letter from Hinks to Mallory, ibid., EE 3/4
18 Ibid.
19 'In Memoriam', *Alpine Journal*, Vol. LXI, 1956.
20 RGS agreement with expedition members, RGS Archives, EE 3/4.
21 Letter from Mallory to his wife, 17 May 1921, Magdalene College Archive.
22 Letter from Mallory to his wife, 24 May 1921, ibid.
23 Letter from Mallory to Geoffrey Young, RGS Archives, EE 3/4.
24 Letter from Mallory to his wife, 21 May 1921, Magdalene College Archive.
25 Letter from Mallory to David Pye, 9 June 1921, quoted in Pye, op. cit., pp 109–10.
26 Howard-Bury, C.K. et al., *Mount Everest: the Reconnaissance*, Edward Arnold, London, 1921, p. 74.
27 Ibid., p. 186.
28 Ibid., p. 192.
29 Letter from Mallory to his wife, 6 July 1921, Magdalene College Archive.
30 Bullock, G.H., 'The Everest Expedition, 1921'. *Alpine Journal*, Vol. LXVII, 1962.
31 Letter from Mallory to his wife, 22 July 1921, Magdalene College Archive.
32 Howard-Bury, op. cit., p. 236.
33 Letter from Mallory to his wife, 22 August 1921, Magdalene College Archive.
34 Letter from Mallory to Young, 9 September 1921, quoted in Robertson, David, *George Mallory*, Faber & Faber, London, 1969, p. 172.
35 Letter from Mallory to his wife, 1 September 1921, Magdalene College Archive.
36 Letter from Mallory to David Pye, 11 November 1921, quoted in Pye, op. cit., p. 122.
37 Howard-Bury, op. cit., p. 260.
38 Bullock, op. cit., p. 305.
39 Howard-Bury, op. cit., p. 269.

CHAPTER SIX

1 Letter from Hinks to Howard-Bury, RGS Archives, EE 13/1.
2 Letter from Hinks to Collie, ibid., EE 11/5.
3 Letter from Mallory to David Pye, 11 November 1921, quoted in Robertson, David, *George Mallory*, Faber & Faber, London, 1969, p. 177.

4 Letter from Mallory to his sister Avie, 10 November 1921, quoted in Robertson, op. cit., p. 177.
5 Letter from Bruce to Hinks, RGS Archives, EE 18/1.
6 Ibid.
7 Ibid.
8 Longstaff, T.G., *This My Voyage*, John Murray, London, 1950, p. 155.
9 Letter from Hinks to Heron, RGS Archives, EE 11/4.
10 Letter from Heron to Hinks, ibid.
11 Unna, P.J.H., 'The Oxygen Equipment of the 1922 Everest Expedition', *Alpine Journal*, Vol. XXXIV, 1923.
12 Letter from Hinks to Bruce, RGS Archives, EE 18/1.
13 Hinks, A.R. (writing anonymously), *Geographical Journal*, Vol. IX, No. V, May 1922, pp 379–80.
14 Letter from Farrar to Hinks, RGS Archives, EE 12/1.
15 Letter from Hinks to Farrar, ibid.
16 Finch, G.I., *The Making of a Mountaineer*, Arrowsmith, 1924, p. 293.
17 Quoted in Robertson, op. cit., p. 183.
18 Morris, John, *Hired to Kill*, Rupert Hart-Davis Cresset, London, 1960, p. 143.
19 Ibid., p. 144.
20 Somervell, T. Howard, 'George Leigh Mallory', *Journal of the Fell and Rock Climbing Club*, No. 6, 1924, pp 385–6.
21 Murray, W.M., *The Story of Everest*, Dent, London, 1953, Appendix 1.
22 Letter from Mallory to his wife, 10 May 1922, Magdalene College Archive.
23 Somervell, T. Howard, *After Everest*, Hodder & Stoughton, London, 1936, p. 52.
24 Letter from Mallory to his wife, 15 May 1922, Magdalene College Archive.
25 From Mallory's report to *The Times*, quoted in Robertson op. cit., p. 191.
26 Ibid., p. 192.
27 Ibid.
28 Bruce, C.G. et al., *The Assault on Mount Everest*, Edward Arnold, London, 1922, pp 208–9.
29 From Mallory's report to *The Times*, quoted in Robertson, op. cit., p. 195.
30 Ibid.
31 Letter from Mallory to his wife, 26 May 1922, Magdalene College Archive.
32 Finch, op. cit., p. 306.
33 Ibid., p. 318.
34 Ibid., p. 323.
35 Letter from Mallory to his wife, 1 June 1922, Magdalene College Archive.
36 Ibid.
37 Letter from Hinks to Bruce, RGS Archives, EE 18/1.
38 Letter from Bruce to Hinks, ibid.
39 Letter from Hinks to Bruce, ibid.
40 Letter from Mallory to David Pye, 1 June 1921, quoted in Robertson, op. cit., p. 199.
41 Diary of T.G. Longstaff, Alpine Club Archives.
42 Bruce, op. cit., pp 282–3.
43 Letter from Mallory to his wife, 9 June 1922, Magdalene College Archive.
44 Somervell, Howard T., op. cit., p. 64.
45 Letter from Charlie Bruce to Hinks, 4 July 1922, RGS Archives, EE 18/1.
46 Letter from Hinks to Collie, 19 July 1922, ibid., EE 11/5.
47 Letter from Hinks to Collie, 21 July 1922, ibid.

48 Letter from Mallory to Younghusband, quoted in Green, Dudley, *Mallory on Everest*, John Donald, Burnley, 1991, pp 110–11.
49 Letter from Younghusband to Mallory, 23 August 1921, quoted in Robertson, op. cit., p. 205.
50 Letter from Collie to Hinks, 25 July 1922, RGS Archives, EE 11/5.
51 Letter from Longstaff to Wollaston, 19 August 1922, quoted in Holzel, Tom and Salkeld, Audrey, *The Mystery of Mallory and Irvine*, Pimlico, London, 1996, p. 124.
52 Ibid., p. 125.
53 Letter from Strutt to Mallory, 2 August 1922, quoted in Robertson, op. cit., p. 203.
54 Geoffrey Young to Mallory, 18 August 1922, ibid., p. 204.
55 Green, op. cit., p. 113.

CHAPTER SEVEN
 1 Letter from Wilson to Larkins, 9 November 1923, RGS Archives, EE 29/5.
 2 Letter from Larkins to Wilson, 10 November 1923, ibid.
 3 Letter from Mallory to his wife, 18 October 1923, Magdalene College Archive.
 4 Letter from Mallory to his father, 25 October 1923, quoted in Robertson, David, *George Mallory* Faber & Faber, London, 1969, p. 211.
 5 Keynes, Geoffrey, *The Gates of Memory*, Clarendon Press, Oxford, 1981, p. 98.
 6 Letter from Ruth Mallory to her husband, 3 March 1924, Magdalene College Archive.
 7 Letter from Mallory to his wife, 8 March 1924, ibid.
 8 Carr, Herbert (ed.), *The Irvine Diaries: Andrew Irvine and the Enigma of Everest, 1924*, Gastons-West Col, Reading, p. 30.
 9 Ibid., p. 71.
10 Letter from Mallory to his wife, 3 March 1924, Magdalene College Archive.
11 Somervell, T. Howard, *After Everest*, Hodder & Stoughton, London, 1936, p. 107.
12 Odell, N.E., 'In Memoriam – Andrew Comyn Irvine', *Alpine Journal*, Vol. XXXVI, No. 229, Nov. 1924, p. 383.
13 Carr, op. cit., p. 80.
14 Ibid., p. 80.
15 Norton, E.F. et al., *The Fight for Everest: 1924*, Edward Arnold, London, 1925, p. 103.
16 Provisions order, RGS Archives, EE 30/4.
17 Letter from Mallory to his wife, 17 April 1924.
18 Carr, op. cit., p. 87.
19 Norton, op. cit., pp 64–5.
20 Carr, op. cit., p. 96.
21 Norton, op. cit., chapter by Bruce, pp 66–7.
22 Norton, op. cit., chapter by Norton, p. 81.
23 Letter from Mallory to his wife, 27 May 1924, Magdalene College Archive.
24 Ibid.
25 Norton, op. cit., p. 103.
26 Norton, ibid., p. 110.
27 Norton, ibid., p. 112.
28 Somervell, op. cit., p. 132.
29 Ibid.
30 Noel, J.B.L., *Through Tibet to Everest*, Edward Arnold, London, 1927, p. 258.
31 Letter from Mallory to his wife, 24 April 1924, Magdalene College Archive.
32 Carr, op. cit., p. 109.

33 Ibid., p. 112.
34 Norton, op. cit., p. 125.
35 Note from Mallory to Odell, 7 June 1924, *Alpine Journal*, Vol. XXXVII, No. 230, May 1925.
36 Note from Mallory to Noel, 7 June 1924, quoted in Noel, op. cit., p. 214.
37 Odell, N.E., in *The Mount Everest Dispatches*, reproduced in *Alpine Journal*, Vol. XXXVI, No. 229, Nov. 1924, p. 223.
38 Ibid., p. 130.
39 Blessed, Brian, *The Turquoise Mountain*, Bloomsbury, London, 1991, p. 35.
40 Norton, op. cit., p. 145.
41 Younghusband, Francis E., *The Epic of Mount Everest*, Edward Arnold, London, 1926, p. 300.

CHAPTER EIGHT

 1 Letter from Mallory to his wife, 24 April 1924, Magdalene College Archive.
 2 Norton's telegram to the Royal Geographical Society (RGS), 11 June 1924, RGS Archives, EE 37/2.
 3 Robertson, David, *George Mallory*, Faber & Faber, London, 1969, p. 250.
 4 Telegram from RGS to expedition, 20 June 1924, RGS Archives, EE 22/1.
 5 Letter from Freshfield to Hinks, RGS Archives, EE 26/5.
 6 A.C. Benson's personal diary, p. 175, Magdalene College Archive.
 7 W.F. O'Connor in a letter to *The Times*, 24 June 1924.
 8 Younghusband, Francis E., *The Epic of Mount Everest*, Edward Arnold, London, 1926, p. 305.
 9 Norton, E.F., 'Mount Everest Dispatches', *Alpine Journal*, Vol. XXXVI, No. 250, November 1924.
10 Letter from Geoffrey Keynes to Ruth Mallory, 21 June 1924, quoted in Robertson, op. cit., p. 253.
11 Letter from Geoffrey Young to Ruth Mallory, 30 June 1924, ibid., p. 254.
12 Letter from Ruth Mallory to Geoffrey Young, undated, RGS Archives, EE 3/4.
13 Somervell, T. Howard, *After Everest*, Hodder & Stoughton, London, 1936, p. 135.
14 Ibid., p. 135.
15 Letter from Norton to Spencer, 28 June 1924, British Library (63119).
16 Letter from Norton to Hinks, 13 June 1924, RGS Archives, EE 31/5.
17 Odell, quoted in Norton, E.F. *et al.*, *The Fight for Everest*, Edward Arnold, London, 1925, p. 143.
18 Letter from Bruce to Hinks, 11 July 1924, RGS Archives, EE 22/1.
19 Longstaff's report, 27 July 1924, ibid., EE 28/7.
20 Letter from Young to Freshfield, August 1924, ibid., EE 26/5.
21 Letter from Freshfield to Hinks, 29 August 1924, ibid.
22 Norton, op. cit.
23 Letter from Young to Freshfield, 10 August 1924, RGS Archives, EE 26/5.
24 Letter from Hinks to *The Times*, ibid., EE 34/8.
25 Blessed, Brian, *The Turquoise Mountain*, Bloomsbury, London, 1991, p. 38.
26 Salkeld, Audrey, *People in High Places*, Jonathan Cape, London, 1991, p. 137.
27 Letter from Bailey to Hinks, RGS Archives, EE 24/2.
28 Letter from Dalaï Lama to Indian government, ibid., EE 26/1.
29 Maurice Wilson's Diary, Alpine Club Archives.
30 Ibid.
31 Ibid.
32 Ibid.

33 Ibid.
34 Ibid.
35 Wang Fu-chou and Chu Yin-hua, 'How We Climbed Chomolungma', Mountain Craft, Summer 1961.
36 Shih Chan-chun, 'The Conquest of Mount Everest by the Chinese Mountaineering Team', *Alpine Journal*, Vol. LXVI, 1961.
37 Ibid.
38 'Nine who Climbed Qomolangma Feng', *Mountain*, No. 46, Nov/Dec 1975.
39 Television interview between author and Ryoten Yashimoro Hasegawa, 10 March 1999.
40 Ibid.
41 Ibid.

CHAPTER NINE
1 Noel, J.B.L., *Through Tibet to Everest*, Edward Arnold, London, 1927, p. 63.
2 Howard-Bury, C.K. et al., *Mount Everest: the Reconnaissance*, Edward Arnold, London, 1921, p. 70.
3 Ibid., chapter by Mallory, p. 192.
4 Dave Hahn, television interview, 1 May 1999.
5 Ibid., 5 May 1999.
6 Conrad Anker, ibid.
7 Ibid.
8 Ibid.
9 Ibid.
10 Jake Norton, ibid.
11 Dave Hahn, ibid.
12 Conrad Anker, ibid.
13 Jake Norton, ibid.
14 Dave Hahn, ibid.
15 Conrad Anker, ibid.
16 Dave Hahn, ibid.

CHAPTER TEN
1 Somervell, T. Howard, *After Everest*, Hodder & Stoughton, London, 1936, p. 137.
2 Jake Norton, television interview, 5 May 1999.
3 Note from Mallory to Noel, 7 June 1924, photograph in Noel, J.B.L., *Through Tibet to Everest*, Edward Arnold, London, 1927, opposite p. 214.
4 Norton, E.F. et al., *The Fight for Everest*, Edward Arnold, London, 1927, chapter VI by Odell, p. 131.
5 Note from Mallory to Odell, 7 June 1924, photograph in *Alpine Journal*, Vol. XXXVII, No. 230 (frontispiece), May 1925.
6 Odell, N.E., 'The Mount Everest Despatches', *Alpine Journal*, Vol. XXXVI, No. 229, Nov. 1924, p. 223.
7 Ibid.
8 Salkeld, Audrey, *People in High Places*, Jonathan Cape, London, 1991, p. 134.
9 Somervell, op. cit., p. 137.
10 Ryoten Yashimoro Hasegawa, television interview, 10 March 1999.
11 Letter from Young to Freshfield, RGS Archives, August 1924, EE 26/5.

Selected Bibliography

Allen, Charles, *A Mountain in Tibet*, André Deutsch, London, 1982.

Anonymous, *Another Ascent of the World's Highest Peak – Qomolangma*, Foreign Languages Press, Beijing, 1975.

Blessed, Brian, *The Turquoise Mountain*, Bloomsbury, London, 1991.

Blodig, Karl, 'Ostertage in North Wales', *Climber's Club Journal*, 1912.

Bruce, C.G. et al., *The Assault on Mount Everest*, Edward Arnold, London, 1922.

Carr, Herbert (ed.), *The Irvine Diaries: Andrew Irvine and the Enigma of Everest 1924*, Gastons-West Col, Reading, 1979.

Dent, C.T., *Above the Snowline*, Longmans, Green & Co, London, 1885.

Desideri, Ippolito, *An Account of Tibet: The Travels of Ippolito Desideri of Pistoia, S.J., 1712–1727*, F. de Filippi (ed.), Routledge, London, 1937.

Finch, G.I., *The Making of a Mountaineer*, Arrowsmith, London, 1924.

Green, Dudley, *Mallory of Everest*, John Donald, Burnley, 1991.

Holzel, Tom and Salkeld, Audrey, *The Mystery of Mallory and Irvine*, Pimlico, London, 1996

Hopkirk, Peter, *Trespassers on the Roof of the World*, John Murray, London, 1982.

Howard-Bury, C.K. et al., *Mount Everest: the Reconnaissance*, Edward Arnold, London, 1921.

Keay, John, *Where Men and Mountains Meet*, Century, London, 1977.

Keynes, Geoffrey, *The Gates of Memory*, Clarendon Press, Oxford, 1981.

Longstaff, T.G., *This My Voyage*, John Murray, London, 1950.

Lubbock, Percy (ed.), *The Diary of Arthur Christopher Benson*, Hutchinson, London, 1926.

Mallory, George H. L., *Boswell the Biographer*, Smith, Elder & Co., London, 1912.

Moorcroft, William, and Trebeck, George, *Travels in the Himalayan Provinces of Hindustan and the Punjab and in Ladakh and Kashmir, in Peshawar, Kabul, Kunduz and Bokhara*, 2 vols, 1837, reprinted Oxford University Press, Karachi, 1979.

Morris, John, *Hired to Kill*, Rupert Hart-Davis Cresset, London, 1960.

Murray, W.M., *The Story of Everest*, Dent, London, 1953.

Noel, J.B., *Through Tibet to Everest*, Edward Arnold, London, 1927.

Norton, E.F. et al., *The Fight for Everest*, Edward Arnold, London, 1925.

Pye, David, *George Leigh Mallory, a Memoir*, Oxford University Press/Humphrey Milford, Oxford, 1927.

Robertson, David, *George Mallory*, Faber & Faber, London, 1969.

Ruttledge, Hugh, *Everest 1933*, Hodder & Stoughton, London, 1934.

Salkeld, Audrey, *People in High Places*, Jonathan Cape, London, 1991.

Somervell, Howard T., *After Everest*, Hodder & Stoughton, London, 1936.

Styles, Showell, *The Forbidden Frontiers: The Survey of India from 1765 to 1949*, Hamilton, London, 1970.

Tyndale, H.E.G., *Mountain Paths*, Eyre & Spottiswoode, London, 1948.

Unsworth, Walt, *Everest*, Allen Lane, London, 1981.

Wessels, C., *Early Jesuit Travellers in Central Asia*, Martinus Nijhoff, The Hague, 1924.

Wilford, J.N., *The Mapmakers*, Junction Press, London, 1981.

Young, Geoffrey Winthrop, *On High Hills: Memories of the Alps*, Methuen, London, 1927.

Younghusband, Francis E., *The Heart of a Continent: A Narrative of Travels in Manchuria, Across the Gobi Desert, Through the Himalayas, and Chitral, 1884–1894*, John Murray, London, 1904.

Younghusband, Francis E., *The Epic of Mount Everest*, Edward Arnold, London, 1926.

Younghusband, Francis E., *Everest: the Challenge*, Nelson & Sons, London, 1936.

Index